What Every Owner, Breeder, and Trainer Should Know

Lowell Ackerman, D.V.M.

Alpine
PUBLICATIONS
Loveland, CO

CANINE NUTRITION:
What Every Owner, Breeder and Trainer Should Know

Library of Congress Cataloging-in-Publication Data

Ackerman, Lowell J.
    Canine nutrition : what every owner, breeder, and trainer should know / by Lowell
Ackerman.
        p.   cm.
    Includes bibliographical references.
    ISBN 1-57779-015-4
    1. Dogs--Nutrition. 2. Dogs--Food. I. Title.
SF427.4.A25   1999   99-21068
636.7'084--dc21   CIP

Many manufacturers secure trademark rights for their products. When Alpine Publications
is aware of a trademark claim, we identify the product name by using initial capital let-
ters.

Neither Alpine Publications nor the author accept any liability for suggested treatments or
diets mentioned herein. Homemade diets are for reference only and should be used only
on the advice of a local licensed veterinarian familiar with the individual animal involved.

This book is available at special quantity discounts for breeders and for club promotions,
premiums, or educational use. Write for details.

1 2 3 4 5 6 7 8 9 0

Cover design by: Bob Schram, Bookends
Coordination & Text design: B. J. McKinney and Tammy Geiger, M.S.

Printed in the United States of America.

CONTENTS

DEDICATION

To the most important individuals in my life—
my wonderful wife Susan, and my three adorable
children: Nadia, Rebecca and David.

With so many varieties and types of dog food available, how can a dog owner make the right choice? It's easier when you learn how to read a label, what nutrients are essential to your dog, and which ingredients provide the best source of those nutrients. Courtesy of PetsMart.

FOREWORD

If there are to be rapid improvements in health, high priority must be given to the detection of nutritional, especially vitamin, imbalances. Man has always been concerned with the interrelationship of food and disease. His intuitive reasoning that the shortcomings of certain foods were associated with various diseases culminated in the concept of vitamins. Nutritional deficiencies, especially those concerning vitamins, underlie numerous diseases; it is also clear that numerous diseases result in nutritional deficits.

In contrast to human studies, little has been done to document the full nutritional profile of animals. This is critical, because the nutritional profile is a mirror for gauging the adequacy of nutritional status and how it can be manipulated to maintain and even enhance an animal's well-being.

In keeping with the dynamics of nutritional progress begun almost 100 years ago, a nutritional revolution is occurring that is armed with an array of vitamins and nutrients that are being used as therapies rather than as nutrients. For example, nicotinic acid (a derivative of niacin) is used to lower cholesterol and triglycerides; vitamins A, E, and C and beta-carotene are being used supposedly to prevent degenerative diseases, cancer, and cardiovascular problems. Vitamins and minerals have grown from being nutritional agents, used in small amounts, to pharmacologic agents, used in amounts fifty to one hundred times greater than nutritionally required. It is exciting to watch this new emerging scenario in which nutrients can play a role different than the strictly nutritional one usually ascribed to them.

Herman Baker, Ph.D.
Professor of Preventive Medicine and Community Health, and Medicine
University of Medicine & Denistry of New Jersey
New Jersey Medical School
Newark, NJ 07107

PREFACE

Welcome to the wonderful world of canine nutrition. Whether you're feeding one dog or one hundred, you need to make important nutritional decisions every day. What food are you going to buy? Does your dog need a supplement? What kind of treats are healthiest for dogs? Where will you turn for the answers to these and other nutritional questions? There is so much conflicting information in the marketplace that it is often difficult to get to the truth about products. If you're one of those people who want to make intelligent decisions about your dog's dietary needs, this book is for you.

Veterinarians and nutritionists agree—there is nothing more important to your dog's health than providing a healthy and balanced diet. And you don't have to be a nutritionist to make sensible choices for your dog. This book will be your guide to feeding your companion throughout his entire life. There are chapters dealing with dietary changes that will help a sick dog and advice on using nutritional supplements that will promote good health. Until now, none of this information has been available in one, concise book.

Your dog relies on you to make intelligent decisions about his diet. After all, his nutrition is entirely in your hands. Your dog trusts you to make these difficult choices, and you should take the responsibility seriously. This book gives you the tools to make good decisions about your dog's nutritional needs so that he is properly nourished for the rest of his life.

Questions to Ponder . . .

Why is reading the label on various pet foods and comparing them not adequate in itself to enable you to make the right choice in deciding what to feed your pet?

If you own several dogs, can you feed the same food to all of them?

Where should you turn for nutritional advice—a veterinarian, the local feed supply salesperson, product literature, or none of the above?

When choosing a food for your pet, what should be your primary objective?

When a label says that a pet food is "complete and balanced," can you trust it to provide adequately for your dog's health and energy needs?

Can you determine the quality and utilization of a dog food by observing your dog's stool?

**Learn the answers to these
and many other nutrition questions
in Chapter 1.**

1
AN OVERVIEW OF NUTRITION

Nutrition is a fascinating subject that interests most pet owners—to a point. You may, at one time or another, question your veterinarian, breeder, groomer, trainer, or salesperson at a pet supply store about which food may be best for your dog. Advertising by pet-food companies inevitably concludes that *their* product is best.

You may also receive mixed signals about nutritional supplements. Most pet-food companies contend that their products provide all the nutrients needed by dogs on a daily basis and that supplements are not needed and may even be harmful. On the other hand, supplements line the shelves in pet-supply stores, so someone must be buying them. Do they have real value, or are they as worthless as the pet-food industry suggests?

Another controversial topic is using the diet to manage certain health problems. Although everyone can appreciate that a low-salt diet would be helpful for a dog with heart disease, can behavioral problems or allergies be managed effectively by dietary modification?

What about additives and preservatives in commercial pet foods? Are they harming your pet, or are they harmless ingredients that keep foods more wholesome? Are "natural" pet foods healthier than regular diets? With all of these questions, where do you turn for help?

Unfortunately, even veterinarians are subject to bias in the information they receive about pet foods. Most of the books available on the subject of canine nutrition have been written by individuals who are in some way affiliated with pet-food companies. While the information in all of these books is valuable, the different conclusions drawn suggest that the answers may not be as clear-cut as they may seem.

You also need to consider the variability in nutrition training received by veterinarians. Only about one-quarter of the veterinary colleges in the United States and Canada have a veterinary nutritionist as a clinical faculty member. In many ways, this is because the American College of Veterinary Nutrition is a recently formed college (1988), which at the time of its founding boasted only eighteen charter diplomates. Many years of specialty training will be needed by residents before this number grows appreciably. In a study published in 1991, only six veterinary colleges offered graduate degrees or residency training in veterinary nutrition. Fortunately, plans are underway to make specialty training in nutrition more accessible to practicing veterinarians.

Still, you would think that nutrition is simply a matter of facts and formulas. If nutrition is a fairly precise science, why are there so many different, and sometimes opposite, opinions floating around? Is there some kind of conspiracy to suppress the true facts? The answers to these questions are yes, because, and no.

Nutrition *is* a fairly precise science, but the interpretation of the facts is controversial. Far from being a conspiracy, this freedom of information allows individuals to draw their own conclusions, sometimes inaccurately and sometimes in a biased fashion. The only defense you have as a consumer and concerned dog owner is to understand the facts and draw your own conclusions. This allows you to bypass the propaganda that you might get from individuals or companies trying to sell you their version of the facts.

WHAT IS NUTRITION?

Nutrition has many definitions, and it clearly has different meanings for different people. Most agree, however, that nutrition is the study of nutrients. Nutrients are substances that are consumed as food and that provide the dietary raw materials for animals to survive and reproduce. Further definition depends on your area of interest.

- If you are a breeder you might consider nutrition as the needed fuel to produce and reproduce animals of desired stature, haircoat quality, or temperament.
- Your veterinarian might regard nutrition as a means of keeping dogs healthy or in managing them optimally if they become ill.
- A chemist might consider nutrition as the conversion of food chemicals to body chemicals.
- A geneticist might think of nutrition as a fundamental requirement for animals to reproduce themselves and contribute genetic material to future generations.

Are any of these definitions incorrect? Not really. They simply reflect viewpoints of people in different situations.

Not all dog owners share the same view of nutrition, and that is why so many different dog foods are on the market. Some people just want a simple food that will meet their dog's nutritional requirements at an economical price. Others buy into the "premium dog food" market because they're convinced that their dogs deserve the best and that these foods are the best because they're more expensive. Would these individuals be surprised to learn that the terms "premium" and "gourmet" are not regulated and therefore can be used with any product? A company's premium line may be the best it has, but there is no law to stop a company from calling any product "premium." You have to know the facts!

THE NUTRIENTS

Nutrients are substances obtained from food and then used by the body for growth, maintenance, and tissue repair.

The Six Families of Nutrients

| Proteins | Carbohydrates | Fat | Vitamins | Minerals | Water |

Within these six families are more than forty-five individual nutrients that are needed by dogs to maintain health. The focus tends to be on protein and on vitamins and minerals. Water, however is the most abundant nutrient in the body and the most indispensable. Dogs can survive a long

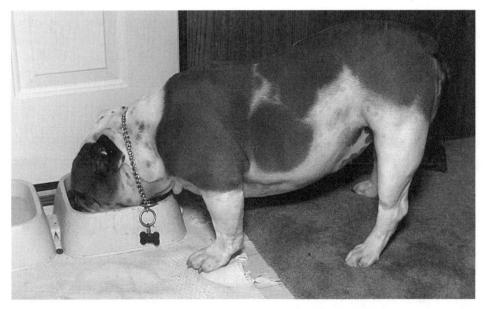

No single diet is adequate for a dog at all of his life stages. Photo by Judith Strom.

time without eating, but if they become more than 12 percent dehydrated, they are unlikely to live very long.

Most foods provide a combination of nutrients. A sirloin steak is not pure protein. It's probably 60 percent water, and the dry-matter content is two-thirds protein and one-third fat. It also contains a small amount of calcium, iron, niacin, and folic acid. Combine it with a baked potato and you add a touch of additional protein, a good carbohydrate source, almost no fat, and some potassium, vitamin C, and dietary fiber. But you still don't have a "balanced" diet. This combination provides you with water, protein, carbohydrates, fats, vitamins, and minerals, but not in the correct proportions. Deficiencies will result if you try to feed this to your dog for very long. This combination contains fat, but not the fat that the body needs. It contains vitamins but is deficient in vitamin A and most of the B vitamins. It contains minerals, but the balance is all wrong for optimal nutrition. Where did you go wrong?

It is important to know the difference between essential nutrients and nonessential nutrients. Essential nutrients *must* be provided in the diet or deficiencies will result. Nonessential nutrients may provide a source of energy, but they are not truly needed for dogs to survive. Therefore, you really can't just look at a dog's diet in terms of nutrients. You must be more specific. There are certain proteins, fats, vitamins, and minerals that are most important, and you must try to provide them in a proper balance to your dog. This is what is referred to as balance in the diet.

Proteins, carbohydrates, and fats are known as energy nutrients—they provide the body with fuel to perform its needed functions. The term "calorie" is used interchangeably with the word "energy" because it is a way of measuring the energy provided by a food source. A given amount of either carbohydrate or protein provides an equivalent amount of energy, but fats provide more than twice as much energy (calories) as proteins or carbohydrates. These energy nutrients, as well as water, are discussed in Chapter 3.

NUTRITIONAL APPROPRIATENESS

One of the biggest misunderstandings about nutrition is assuming that the ingredients in the food determine its ultimate value. Ingredients are substances such as chicken, beef, soy, corn, and lamb. The confusion arises when you examine *ingredients* rather than nutrients. Remember—nutrients are water, proteins, carbohydrates, fats, vitamins, and minerals. The specific nutrients are what meet your dog's daily nutritional needs. The *quality of a diet* is therefore determined by the appropriate blend of nutrients, *not* ingredients. The ingredients are important in that they contribute to other aspects of the food, such as palatability (taste), digestibility, and cost.

Palatability is important because if the food is not eaten, it really doesn't matter *how* nutritious it is. One of the biggest problems with clinical nutrition is that you may buy a dog food based on your preferences, not on those of your dog. You might be surprised to know that if a sirloin steak and a plate of chicken guts is offered to a dog, he will probably select the guts over the steak. Most commercial dog foods are formulated to appeal to owners because they are the ones who make the purchase. Dogs prefer foods that are "smelly," but companies formulate diets that are not offensive to people. Dogs do not select foods based on shapes or colors, yet dog-food companies manufacture shapes and colors of food that, again, are most attractive to people. This is a major hurdle if you ever want companies to make foods with your dog—not you—in mind.

Digestibility of the food is also important. If the food is palatable and eaten readily, it is a waste if the food cannot be digested adequately. This is a problem with the very cheap diets that contain a lot of cereal grains and fiber as a cost-cutting measure. If you look at the pet-food label, you will find that these foods may meet nutritional recommendations but that the nutrients may not be able to be used. The real trick to making a quality dog food is to process ingredients properly so that the nutrients are digested readily. If this is done, cereals, fruits, and vegetables can be as satisfactory as meats in a dog's diet.

Associated with digestibility of a diet is the stool produced by the dog. Do the firmness and color of the stool really tell you anything about the nutritional quality of the diet? Some pet-food companies would like you to believe this, while other companies contend that stool quality is a feature of the nonnutritional composition of a diet. For example, beet pulp as a dietary ingredient has very little nutritional benefit for dogs. It may be added to a ration because it absorbs up to six times its weight in water, making stools drier and more compact. If enough beet pulp is added to a diet, it actually interferes with the absorption of needed nutrients, although the stool looks great. You have to know the facts!

Also related to digestibility is nutrient utilization, or the biological value of the food. How do you know that what you're feeding is actually being digested, absorbed, and utilized? This information is provided by digestibility trials. Dogs are fed measured amounts of the food, usually for a two-week period, and their stools and urine are analyzed for unused nutrients. In this way, you can specifically determine the nutrients that go into the dog and the ones that come out the other end unused. The higher the digestibility of individual nutrients, the more efficiently they are utilized by a dog. This type of study provides two useful statistics, the digestible energy and the metabolizable energy of a dog food. The digestible energy is the total energy (calories) provided less those that appear in the stool. The metabolizable energy (ME) is the total energy (calories) provided, less those that appear in the urine as well as in the stool. This ME is that which is ultimately utilized by the body's tissues. Testing for metabolizable energy is costly and requires special facilities. Because the original studies have already been done, there already are suitable formulas for approximating ME, if not providing exact values.

Calculating the metabolizable energy of a dog food is useful because many nutritionally useless ingredients are included in dog food that are not apparent by reading the label. This makes it very difficult to compare dog foods meaningfully by looking only at the analysis on the label. It also makes it difficult to compare canned, dry, and semimoist diets.

DAILY REQUIREMENTS

There is much talk of daily requirements of nutrients, but there is as much variability in canine requirements as there is in people, and probably more so. Two people of equal weight may have vastly different needs for energy (calories). Consider the individual who consumes a regular meal and gains weight with the individual who can eat all day and never gain an ounce. How about the individual who eats junk food, smokes, and abuses alcohol but is perpetually healthy versus the health-food addict that is continually ill?

You cannot expect your dog to be any different. Your dog is an individual, and no formula can exactly predict his nutritional needs constantly, throughout his entire life. No factor can predict optimal levels of nutrients for any animal. Dogs, like people, have individual requirements that need to be addressed if they are to remain healthy. Be wary of any published requirement that applies to all dogs. You can't really expect a five-pound Chihuahua to have the same requirements as a one-hundred-and-fifty-pound Great Dane. It is not likely that the Great Dane would have to eat thirty times as much as the Chihuahua to gain the same nutritional benefit. Nor would you expect an Afghan Hound with a long, luxurious coat to have the same nutritional needs as a short-coated Greyhound. The brachycephalic breeds, those with "squashed faces" such as the Bulldog, Pug, and Boston Terrier, also have dental patterns that may dictate which foods they ingest best. Several breeds have potential metabolic concerns. Siberian Huskies and Alaskan Malamutes sometimes require higher levels of zinc than other breeds. Dalmatians may require a low-purine diet to avoid urinary-tract stones and skin problems. Bedlington Terriers may accumulate copper in their livers, resulting in toxicity. Giant Schnauzers may be prone to vitamin B_{12} deficiency, and Miniature Schnauzers may be prone to high blood triglyceride and cholesterol levels. These are just some breed peculiarities. Nutritional requirements are based on averages. The National Research Council's report on minimum nutrient requirements of dogs is based on dogs weighing ten kilograms (twenty-two pounds). The puppy studies were based on three-kilogram (six-and-one-half-pound), growing Beagle puppies.

Your obligation as a dog owner is to understand dietary requirements and to make sense of the contradictory information. This means learning the issues and some scientific-sounding words. For instance, you must be aware of the ultimate bioavailability of nutrients in the diet, and you need to know that the actual numbers might be different than those on the label.

It's one thing to put an ingredient in the food and another thing for that ingredient to be adequately digested, absorbed, and utilized. The ultimate usefulness is called "bioavailability." You could feed your dog a leather wallet and claim "protein," a piece of wood and claim "carbohydrate," and diesel oil and claim "fat." You could even prepare them in proper proportions so that on a label they would appear "balanced." This, however, is no assurance that your dog is receiving adequate nutrition.

Surely the nutritional requirements for dogs are not subject to debate. Doesn't some government agency conduct studies to assure that the actual requirements for dogs are known, beyond doubt? Unfortunately, the subject of daily requirements may be as confusing as the different meanings of nutrition. There is also a significant difference between minimal daily requirements (MDR), the amount needed to prevent deficiencies, the recommended daily allowances (RDA), and the optimal daily recommendations for each individual dog.

The National Research Council (NRC) is the working arm of the National Academy of Sciences, the National Academy of Engineering, and the Institute of Medicine. It is not a part of the United States government, nor does it do any of its own research. It is not an enforcement agency for pet-food companies. What the NRC does is compile research done by others. Its committee on animal nutrition identifies problems and needs in animal nutrition but does none of the research or testing of actual dog foods. Nor does it develop or enforce federal or state regulations.

The NRC periodically publishes "Nutrient Requirements of Dogs," the last one being in 1985 (see Appendix). This latest publication is vastly improved from previous efforts. It was recognized that protein percentages could be misleading, and the requirements were changed to specific amino acids. This report also specified that the amounts should be considered "minimum requirements," not "recommended allowances." Most of the NRC requirements are based on preventing deficiencies in dogs kept under experimental conditions. As such, they are only loosely related to real-world circumstances.

The NRC publications will be updated in 1999 or 2000 and will combine the requirements for dogs and cats into a single report (www4.nas.edu/ banr/ba.nsf). The new report will provide updated estimates of requirements for all nutrients and will contain discussions of nutrient metabolism, toxicity, deficiency, and nutritionally-related disease in both dogs and cats. Information of the impact of physiologic status, temperature, breed, age, and environment on nutrient requirements will also be included.

Although the NRC is a valid and useful organization, dog foods based on these minimal requirements are not necessarily the best for your dog. In some ways, this is like calculating how little gasoline an engine needs to keep it running for that day. It might continue to run on low volumes but probably not optimally or at peak performance. Even the pet-food companies are aware of this fact and are looking for viable alternatives that can set an industry standard.

Abbreviations You Need to Know

MDR   **Minimum daily requirements –**
             the amount needed to prevent deficiencies

RDA   **Recommended daily allowances –**
             the optimum daily recommended amount per dog

NRC   **National Research Council –**
             compiles research on animal nutrition done by others, but
             does no testing and does not regulate pet food manufacturing

AAFCO   **Association of American Feed Control Officials –**
             designs and regulates testing protocols

CNE   **Canine Nutrition Expert (subcommittee of AAFCO) –**
             formulated nutritional requirements for amino-acid levels, etc.

PFI   **Pet Food Institute –**
             national trade association of pet-food manufacturers
             formulated nutrition requirements referred to as NAP

The Association of American Feed Control Officials (AAFCO) is an advisory body of representatives from the various states that provides additional useful information about diets. It does not police the industry but offers testing procedures in which diets are fed to healthy dogs on a long-term basis and evaluated periodically (www.uky.edu/agriculture/regulatoryservices/aafco.htm). To be declared a complete and balanced diet for a particular life stage (e.g., maintenance, growth, reproduction), AAFCO has designed testing protocols that must be performed before the particular label claim may be made. Companies that subscribe to this protocol will list on their labels "substantiated by testing performed in accordance with the procedures established by the AAFCO." AAFCO regulations give manufacturers the option of conducting feeding trials to verify their claims or relying on laboratory analysis of the food. Unfortunately, testing the food alone only means that the ingredients are there. It doesn't mean that they are actually absorbed by dogs and can be used for the purposes intended.

In 1990, the AAFCO Canine Nutrition Expert (CNE) subcommittee was formed and subsequently revised the nutritional-profile requirements for dog foods. One of the major breakthroughs was looking at amino-acid levels rather than at percentages of protein in the diet. The committee also established maximum levels for calcium, phosphorus, fat-soluble vitamins, and many trace elements. The value of these changes will become more apparent as you read this book.

Even newer requirements (1992) were designed by the Pet Food Institute. These are referred to as the Nutrition Assurance Program (NAP). The Pet Food Institute is the national trade association of dog- and cat-food manufacturers. Participating pet-food companies must document the performance of each product they submit. Only one product in a family (e.g., canned, semimoist, dry) must be successfully tested, however. Only an abbreviated analytical profile must be conducted for most other products manufactured by a company. These minimal nutritional profiles must equal or exceed the nutritional profile of the successfully tested product within that family to comply. This means that if a pet-food manufacturer makes ten different canned dog foods, only one needs to successfully pass AAFCO feeding trials. If the laboratory nutrient profiles of the company's other products meet or exceed those of the canned food tested, they also will pass the test and can state this on their labels.

Under this program, only live-animal feeding tests are accepted as proof of nutritional adequacy, and the trials must be performed in accordance with AAFCO protocols. Testing must be repeated every two years or at the time of a significant formula change. The thrust of this program is to ensure that animals will not be harmed by the diet and that it actually will support the stage of life claimed. The program does not examine the relationship of the diet to long-term health or to disease prevention. Products meeting this claim will list on the pet-food label "Animal feeding tests using AAFCO procedures show that (Brand) provides complete and balanced nutrition for (life stages)."

The Canadian Veterinary Medical Association (CVMA) took the situation one step farther. It developed the Pet Food Certification Program to test a manufacturer's products and to certify those products as meeting CVMA standards. To comply, products are tested by the CVMA, feeding trials are performed, and the product is monitored to ensure that it continuously meets CVMA's high standards for composition, digestibility, and palatability (www.vpei.ca/~cvma/petfood.htm). In many ways, this is superior to the AAFCO standards and far superior to the NRC stan-

---

Remember

Optimal diets contain a balanced range of nutrients suitable for different phases of a dog's life, including health, old age, breeding, growth periods, showing, competing, and even illness. You really cannot expect one food to meet all of these different needs. Chapter two focuses on actual nutritional needs and how they change throughout a dog's life.

dards, because it puts an impartial but trained veterinary association in a watchdog role for the pet-food industry. Participation is voluntary, but foods that are successfully evaluated can claim certification by the Canadian Veterinary Medical Association. Unfortunately, there is no pet-food supervisory division of the American Veterinary Medical Association. Perhaps the best qualified group in the United States to attempt regulation is the American College of Veterinary Nutrition (ACVN). Members of the college are usually asked to participate in AAFCO and PFI projects, but for the time being, the watchdog of the industry continues to be the industry itself.

NUTRITIONAL LINGO

To make life easier as you read this book, take the time to learn a few of the terms important in the field of nutrition. After all, nutrition is a science and must take into account anatomy, chemistry, physiology, immunology, genetics, and medicine.

AMINO ACID

Amino acids are the building blocks of protein. When protein is consumed it is broken down into amino acids that are then absorbed by the body. These amino acids are used to create the specific proteins that the body needs most.

Two types of amino acids relate to the daily needs of a dog. The body can make some amino acids on its own, and it doesn't matter if they are included in the diet. These are known as the dispensable, or nonessential, amino acids. On the other hand, the body *does* need specific amino acids that it cannot manufacture itself. These must be included in the diet and are referred to as essential amino acids. If one or more essential amino acids are not adequately provided in the diet, they are considered "limiting" amino acids.

ANTIOXIDANT

Antioxidants are compounds that prevent damage caused by oxidation, the process whereby oxygen actually causes problems in tissues. For example, fats go rancid without antioxidants because the oxygen breaks down the fats and spoils them. The same thing can happen in the body. All of the cells in the body have surrounding membranes that contain fat. Harmful oxygen (see free radicals) can damage these membranes, and this process is associated with the onset of many degenerative diseases, including heart disease, arthritis, and cancer.

Antioxidants can be natural or synthetic. There are natural antioxidants within the body responsible for "scavenging" harmful by-products. Most of these are enzymes such as superoxide dismutase. Vitamin A, beta-carotene, vitamin C, and vitamin E are natural antioxidants included in our diets. Because of their antioxidant effects, they are often recommended as aids (not cures) for degenerative disorders. In fact, they probably can play an even larger role in preventing these conditions than they do in treating them. Many other synthetic antioxidants are added to dog foods as preservatives to stop the fats in the ration from going rancid. These include ethoxyquin, butylated hydroxytoluene (BHT), and butylated hydroxyanisole (BHA).

BIOAVAILABILITY

Bioavailability is the term used to describe the ultimate usefulness of nutrients in a food source. Some ingredients may contain ample amounts of nutrients, but for some reason or another, those nutrients do not get digested, absorbed and utilized as intended. Bioavailability tells you the difference between the nutrient content of a food and its ability to deliver those nutrients so that they can be used.

Bioavailability takes into account many variables. For example, red iron oxide is commonly added to dog foods to make them look meaty. Red iron oxide, however, exists in a form where the iron is almost completely unusable by dogs for nutritional purposes. Therefore, although dogs need iron in their diet, red iron oxide may contain iron oxide but not in a bioavailable form useful to dogs. Similarly, soybean oil contains vitamin E but in a form (gamma tocopherol rather than alpha tocopherol) that is only poorly utilized by dogs, if at all. When you keep in mind that the ultimate purpose of feeding your dog is to make sure that appropriate nutrients are delivered, bioavailability becomes a most important concept.

CALORIE

Everyone is familiar with the calorie, a unit of energy, and is aware that foods have different caloric values. Food substances possess chemical energy that can be used by the body (once digested) for various purposes. Although the term "calorie" is used loosely, in nutrition it is often used incorrectly. A calorie is actually the amount of energy required to heat a gram of water one degree centigrade. This, of course, is a very small number. When the term "calorie" is used in nutrition, it really implies kilocalories, or 1,000 calories. It's sort of like watts and kilowatts. When you say a teaspoon of sugar is 16 calories, the truth is that it is 16 kilocalories, or 16,000 calories.

With the confusion between calories and kilocalories, many countries have gotten away from the term altogether. Instead, the new international system (SI) prefers the term "Joule." Because the United States is a long way from adopting the metric system, conversion to this new international system is not likely to be quick for Americans. So, calories (really kilocalories) will still be around for some time to come.

CARBOHYDRATES

Carbohydrates consist of sugars, starches, and fiber. The sugars are often referred to as simple carbohydrates, while the longer chains of sugars found in starches are referred to as complex carbohydrates. Dogs do not require any carbohydrates in their diets, yet carbohydrates are frequently used to provide energy (calories) and to add bulk.

Complex carbohydrates are digested slowly and are then converted to sugar in the body. Sugars are digested more quickly, and because they are so bioavailable, they will be converted to fat if the body doesn't use their energy quickly. Carbohydrates, however, are no more fat-promoting that proteins. Carbohydrates and protein provide equivalent amounts of energy (calories).

ENZYMES

An enzyme is a protein that helps make things happen. It "drives" chemical reactions without changing significantly itself. For nearly every chemical process that occurs in the body, there are specific enzymes to guide the process. An automobile is a good comparison. A car is a car, whether it's moving or not. If it is in working condition and if it has fuel, it can serve as a form of transportation. To convert the car from a piece of machinery to a form of transportation, you need to place a key in the ignition. This key functions similarly to an enzyme. It makes the reaction happen without changing dramatically itself.

A related term, coenzyme, is used in nutrition to describe nonenzymes that help make things happen. Vitamins frequently fulfill this role. For example, many of the B vitamins and several minerals work closely with specific enzymes. Coenzyme Q is a specific coenzyme that functions within the mitochondria of every cell in the body. It belongs to the same family (quinones) as vitamin K.

FATTY ACIDS

Fat is a nutrient in the diet. As a source of energy (calories), it provides two and one-fourth times as much energy as proteins or carbohydrates. Fatty acids are the actual nutritional derivatives of fats, and these are usually described as saturated, monounsaturated, or polyunsaturated based on their chemical structure. Most of the saturated fats come from animal sources and can cause problems in dogs, just as they do in people. The polyunsaturated fats come from plant oils and include the essential fatty acids—those required in the diet as an absolute need. For the dog, linoleic acid is often described as an *essential fatty acid*. The other fatty acids are not needed for specific nutritional reasons but contribute their energy (calories) toward daily requirements.

The omega-3 fatty acids are derived from alpha-linolenic acid and are found in fish, plants and marine oils. The omega-6 fatty acids are derivatives of linoleic acid and are found in plants such as evening primrose and borage. These omega-series fatty acids are used therapeutically in people and pets for helping to treat a variety of disorders.

FIBER

Dietary fiber is that part of the plant material that resists digestion, although at least some of the fiber can be digested by dogs. Water-soluble fiber is more commonly found in fruits, oats, barley, and legumes, and water-insoluble fiber is found in larger amounts in vegetables, wheat, and most grains. High-fiber diets are often suggested for overweight pets or for those suffering from digestive problems or diabetes mellitus.

Fiber levels in the common dog foods range from 2 to 4 percent. The new "Lite" foods can contain in excess of 20 percent fiber. These levels of dietary fiber can increase the bulk of the food and give the dog a "full food feeling" with a much lower dietary energy intake. This is not entirely without risk, because fiber can also reduce the digestibilities of protein, carbohydrates, fats, and some vitamins and minerals.

FREE RADICALS

Free radicals are harmful agents that are produced when cells are damaged. Most are damaging by-products of oxygen and are often referred to as oxygen-derived free radicals. The problem with free radicals is that they set up a chain reaction of damaging effects. Evidence supports the theory that free radicals contribute to many degenerative diseases, including heart disease, arthritis, and even cancer.

Free radicals are produced by several factors, including exposure to radiation, smoking, ingestion of saturated dietary fats, and exposure to excessive ultraviolet light. Natural "scavengers" in the body, such as superoxide dismutase, remove free radicals when they are encountered. When the system is overtaxed, however, free radicals do more damage than can be prevented or repaired.

To diminish the adverse effects of free radicals, antioxidants have a protective role. Natural antioxidants found in the diet include beta-carotene, vitamin A, vitamin C, selenium, and vitamin E.

METABOLIZABLE ENERGY (ME)

The metabolizable energy (ME) of a dog food describes how much of the dog food can actually be used by the dog for energy (calorie) purposes. It is the difference between the energy (calorie) content of the food being fed and the amount lost in the urine and feces.

The ME of a dog food can be approximated if the protein, carbohydrate, and fat contents of the food are known. Vitamins, minerals, and water do not provide calories in the diet. Fat provides more than twice as many calories as either proteins or carbohydrates, and this is reflected in the formula. This calculation is a great equalizer for comparing dog foods and forms of food (e.g., canned, dry, semimoist). The final number is expressed as kilocalories of metabolizable energy per hundred grams of food. This also allows you to calculate the number of calories in the diet supplied as protein, fat, and carbohydrate.

MINERALS

Minerals are inorganic nutrients that originate in the soil rather than in plants or animals. Plants acquire minerals from the soil in which they grow and from the water used to irrigate these plants. Animals acquire minerals in water and by consuming plants or other animals.

The minerals are often subdivided into macrominerals (macroelements) and microminerals (trace elements), depending on the amounts needed in the diet. Much is known about the needs for macrominerals such as calcium and phosphorus, but the amount of trace minerals needed is a matter of debate. Obviously, not all minerals are essential, and some are downright harmful. Arsenic, mercury, and tin are all minerals, but they're hardly considered healthful. On the other hand, fluorine may have a positive effect on the teeth, but you wouldn't expect a deficiency if it were not provided in the diet or water supply.

NITRIC OXIDE PATHWAY

Not to be confused with nitrous oxide (laughing gas), nitric oxide is made by cells from the amino acid L-arginine by a family of enzymes known as nitric oxide synthases. This metabolic route has come to be known as the L-arginine-nitric oxide pathway and its ultimate importance is only now being realized. For example, nitric oxide is responsible for blood vessel tone and thus is critical for regulating blood pressure. In the central nervous system, nitric oxide is a neurotransmitter that performs several functions, including the formation of memory.

Nitric oxide also contributes to the ability of platelets to stick to one another and regulates the contractions of the heart. Emerging evidence suggests that some diseases are related to defects in the generation or action of nitric oxide. In addition, nitric oxide is produced in large quantities during host defense and immunologic reactions; it thus plays some role in nonspecific immunity. As if that's not enough, nitric oxide is involved in the development of conditions such as inflammation, septic shock, and cirrhosis.

It is thus clear that nitric oxide is an important mediator of many body processes and immune mechanisms. Current research suggests that the L-arginine-nitric oxide pathway is involved in a number of degenerative processes, such as arthritis and heart disease. Nitric oxide is important to nutritionists because it is formed by an important amino acid and appears to be susceptible to manipulation by some dietary factors. Manipulation of nitric oxide has already proved clinically successful for a variety of human diseases and it is hoped increased control in heart disease and arthritis in the dog and human won't be far away.

PROTEINS

Proteins are chemical compounds made up of chains of amino acids. Some proteins are structural in nature (e.g., collagen), others may function as hormones (e.g., insulin), while others are considered enzymes.

There is no dietary requirement for protein in dog food. The only absolute requirement for dogs is for specific amino acids, known as the essential amino acids. These compounds are provided by protein in the diet. This is confusing because most dog-food labels list only ingredients and percentages of protein, fat, carbohydrate, and fiber. The percentage of protein in the diet is somewhat irrelevant, and you can only hope that the pet-food manufacturers know enough about a dog's nutritional needs to include all the essential amino acids.

VITAMINS

Vitamins are organic substances required in the diet. Most of the vitamins are not single compounds but are really groups of chemicals with similar structure and function. For instance, vitamin E is used to describe the tocopherols, yet it is alpha tocopherol that provides most of the benefits attributable to vitamin E.

The vitamins are often subdivided into fat-soluble and water-soluble varieties. The fat-soluble vitamins are A, D, E, and K. The water-soluble vitamins are C and the B vitamins. Vitamin C is not a true "vitamin" in the dog, because dogs can make their own, even if fed a vitamin C-deficient diet.

The alphabetical names for the vitamins (e.g., vitamin B_6) have some historical interest but are less commonly used now because the chemical nature of the vitamins is better understood and the differences between them are recognized. "Thiamin" says much more than does the impersonal "vitamin B_1."

Provitamins are nutrients that are converted in the body to vitamins. The best example is beta-carotene, which is a form of plant pigment that is converted by the liver to vitamin A.

IN SUMMARY

There are six families of nutrients: proteins, carbohydrates, fats, vitamins, minerals, and water. Within them are more than forty-five individual nutrients that are needed by dogs to maintain health.

Essential nutrients are those which must be provided in the diet or deficiencies will result.

The quality of a diet is determined by the appropriate blend of *nutrients,* not by the ingredients.

Most dog foods are made to smell and look appealing to people, not dogs.

Digestibility is a measure of the way the nutrients are absorbed and utilized. Many foods meet nutritional recommendations but the nutrients may not be able to be used. This makes it difficult to compare dog foods meaningfully by looking at the analysis on the label.

Dogs have individual nutritional requirements, as well as different requirements at various life stages and to meet different work or stress levels. No one food is suitable for all stages of a dog's life.

The ultimate purpose of feeding your dog is to make sure that appropriate nutrients are delivered and utilized. Bioavailability is the term used to describe the ultimate usefulness of nutrients in a food source—the difference between the nutrient content and its ability to deliver those nutrients so they can be used.

Carbohydrates, consisting of sugars, starches, and fiber, provide energy amounts equivalent to protein in the dog's diet.

Enzymes are proteins that help make things happen. For nearly every chemical process that occurs in the body, there are specific enzymes to guide the process.

Fat is a source of energy. Saturated fats, most of which come from animal sources, can cause problems in dogs just as they do in people. Linoleic acid from plant sources is an essential fatty acid for the dog.

ADDITIONAL READING

Bebiak, D.M., Lawler, D.F., and Reutzel, L.F., "Nutrition and Management of the Dog." *Veterinary Clinics of North America: Small Animal Practice,* 1987; 17(3): 505-533.

Brown, R. G., Atkinson, J., Barrett, D. (Eds.), *CMVA Desk Reference Manual on Nutrition,* 1993: 98 pp.

Burger, I. (Ed.), *The Waltham Book of Companion Animal Nutrition.* Pergamon Press, Oxford, 1993; 136 pp.

Case, L.P., Carey, D.P. Hirakawa, D.A., *Canine and Feline Nutrition: A Resource for Companion Animal Professionals.* Mosby, St. Louis, Missouri, 1995; 455 pp.

Dzanis, D.A., "Watchdogging Pet Food Claims and Labels." *Veterinary Forum,* October 1992; 43-44.

Earle, K.E., "Feeding for Health." *Pet Nutrition in Practice.* Waltham Symposium No. 13, March 1989; 4-8.

Edney, A.T.B. (Ed.), *The Waltham Book of Dog & Cat Nutrition,* 2nd ed. Pergamon Press, Oxford, 1988; 143 pp.

Ekedahl, D.H., "Is a Nutrition Assurance Program Necessary?" *Veterinary Forum,* October 1992; 44-45.

Gaines Professional Services. *Basic Guide to Canine Nutrition.* General Foods Corporation, 1977; 98 pp.

Gey, K.F., "Prospects for the Prevention of Free Radical Disease, Regarding Cancer and Cardiovascular Disease." *British Medical Bulletin,* 1993; 49(3): 679-699.

Lewis, L.D., Morris, Jr., M.L., Hand, M.S., *Small Animal Clinical Nutrition III.* Mark Morris Associates, 1987.

Lonsdale, T., "Feeding vs Nutrition—Have We Lost the Plot in Small Animal Dietetics?" *Australian Veterinary Practitioner,* 1993; 23(1): 16-19.

Moncada, S., Higgs, A., "The L-arginine-nitric oxide pathway." *The New England Journal of Medicine,* 1993; 329(27): 2002-2012.

Pet Food Institute: Nutrition Assurance Program–PFI Handbook. Pet Food Institute, Washington, D.C., 1994; 72 pp.

Ralston Purina Company, *Nutrition and Management of Dogs & Cats.* Ralston Purina, 1987.

Thatcher, C.D., "Answer Nutritional Trend with Improved Education." *Veterinary Forum,* October 1992; 24-25.

Wills, J.M., Simpson, K.W. (Eds.), *The Waltham Book of Clinical Nutrition of the Dog and Cat.* Pergamon Press, Oxford, 1993; 136 pp.

Questions to Ponder . . .

When is the appropriate time to wean puppies?

Should I supplement my growing puppy with calcium or vitamin D?

What kind of maintenance diet should my dog graduate to after puppy food?

What is the difference between maintenance diets and geriatric diets?

When should I switch my older dog to a senior diet?

When should I begin feeding a higher quality food to my pregnant bitch?

What are the exact protein, fat and carbohydrate requirements that my working dog needs?

Are there any different nutritional requirements for my injured dog?

**Learn the answers to these
and many other nutrition questions
in Chapter 2.**

2
NUTRITIONAL NEEDS AT DIFFERENT LIFE STAGES

Dogs are very versatile when it comes to meeting their dietary needs. They are not strict carnivores by nature. They do have teeth for tearing flesh and their digestive tracts are short and simple, but they do not have a strict requirement for meat in their diet. Meat protein is easier for dogs to digest and contains more optimal blends of amino acids from which proteins are made. In the 20,000 or so years that dogs have been man's companion, however, they have gradually become accustomed to the foods we eat, and have lost their need to be strict carnivores. By comparison, the cat is still a strict carnivore and must receive animal protein in its diet.

Nutritional needs for a dog change during his lifetime. Nutrients that are critical when he is a pup are less important when he reaches adulthood. A bitch has different needs when she is pregnant or lactating than when she is spayed or not used for breeding. Finally, as your dog ages, his nutritional needs also change. Superimposed on this is the realization that other factors such as sporting competition, the show circuit, and disease have an impact on nutrition.

FEEDING THE NEWBORN PUPPY

Soon after pups are born, they should begin nursing their mother. Their level of nutrition will parallel that of the dam. Pups must nurse extensively during the first twenty-four hours because that is when they receive the antibody-rich colostrum from their mother. Colostrum helps protect them from infection for the first two to three months of life. Pups should be allowed to nurse for at least six weeks before they are completely weaned from their mother. Supplemental feeding may be started by as early as three weeks of age.

It is critical that puppies nurse effectively. The energy needs of growing pups are nearly three times what they are for an adult when compared on the basis of metabolic body size. Small or weak pups must be closely supervised because they may appear to nurse yet can eventually weaken and die. If they nurse ineffectively, they may ingest only air, not milk. If the bitch has limited milk supplies, it is best to let the smallest pups drink their fill and supplement the larger ones with milk replacer. Weak puppies that do not improve within a few hours must be tube fed or given some other method of supportive therapy.

ORPHANED PUPPIES

If puppies are orphaned before six weeks of age and no nursing foster bitch is available, you need to take full responsibility for the pups' nutrition. These puppies may not grow as rapidly or as strongly as naturally reared pups but, if properly managed, they should be healthy and normal within a few months. Most pups, reach fifty percent of their mature weight by sixteen to twenty weeks of age. The age at which they reach their final weight, however, varies with the breed, type of diet, and amount of calories consumed on a daily basis.

Orphaned puppies need to be reared on a towel-covered heating pad to mimic the moist heat provided naturally by the bitch. Place the heating pad so that the pups can avoid it if they get too hot. A hot-water bottle can also be used but will require frequent reheating. Keep a thermometer near the pups so that the ambient temperature can be monitored and adjusted as necessary. If the room is not humidity controlled, pans of water will be needed near the area to provide a desired relative humidity of near 50 percent.

Orphan puppies should be fed a commercially available canine milk replacer. Cow's milk is inferior to canine milk replacer because bitch's milk contains less lactose and more milk fat. Cow's milk also has more carbohydrate and less protein than does bitch's milk. There has been some recent concern that canine milk replacers might cause cataracts in pups. Several theories have been proposed, including low levels of the important amino acid arginine and a problem with certain forms of sugar. The risk is highest in pups given milk replacer exclusively at less than one week of age. Ideally, pups should consume bitch's milk exclusively for the first few weeks of life so they ingest adequate amounts of important nutrients, antibodies, enzymes, and hormones from the dam. Milk replacer should be given to pups less than one week of age only if no bitch's milk is available. If the bitch has no milk, milk replacer is still preferred to cow's

The needs of growing puppies are different from those of adult dogs Photo © Click the Photo Connection.

milk. If the bitch has limited milk supplies, it is best to let the smallest pups drink their fill and supplement the larger ones with some milk replacer. Avoid the temptation to prepare elaborate formulations combining ingredients such as milk, baby cereal, eggs, meat, vitamins and minerals. They are expensive and time consuming and, for the most part, inferior to commercial milk replacers. There is much more likelihood of introducing a nutritional imbalance with these formulations unless you are confident that you can indeed prepare a balanced ration.

Young orphaned pups need to be bottle-fed. Special pup-size feeding bottles are commercially available. Hold the pup in your hand with the head tilted up during feeding. Do not feed the formula too quickly because there is a danger of the food ending up in the lungs. This can cause a very dangerous situation called aspiration pneumonia. Very young pups may need to be tube fed. You veterinarian will give you instructions on how to perform this procedure. After feeding, "burp" the puppies in the same manner as you do a baby. This helps relieve trapped gas.

When pups are accustomed to bottle feeding, they can normally be maintained with feedings every six hours. This needs to be individualized depending on the pups and their specific needs. More frequent feedings are sometimes necessary, but pups need their sleep, and too many feedings can be stressful and counterproductive.

By two or three weeks of age, pups can drink milk replacer from a shallow pan to augment their bottle feeding. You can encourage them to drink from the pan by soaking a finger in the liquid, letting them suckle, then leading them to the pan. The milk must be fresh and warm and the pan scrupulously clean. After the pups have been allowed to lap milk replacer for several days, add some solid food to the milk pan. Once food has been introduced, it is important to provide fresh, clean water on a regular basis. Eventually, phase out the bottle-feeding over several days. Pups can then be gradually converted to puppy food by seven to eight weeks of age.

FEEDING THE GROWING PUPPY

By two months of age, pups should be fed puppy food. They are in an important phase of life—growth! Skeletal development is at its peak for the first six months of life. Nutritional deficiencies and/or imbalances during this period are more devastating than at any other time. During this phase, your dog develops a functioning immune system, dramatically adds bone and muscle mass, and he learns all about his new environment, developing proper socialization behaviors all the while. There is no more critical time to ensure proper nutrition.

This is not the time to scrimp on nutrition. Puppies in their active growth phase should be fed a high-quality diet that meets their specific nutritional needs. Purchase a food specially designed for this growth period, and be certain that feeding trials have been conducted by the manufacturer. Keep pups on this diet until twelve to eighteen months of age, depending on the breed. Many large breeds do not mature until eighteen months of age and so benefit from a longer period on these rations.

When it comes to feeding schedules, most puppies do best being fed at specific times throughout the day rather than having food available at all times. Put the food down for twenty to thirty minutes, then remove it until the next feeding. Pups initially need to be fed two to three meals daily until they are three to four months old. By three or four months of age, many puppies can be fed three meals daily. Continue this schedule until they are twelve to fifteen months old, then feed twice daily when they are converted to adult food.

Dietary Needs of Growing Puppies

Feed high-quality food formulated for growth.
Establish a regular feeding schedule at frequent intervals.
Do not overfeed.
Avoid supplementation.

It is important for pups to receive regular feedings, but it is just as important that they not be overfed. Puppies that are overfed, especially the large breeds, are more prone to bone diseases when they grow too fast or become overweight. Keep pups lean and healthy during their growth phase, and disorders such as hip dysplasia and osteochondrosis are less likely to occur.

It should come as no surprise that the nutritional needs of pups are different from those of adults. Even the amino acids needed are different, and pups require much more arginine than adults. They also require many more calories. Vitamin and mineral imbalances can be disastrous for a puppy. Vitamin E deficiency can cause muscle degeneration in

PURINA
BODY CONDITION SYSTEM

1 EMACIATED Ribs, lumbar vertebrae, pelvic bones and all bony prominences evident from a distance. No discernible body fat. Obvious loss of muscle mass.

2 VERY THIN Ribs, lumbar vertebrae and pelvic bones easily visible. No palpable fat. Some evidence of other bony prominence. Minimal loss of muscle mass.

3 THIN Ribs easily palpated and may be visible with no palpable fat. Tops of lumbar vertebrae visible. Pelvic bones becoming prominent. Obvious waist and abdominal tuck.

4 UNDERWEIGHT Ribs easily palpable, with minimal fat covering. Waist easily noted, viewed from above. Abdominal tuck evident.

5 IDEAL Ribs palpable without excess fat covering. Waist observed behind ribs when viewed from above. Abdomen tucked up when viewed from side.

6 OVERWEIGHT Ribs palpable with slight excess fat covering. Waist is discernable viewed from above but is not prominent. Abdominal tuck apparent.

7 HEAVY Ribs palpable with difficulty, heavy fat cover. Noticeable fat deposits over lumbar area and base of tail. Waist absent or barely visible. Abdominal tuck may be absent.

8 OBESE Ribs not palpable under very heavy fat cover, or palpable only with significant pressure. Heavy fat deposits over lumbar area and base of tail. Waist absent. No abdominal tuck. Obvious abdominal distention may be present.

9 GROSSLY OBESE Massive fat deposits over thorax, spine and base of tail. Waist and abdominal tuck absent. Fat deposits on neck and limbs. Obvious abdominal distention.

This Body Condition System was developed and tested at the Purina Pet Care Center and has been documented in the following publications:
Laflamme DP. **Body Condition Scoring and Weight Maintenance.** Proc N Am Vet Conf, Jan 16-21, 1993, Orlando, FL, pp 290-291
Laflamme DP, Kealy RD, Schmidt DS. **Estimation of Body Fat by Body Condition Score.** J Vet Int Med 1994; 8:154.
Laflamme DP, Kuhlman G, Linder DF, Kealy RD, Schmidt DA. **Obesity Management in Dogs.** J Vet Clin Nutr 1994; 1: 59-65

pups, while choline deficiency can interfere with liver function. Pantothenic acid deficiency impairs the growth rate, and fewer antibodies are produced when pups are exposed to viruses. Vitamin D deficiency can result in osteoporosis, while vitamin A deficiency can cause abnormal bone development, eye and skin problems, and a greater susceptibility to infection. All of these can be prevented by providing a high-quality diet designed specifically for this important growth phase.

One pitfall to be avoided is supplementing pups with protein, vitamins, or minerals. It is easy to become overzealous with supplements, but this is not wise. Most of the mistakes are made with supplements containing calcium, phosphorus and/or vitamin D. You may think that these supplements will help your growing puppy by adding to his calcium resources. After all, children are encouraged to drink milk to build strong bones and teeth. Why not pups? The reason is because growth rations have been formulated with an ideal ratio of calcium to phosphorus, usually around 1.3 parts calcium to every 1 part phosphorus. This is the optimal ratio for healthy bone growth. This can be quickly unbalanced by providing calcium, phosphorus, vitamin D, or combinations. There is more than adequate proof that these supplements are responsible for many bone deformities seen in growing dogs. Avoid the temptation to supplement. If you really must supplement, select moderate amounts of the water-soluble vitamins (vitamin C and the B vitamins) instead of the minerals or fat-soluble vitamins. If you must select a fat-soluble vitamin for supplementation, use vitamin E rather than vitamins A, D or K.

Now is the time to ensure optimal nutrition and create proper eating habits that will last a lifetime. Learn how to feed pups amounts that won't make them fat, but don't deprive them either. And, don't try to second-guess nature by supplementing the diet with potentially dangerous nutrients, even if it appears to make sense on the surface. This is definitely not the time to make mistakes with your dog's nutrition.

FEEDING THE ADULT

When pups become adults, they enter a new nutritional phase—maintenance. Once they've finished growing, the "growth" diets provide more calories and protein than they really need. If they continue on the growth diets, they may become obese. The goal is to switch them to a maintenance ration that is balanced correctly for this phase of life.

The term "maintenance" is used loosely, but it is important to understand what is really meant by it. Dogs require maintenance rations when they are living a comfortable and relatively stress-free existence as a house pet. A dog staked by a four-foot-long chain in the backyard is not being "maintained." A dog tossed outside at night in the cold to patrol a lot is also not being "maintained." The maintenance energy requirements (MER) can be calculated with a mathematical formula for dogs that are not kept as house pets. This book is dedicated to the caring dog owner, however, and these exceptions will not be discussed.

There are many choices when it comes to selecting a maintenance diet. Most commercially available foods are combinations of animal-based and plant-based ingredients. The animal-based ingredients are tastier for dogs and easier for them to digest, but the plant-based ingredients are cheaper. To be cost-effective, most commercial dog foods blend ingredients from both plant and animal sources.

In general, dogs can do well on maintenance rations containing predominantly plant- or animal-based ingredients as long as that ration is specifically formulated to meet maintenance-level requirements. This contention should be supported by studies performed by the manufacturer in accordance with American Association of Feed Control Officials (AAFCO). In Canada, these products should be certified by the Canadian Veterinary Medical Association to meet maintenance requirements.

There are many criteria by which you might select a dog food for maintenance purposes. A dog that is fairly sedentary, has finished growing, is not in competition, and is not being used for breeding can accommodate varying amounts of dietary fat, protein, and carbohydrate. They are the classic low-stress dogs for which the maintenance requirements were designed. These dogs do well on most commercial or home-made diets. In fact, it is probably a mistake to feed these animals super-premium dog foods because they tend to become obese.

Many manufacturers of premium dog foods market their products on the basis of ingredients. Most of the super-premium diets have a higher content of meat and meat by-products. Most of the cheaper brands of dog food have a higher content of cereal. It is not always easy, however, to tell the difference by looking at the pet-food label. For instance, the

Maintenance rations are intended to meet the minimum requirements for stress-free house pets. Photo © Click the Photo Connection.

label may read "chicken, corn-gluten meal, ground corn, . . ." and so on, leading you to believe that chicken is the main ingredient. In fact, by dividing corn into individual ingredients such as ground corn, corn-gluten meal, corn flour, and corn bran, the total cereal content of the diet may be camouflaged. You think you're feeding a predominantly chicken-based diet when cereal is actually the primary ingredient. Canned pet foods contain more than 75 percent water, yet this can also be confusing when you examine the label. It may list chicken or beef as the main ingredient but when you examine the analysis, it lists "moisture" at about 78 percent.

Dietary Needs of Adult Dogs

Choose the dog's food based on his activity and stress levels. Food should be easily digestible and provide nutrients slight above minimum requirements.

There's nothing wrong with feeding a cereal-based diet to dogs on maintenance rations, and this is the most economical diet. Unfortunately, corn is low in certain essential amino acids, and this must be remedied by complementation, a process combining different protein sources to provide a suitable blend that *does* meet requirements. In the least expensive brands, this can often be done by selecting soy as a vegetable protein source. Most dogs tolerate soy well, but some dogs are soy intolerant and do not do well on these rations. Certain breeds, such as the Irish Setter, the Siberian Husky and the Chinese Shar-Pei have a higher incidence of soy intolerance, although any breed is susceptible. Soy also contains some sugars (e.g., raffinose, stachyose) that are *not* digestible by dogs but that *are* digestible by bacteria. As a result, the sugars may get digested by microbes in the colon, producing gas. This may contribute to flatulence or "windiness" in a dog. Other ingredients in soy can also be problematic if the food is not processed adequately.

Keep in mind that maintenance rations meet only the minimum requirements for stress-free house pets. There are many stressful situations that can change a dog's nutrient requirements from maintenance levels to above-maintenance levels. Dogs housed outside in cold weather, dogs that are exercised extensively, dogs that are used for breeding, and dogs that are ill often will benefit from eating foods that provide more than just minimum requirements. Also, most of the dogs that are first switched from puppy foods to maintenance foods still have some growing to do. It is therefore recommended that you feed your dog a diet that contains easily digested ingredients that provide nutrients at least slightly above minimum requirements. Typically, these foods will be intermediate in price between the most expensive, super-premium diets and the cheapest generic diets. Select diets that have been substantiated by feeding trials to meet maintenance requirements, that contain wholesome ingredients, and that are recommended by your veterinarian. Don't select a food based on price alone, on company advertising, or on total protein content.

FEEDING THE AGING DOG

Dogs are considered elderly when they have achieved 75 percent of their anticipated life span. This obviously differs for each breed. A Great Dane may be considered old at six years of age, while a Poodle may not be seen as elderly until ten years of age. And, there is so much variability between individual dogs that even breed generalizations are merely guidelines. It is important to recognize the needs of these "senior" pets before the onset of age-related problems, while nutrition can still provide the best preventive medicine.

As a dog ages, his metabolism slows. There is a decreased sense of thirst that can result in dehydration if not detected. At the same time, if maintenance rations are fed in the same amounts and metabolism is slowing, weight gain is common. Obesity is the last thing you want to contend with in an elderly pet, because it increases the risk of other health-related problems. On the other hand, an elderly dog may lose weight, and this is not good either. The older dog doesn't have as acute a sense of smell as he had when he was younger. Dental problems also plague him. Approximately 85 percent of dogs over four years have periodontal disease. This can result in painful chewing, infection and tooth loss. All of these conditions can contribute to undesirable weight loss as your dog ages. Dental health care is an important part of overall wellness. Don't wait until your dog is old to consider the impact of routine dental care.

As dogs age, most of their organs do not function as well as they did in youth. In the digestive system, the liver, pancreas, and gallbladder do not work at peak capacity. The intestines have more difficulty extracting all the nutrients from the food consumed. The colon doesn't have the motility that it used to have, and constipation becomes more common. In the cardiovascular system, the heart has been beating relentlessly for years and is more likely to show the effects of overwork. The blood vessels aren't as flexible anymore, and the heart valves are not as efficient. The kidneys contain a finite number of filtering units that are not replaced as they succumb. A gradual decline in kidney function is considered a normal part of aging.

A responsible approach to geriatric nutrition is to realize that degenerative changes are a normal part of aging. The goal is to minimize the potential damage by taking appropriate measures while your dog is still well. If you wait until your elderly dog is ill before you change his diet, the job will be much harder.

A geriatric diet often provides fewer calories per serving than the growth or maintenance rations to accommodate a slower metabolism. If the energy content of the diet is not restricted, but a dog exercises less, then he will become obese. Of course, this is not true for *all* senior dogs. If your dog loses weight with age, you may need to increase the calorie content of his diet. If you dog tends toward obesity, however, you will need to reduce the fat and protein contents of the diet and provide more calories in the form of easily digestible carbohydrates. Older dogs benefit from essential fatty acids like linoleic acid but have little need for saturated fats or other oils. If you provide high-quality vegetable oils (safflower oil, flaxseed oil), you will meet the essential fatty acid requirements. These oils also allow for the absorption of the important fat-soluble vitamins.

Most elderly dogs do better on diets that are easily digested. Geriatric diets are typically low in fiber because dogs have a difficult time absorbing fiber. There are some medical conditions that benefit from fiber, including diabetes mellitus, colitis, and constipation, and a geriatric diet can be augmented with psyllium (*Metamucil*) or pectin if your dog requires a higher fiber content. Because the digestive system becomes less efficient as a dog ages, a diet that is more digestible is also more likely to provide needed vitamins, minerals, amino acids, and essential fatty acids.

Older dogs don't need *more* protein in their diet, but they do benefit from *better-quality* protein. The protein content of the diet is only a source of essential amino acids. Protein is typically hard to digest and requires metabolism in the liver and filtering by the kidneys. All of these functions can be impaired in the older dog. Your goal is to provide lower levels of total protein (typically fourteen to twenty-one percent of dry matter) but higher levels of the essential amino acids. You need to provide your aging dog with the proteins that *do the most good*. If you severely limit protein in your elderly dog's diet, especially if he is losing weight, you can induce protein deficiency and adversely affect immune function and enzyme activity.

It is very important to understand the dynamics of vitamin and mineral nutrition in the older dog. Older dogs need higher levels of vitamins A, B_1, B_6, B_{12}, and E than they did when they were younger. Zinc is also needed to help with body repairs and to bolster the immune system. Most maintenance diets are much too high in sodium (salt) for the geriatric dog and the levels are restricted in the "senior" diets. These diets also take into account the changing dynamics of calcium and phosphorus metabolism and slightly reduce the phosphorus content to lessen the workload of the kidneys.

There are many options for feeding your senior dog. Ideally, you should change his diet when he is still healthy and has not slowed down too much or become ill. Switch him to a senior diet when he has achieved about seventy-five percent of his expected life span, or when recommended by your veterinarian. This may stall the onset of heart, kidney, and digestive disorders by being more "user-friendly" and not overtaxing his system. For example, a low-protein diet may not prevent kidney disease, but it certainly is easier to handle for a dog experiencing any impairment of kidney function. The diet should contain ample amounts of the amino acids that dogs require and lesser amounts of the ones deemed dispensable. A low-salt diet won't necessarily prevent heart disease, but it is certainly helpful in dogs with impaired cardiac efficiency.

Elderly dogs need to be treated as individuals. While some dogs benefit from the nutrition found in "senior" diets, others might do better on the highly digestible puppy and super-premium diets, which provide an excellent blend of digestibility and amino acid content. Unfortunately, many are higher in salt and phosphorus than the older dog really needs.

It is *not* advisable to continue to feed your elderly dog maintenance rations even if you cut down the amount you feed to limit calories. Maintenance rations were formulated to meet minimum requirements for stress-free house pets. Advancing age is a definite stress on the system, and maintenance rations do not optimally meet the protein, fat, vitamin and mineral requirements of an aging dog. If you must feed this diet for economic reasons, give your dog a daily vitamin-mineral supplement designed for "seniors." These supplements are typically rich in the B vitamins and the antioxidant nutrients vitamin A, vitamin C, vitamin E, and selenium, as well as zinc. There is also a good argument for providing high-quality table scraps to the very senior dog that tends to lose weight. Freshly prepared chicken, beef, organ meats, and cooked grains and vegetables can provide a tasty and nutritious treat for dogs that may not be eating enough of their own food. At this time of life, there is no point in being hard-nosed about the evils of table scraps unless there is a medical reason for doing so.

FEEDING THE PREGNANT OR NURSING BITCH

Care of the pregnant or nursing bitch presents certain nutritional challenges which must be considered and met. Prior to being bred, the bitch should be in good body condition, not too thin and definitely not obese. She should be in excellent dietary status to enhance the chances of conception and then maintained on an increasing nutritional plane as her body strives to meet the needs of pregnancy and then lactation (milk production). It is important to understand that the nutrient requirements may increase as much as four times over usual adult maintenance levels. Providing proper nutrition to the reproducing dam directly influences the quality of the milk she produces, the survival of the pups, and their birth weight.

Usual maintenance diets are not suitable for the pregnant or lactating bitch. They do not provide enough energy to meet her needs on a daily basis. The diet must be complete and balanced for this stage of life and provide at least 1600 digestible calories for every pound of food fed. This type of diet should be introduced before the fourth week of pregnancy when nutritional demands begin to skyrocket. Acceptable diets usually contain more meat than do regular diets, and only certain super-premium and canned dog foods actually meet these criteria. Many commercial canned cat foods also meet the criteria and are useful in toy and miniature breeds of dogs. These claims should be supported by actual feeding trials, not just lab analysis. With regular maintenance diets, the bitch is unlikely to consume enough food to meet her actual needs. It is also difficult to "supplement" regular maintenance diets to be suitable for pregnancy and lactation. If this option is an economic necessity, it will be necessary to add eggs, meat (with fat) or small amounts of super-premium canned dog foods or cat foods to the ration.

Dietary Needs of Pregnant/Nursing Bitches

Choose a feed that supplies at least 1600 calories per lb. of food and that is high in meat content.

Expect bitches to consume up to 40% more than their normal ration during the latter half of pregnancy.

Most bitches do not show appreciable weight gain until into their fourth week of pregnancy (gestation). Over the final month of pregnancy, it is not unusual for food consumption to increase by 40 percent. As the pups occupy more and more area in the abdomen, the bitch will appreciate being fed several small meals throughout the day rather than one or two large ones. During the final 2 weeks of pregnancy the pups, placenta, fluids, and developing mammary glands all contribute to additional weight gain. Within a day or two of littering, however, it is not unusual for the bitch to lose her appetite. It normally is recovered within a day after whelping. It is important that the bitch not be underweight or overweight at this time. Underweight bitches may have difficulty meeting the nutritional needs of the pups after whelping. Overweight bitches have more trouble with delivery, have less efficient lactation and increased risk of complications for the puppies and themselves.

After whelping, the dam has an additional nutritional drain. She now has attentive pups hungering for her milk and the challenge of meeting her own needs in the process. She may not have time or inclination to leave the pups so care must be taken to make her food and water accessible, palatable, and laden with energy (calories). As the pups grow so does her need to provide for their nutritional needs. This reaches a zenith when they are about 3-4 weeks of age, at which time she may be consuming 2–4 times the amount of calories she did when she wasn't pregnant. After this time the pups start to take more of an interest in solid food and demand for milk then diminishes. When the pups are fully weaned at 6 weeks of age, the food consumption of the dam is down to about 50 percent above non-pregnant levels and continues to diminish.

Nutritional supplementation can be helpful during pregnancy within very strict guidelines. It is much better to provide a wholesome, well-balanced diet than to predict the benefits of nutritional supplements. A good choice would be a "senior" vitamin-mineral supplement that includes the B vitamins, vitamin E and zinc. Supplements containing significant amounts of calcium, phosphorus or vitamin D should only be given under the direction of a veterinarian.

FEEDING THE STUD DOG

With so much attention focused on the brood bitch, sometimes the stud dog gets short-changed. Males need proper nutrition too if they are going to perform reproductively at their best. Dogs shouldn't be too thin, or too fat, but being normal to slightly overweight is best. Dogs that are too thin or too fat often have medical problems that could affect their ability to properly mate and impregnate a bitch. The amount and type of food fed should be adjusted, before breeding, to bring the male in optimal body condition.

Most stud dogs can be maintained on moderately priced dog foods and do not require the energy-dense foods fed to the brood bitch. However, check the label and make sure the ration has been assessed by feeding trials (AAFCO or CVMA). The diet should be fed so that the dog maintains optimal body condition, not necessarily the recommended level on the label. Stud dogs are individuals and some may require more or less than recommended to maintain optimal body condition.

Currently, research is underway to examine in more detail the role of specific nutrients in sperm development. For example, deficiencies of beta-carotene and vitamin A have resulted in testicular degeneration in other species; ascorbic acid may be involved in normal sperm production; pyridoxine is involved in the release of pituitary hormones; chromium is important in maintaining the integrity of nucleic acids; and zinc has been reported as a cause of testicular degeneration in some species. However, there is not enough research done in the dog to make any specific recommendations.

Avoid the temptation to supplement the stud's diet, although some healthful meat and vegetables isn't a bad idea. Most vitamin-mineral supplements will not perk up the sperm, and some have definite adverse effects. A standard one-a-day vitamin is fine, but high doses of specific nutrients are not recommended.

FEEDING THE SHOW DOG

The requirements for feeding a show dog are significantly different from those for a field-trial dog and also different from the typical maintenance ration for a sedentary house pet. The goal of feeding the show dog is to optimize the physical characteristics of the dog, not meet its minimum

Twelve-year-old Shetland Sheepdog shown after winning the Veteran Bitch Class. Photo by Koehler.

dietary requirements. Most breeders are adamant about the foods they will and won't feed their dogs. When they sell puppies, they often provide dietary recommendations for "what works for them." Whether there is any scientific rationale for the choice often takes a back seat to personal experience. Even poorly balanced diets may produce a champion and this attests more to the resiliency of dogs than to the intuitiveness of breeders.

Most show dogs benefit from a blend of protein, fat and carbohydrate and do not need the energy-dense format found in performance diets. These performance diets often provide too much fat, and the wrong kind of fats to promote good skin and haircoat. A maintenance ration containing "wholesome ingredients" should be provided and it needn't be high in protein, fat, or carbohydrate. These dogs truly benefit from a "balanced" ration, not one of extremes.

Most dog foods intended for show dogs are primarily meat-based. Soy protein contains much indigestible fiber and some highly-bred canines do not tolerate soy as well as meat. Chicken, beef, pork, and lamb are all well digested by dogs. If these ingredients make up the protein basis of the dog food, a high-protein ration is not needed. Meat protein provides ample amounts of the essential amino acids that are required. If there is too much meat in the diet, the content of saturated fat will also increase and this is counterproductive to enhancing the skin and hair coat. By incorporating easily digestible carbohydrate into the diet, such as rice, potatoes or corn starch, calories can be provided without relying on high levels of fat or protein.

Supplementation of foods intended for show dogs is commonplace and so there is no point in recommending against it. It is better to discuss options for sensible supplementation that does not "unbalance" a balanced ration. If the starting point is a good-quality "maintenance" ration rather than a performance ration, better results will be seen with or without supplementation.

Fat and oil supplements are commonly given to dogs and the show dog is no exception. Unfortunately, these fats and oils are often poorly formulated and provide more calories than essential nutrients. The purpose of supplementing with fats is to provide the essential linoleic acid to the diet. The best source of this fatty acid is safflower oil or flaxseed oil. Corn oil is only about 50 percent linoleic acid and the other vegetable oils contain even less. It is cheaper and more effective to purchase safflower or flaxseed oil directly rather than the vegetable oil mixtures found in pet supply outlets. Don't overdo it—add no more than a tablespoon per day to the food. Another fatty acid that might be helpful to skin and haircoat is gamma-linolenic acid found in evening primrose oil or borage oil. These can be found in health food stores or from your veterinarian. Veterinary products often combine the plant oil with marine oil for added benefit; the combination product is not currently available from health food stores.

Protein supplements are not needed for the show dog and can be harmful. The real need is for essential amino acids which are present in the protein source itself. All protein ingested is "broken down" first to individual amino acids. The most important amino acids for skin, haircoat, and claws (nails) are the sulfur-containing methionine, cysteine and cystine. Additional protein in the diet can not be stored and will be converted to fat or excreted by the kidneys.

Vitamins and minerals are important to healthy skin and fur but indiscriminant supplementation is unlikely to be beneficial. A general "stress" vitamin-mineral supplement is helpful as it provides a broad spectrum of important B vitamins and antioxidants such as vitamin A (or beta-carotene), vitamin C, vitamin E and selenium. It is unwise to supplement with additional calcium and phosphorus because this frequently results in bone deformities in growing dogs.

Many other supplements are used by breeders that have no scientific rationale. Some of the most common are brewer's yeast and kelp. Brewer's yeast is a good source of B vitamins but it also lacks the much-needed vitamins A, C and E. Despite the contentions of many to the contrary, scientific studies of brewer's yeast have not found it to repel fleas. Kelp is a type of seaweed and is indeed a rich source of vitamins and minerals. It is not nutritionally complete on its own but does provide several useful amino acids in addition to the vitamins and minerals. In most cases, if a dog improves on brewer's yeast or kelp, it indicates that the dog food being fed previously was not properly fortified. In this instance, it is usually more cost-effective to switch to a better diet that to continue supplementing with these products.

FEEDING THE WORKING OR COMPETING ANIMAL

The needs of the canine athlete are significantly different from those of the typical sedentary house pet. The stresses, both physical and mental, that these dogs experience increase their requirements for most nutrients. Their need for energy (calories) may be even greater than that of the pregnant and lactating bitch.

The canine athlete often requires "performance" rations that provide calories in a very energy-dense ration. These diets should contain a minimum of 1900 kcal of metabolizable energy per pound of food fed. These diets tend to be high in fat and readily digestible. When possible, complex carbohydrates also provide an important source of energy but for some rations that are extremely energy-dense, there may not be room for that much carbohydrate. Since there is no absolute requirement for carbohydrate in the diet, protein needs must be met first, and then those for fat. Because these diets are energy-dense, competing animals don't need to eat as much to meet their needs. Because they don't eat as much, it is important that these diets also be high in the critical vitamins, minerals, and amino acids or deficiencies could result.

Animals that exercise at supramaximal levels (e.g., racing greyhounds) are no longer engaging in aerobic exercise. These animals have anaerobic breakdown of glycogen (storage form of glucose) and lactic acid

The ability to perform well in a particular activity or event is closely tied to the dogs' nutrional needs. Dogs performing in ring competitions do not have the high energy requirements that racing greyhounds have, and dogs running in endurance races have significantly different needs than sprint racing dogs. Left: Wire Fox Terrier retrieving over a high jump. Photo by Judith Strom. Below: Sled dogs racing. Photo by B.McKinney.

accumulates in the muscle. Because the muscles use more energy than the aerobic system can provide, the muscles can experience "oxygen debt." In contrast, dogs performing in ring competitions and agility trials do not suffer from this oxygen debt. The diet fed to racing greyhounds should also contain a reasonable amount of highly-digestible carbohydrate to enable prompt restoration of muscle glycogen levels following racing and training.

Dogs running endurance races have significantly different requirements than racing greyhounds. During an endurance test, fatty acids provide the most energy to muscle cells. This depends on the dog being appropriately trained, fed a diet high in fat, and having high blood levels of fatty acids. Fat also provides most of the energy for dogs to withstand cold temperatures. Meat tends to be high in fat, but racing dogs benefit from other fatty acids. Coconut and palm oils can be absorbed without much digestive effort and without the participation of bile secretions. Fish oils are also important, and are thought to decrease inflammation in the intestines, which is common with high-calorie diets.

Huskies tend to have lower maintenance energy requirements than breeds of similar weight. Sled dogs trained for endurance can maintain a pace of 10 miles per hour for 10-14 hours a day for several days. To do this, their diets must consist heavily of fats. However, their caloric requirements change depending on their level of activity. The maintenance requirement for a 45-pound husky not in training is about 1000-1200 Kcal of ME; this increases by about 15-20% during light training (3-5 miles per day), by about 70% during moderate training (6-12 miles per day) and effectively doubles during heavy training (20 miles per day). However, during stressful events like the Iditarod, the requirements increase by a factor of seven or eight. Since it is unwise to quickly change the diet, gradual changes must be made to the diet throughout the training and racing schedule to meet the requirements of the dogs without causing digestive upset. Most racing diets provide about 35% fat, 25% carbohydrate, and 40% protein. Recent research suggests that dogs fed 40% of their calories as protein fare better during strenuous training than dogs fed diets with less protein. However, amino acids play a very minor role in muscular work. Feeding a high fat diet during training (60% fat, 25% protein, 15% carbohydrate) seems to accustom a dog's muscles to burn fat more efficiently and spare carbohydrate use. A carbohydrate "snack" during rest periods seems to enhance muscle glycogen repletion.

As a general rule, working dogs need a 10% increase in their caloric intake for every hour of work activity. Thus, in a typical full day's event, an increased caloric intake of 40-50% is required. Also, as the exercise becomes more prolonged rather than intense, the fat content of the diet should go up and the carbohydrate portion should go down. Similarly, the protein content should increase from 34% during brief, intense exercise, to 40% during competition or prolonged work. This can be accomplished, in practical terms, by feeding a restricted amount of premium dog food during idle times, and increasing the amount or supplementing with meat or high-protein canned food during periods of activity. Sudden changes to high-protein, high-fat diets from maintenance rations are not recommended and can interfere with performance.

Human athletes sometimes train with dissociated diets designed to transiently produce a glycogen overload. This should not be done in greyhounds because it can cause a condition called rhabdomyolysis (tying up) which damages cells and tissues. To prevent excessive lactic acid buildup and avoid glycogen overload in the muscle, racing greyhounds should be fed a balanced diet (e.g., 40% nitrogen-free extract, 30% fat, and 30% protein). Simple sugars should not be fed, and about one-quarter of the fat intake should be provided as palm, coconut and fish oils. A maintenance diet for non-racing greyhounds should provide about 27% protein, 10% fat, 3% fiber, and 55% carbohydrate.

Dietary Needs of High Performance Dogs

Feed a balanced "performance" ration with a significant amount of the calories in the form of complex carbohydrates such as corn, wheat, rice, and potatoes.
Dogs performing at exertion levels need additional fat. This allows them to consume more calories without eating twice as much food.
Do not feed high-fat diets to average canine athletes.
Feed a diet high in, or supplement with, stress formula vitamins and minerals.

Working dogs tend to fatigue when lactic acid levels accumulate in their bloodstream. This tends to occur when dogs get excited or get exhausted. It is therefore best if racing huskies and dogs involved in hunting, tracking, field trials or ring competitions be kept quiet before competing.

The ideal diet for dogs competing in field events is a balanced "performance" ration that provides a significant amount of the calories in the form of complex carbohydrates such as corn, wheat, rice, and potatoes. This is the same strategy used by human athletes. For those dogs that perform at exertion levels well above those of the regular canine athlete (e.g., sled dogs), most of the energy will need to be provided as fat. Since fat provides more than twice as many calories as carbohydrate and protein for the same size serving, this regimen allows dogs to receive more calories without eating twice as much food. High-fat diets are not recommended for the average canine athlete. Inappropriately feeding these diets to regular athletes may cause digestive upset, diarrhea, and vomiting. Also, high-fat diets should never be fed to dogs with susceptibility to pancreatitis. Ask your veterinarian if you are not sure. These diets should be reserved for dogs performing exceptionally strenuous tasks.

Dietary supplementation may be useful in the canine athlete to help minimize the harm done by these stressful events. A vitamin-mineral supplement is advised, especially those formulated for "stress" purposes. These supplements usually provide B vitamins, zinc and the all-important antioxidant nutrients, vitamin A, vitamin C, vitamin E, and selenium. Additional supplements to be considered are chromium (GTF) and specific amino acids such as glutamine, ornithine, dimethylglycine, and carnitine.

FEEDING THE CONVALESCING DOG

When dogs are recovering from injury or surgery, they need additional calories and protein to help in the healing process. After all, wound healing, tissue repair and fighting infection are a major stress on the body. This increased need often occurs at the same time that animals may have a diminished appetite, so intervention is sometimes critical.

Getting extra protein and calories into a recovering dog can be challenging. They often don't have a full appetite so it is important to get them the needed nutrients in a calorie-dense format. This has already been done in human medicine, and several products available at pharmacies and grocery stores (e.g., Ensure, Isocal) are suitable for dogs in the short term. Specific canine enteral products are available from veterinarians. These products are like milk shakes and can be offered to recovering dogs as a drink treat. Sometimes a more inventive approach is needed.

These enteral products can be used to topdress the regular diet and can be made into a gruel by mixing with canned dog food. A kitchen blender is useful for creating just the right consistency for each individual dog. For those that can't be coaxed into self-feeding, the liquid or gruel combination can be administered carefully by syringe. "Careful" is a key word because forcing food into the throat can result in aspiration pneumonia. A dog that truly won't eat should be enterally (or parenterally) fed at a veterinary hospital. As dogs start to recover and are more interested in eating, high-quality snacks like boiled eggs and cottage cheese can be offered to help the process further along.

IN SUMMARY

Skeletal development is at its peak during the first 6 months of life. Thus, puppies should be fed puppy food until at least 12-18 months of age depending on the breed.

Vitamins and minerals including calcium, phosphorus, and vitamin D, must be fed at proper ratios to provide normal bone and muscle growth in the growing puppy.

Cereal diets may contain high concentrations of soy. Your dog should be watched closely for soy intolerance.

Better quality or more easily digestible protein sources are important in geriatric diets. The diet should be lower in total protein and high in essential amino acids.

Older dogs need larger amounts of vitamins A, B_1, B_6, B_{12}, and E, as well as increased amounts of zinc. The phosphorus content in the diet should be lower.

Nutritional needs of the pregnant bitch do not increase until about the fourth week of gestation. Her nutritional needs gradually increase throughout lactation and reach its highest level when the puppies are approximately 3-4 weeks of age.

Linoleic acid is the amino acid that is responsible for a healthy coat and good skin condition. The best source of linoleic acid is found in safflower oil or flaxseed oil.

The working dog's diet is composed of more readily digestible fat for energy, and increased amounts of vitamins, minerals, and amino acids.

Working dog diets can differ greatly depending on the type of work the dog is doing. A Greyhound uses an abundance of energy in a very short period of time using non-aerobic metabolism while a husky is an endurance animal and needs energy for a very long period of time using aerobic metabolism.

ADDITIONAL READING:

Alexander, J.E., Wood, L.L.H., "Growth studies in Labrador retrievers fed a coloric-dense diet: time restricted versus free-choice feeding." *Canine Practice,* 1987; 14(2): 41-47.

Bebiak, D.M., Lawler, D.F., and Reutzel, F.L., "Nutrition and management of the dog." *Vet. Clin. N. Am. Sm. Anim. Pract.*, 1987; 17(3): 505-533.

Brown, R.G., "Gastrointestinal upsets with high performance diets." *Can Vet J,* 1987; 28(7): 419-420.

Donoghue, S., "Providing proper nutrition for dogs at different stages of the life cycle." *Vet. Med.,* July 1991; 728-733.

Downs, L.G., Bolton, C.H., Crispin, S.M., Wills, J.M., "Plasma-lipoprotein lipids in 5 different breeds of dogs." *Research in Veterinary Science,* 1993; 54(1): 63-67.

Grandjean, D., Paragon, B.M., "Nutrition of Racing and Working Dogs. Part I. Energy Metabolism of Dogs." *Compendium on Continuing Education for the Practicing Veterinarian,* 1992; 14(12): 1608-1615.

Grandjean, Paragon, B.M., "Nutrition of Racing and Working Dogs. Part II. Determination of Energy Requirements and the Nutritional Impact off Stress." *Compendium on Continuing Education for the Practicing Veterinarian,* 1993; 15(1): 45-56.

Grandjean, D., Paragon, B.M., "Nutrition of Racing and Working Dogs. Part III. Dehydration, Mineral and Vitamin Adaptations, and Practical Feeding Guidelines." *Compendium on Continuing Education for the Practicing Veterinarian,* 1992; 14(12): 1608-1615.

Grandjean, D., Valette, J.P., Jouglin, M., et al., "Dietary supplementation with L-carnitine, vitamin-C and vitamin B-12 in sports dogs—experimental study with sled dogs." *Recueil de Medecine Veterinaraire,* 169(7); 543-551.

Hinchcliff, K.W., Olson, J., Crusberg, C., et al.," Serum biochemical changes in dogs competing in a long-distance sled race." *Journal of the American Veterinary Medical Association,* 1993; 202(3): 401-405.

Markham, R.W., and Hodgkins, E.M., "Geriatric Nutrition." *Veterinary Clinics of North America,* 1989; 19(1): 165-181.

Monson, W.J., "Orphan Rearing of Puppies and Kittens." *Veterinary Clinic of North America,* 1987; 17(3): 567-576.

Paragon, B.M., Granjean, D., "Ration formulation for the female dog during the reproductive period." *Recueil de Medecine Veterinaire,* 1993; 169(4): 223-230.

Rasmussen, K.M., "The influence of maternal nutrition on lactation." *Annual Review of Nutrition,* 1992; 12: 103-117.

Sokolowski, J.H., "Dietary Management of the Dog: Nutrition for Life." *Compend. Contin. Educ. Pract. Vet.,* 1982; 4(11): 920-924.

Questions to Ponder . . .

Why is meat not a quality protein source? Which sources are better?

What is a common problem some dogs have with soybeans in the diet?

How are omega-3 and omega-6 fatty acid supplements stored and why?

Would you feed a sedentary dog a diet high in animal fats? Why or why not? What would be better?

High fiber or "lite" diets should only be fed for a limited time and under veterinary supervision. Why?

Fats are stored as fat. How do proteins and carbohydrates end up being stored as fats?

What are some healthy choices for home prepared meals?

**Learn the answers to these
and many other nutrition questions
in Chapter 3.**

3
BASIC NUTRITIONAL COMPONENTS

$\mathbb{P}$roteins, carbohydrates, and fats are the basic nutritional components that provide energy in the diet. If food is considered fuel, then proteins, carbohydrates, and fats provide the energy in that fuel. Of course, vitamins and minerals are important as well, but the proteins, fats, and carbohydrates in the diet are what provide the energy (calories) to meet the daily needs of your dog. Water is critical too, because perhaps 70 percent of a dog's body is made up of water. But never underestimate the importance of proteins, carbohydrates, and fats in helping your dog to use the foods he eats for his own needs.

There are many misconceptions about the relative merits and detrimental effects of proteins, carbohydrates, and fats. Proteins are often regarded as "good" nutrients, fats as "bad," and most people don't know *what* to think about carbohydrates. The fact is, each of these items has its beneficial as well as detrimental aspects when considering dog nutrition. No one ingredient should be considered better than another.

PROTEINS

Proteins are given the most attention in any discussion of nutrition, but you might be surprised to learn that dogs have no real protein requirement at all. It's true! There's protein in eggs, milk, beef, and soy but also in fur, beaks, hoofs, and leather. Clearly, not all protein is created equal, and it is not fair to say that a dog requires 22 percent protein in his diet to keep him healthy. The *real* requirement is for *amino acids* from which the body can create its own proteins. When diets contain very high-quality protein, adult dogs require between 4 percent and 7 percent of their metabolizable energy to be supplied as protein. Growing puppies need significantly more, between 17 percent and 22 percent of their metabolizable energy.

Amino acids are considered the building blocks of protein. These nitrogen-containing compounds link up with one another to form simple and complex proteins, usually 100 to 300 amino acids in each protein molecule. When a dog eats protein-containing foods, the protein is broken down during digestion and the amino acids are absorbed from the intestines to be reused for the body's own needs. Many of the amino acids found in the body are not even required in the diet. Most are produced in the body from other amino acids that are consumed. Some amino acids are critical, however, and must be supplied in the diet. These are called essential amino acids. If your dog is deficient in them, he can experience problems, regardless of the total concentration of protein in the diet.

Protein serves other purposes as well. It provides a source of energy (calories), although less efficiently than either fats or carbohydrates. For instance, fats provide more than twice as much energy as equal amounts of protein or carbohydrates. Most forms of carbohydrates are easier for the body to digest and absorb than protein, which means that protein can provide equivalent amounts of energy but will consume more energy in the process.

There are reasons other than amino acid content and energy to include protein in the diet. Protein, especially animal protein, tends to make diets tastier. When heated in the presence of either carbohydrates or fats, proteins develop "reaction flavors" that increase the palatability of the diet. In dry dog foods, the protein can contribute to the structural integrity of the feed, while in canned foods it contributes to the texture. Because meats frequently lose their shape and texture when processed for pet foods, most "chunks" are actually texturized vegetable proteins.

It is also important to realize that dogs do not need meat to survive and thrive; they are not strict carnivores by nature, as is the cat. They are sometimes described as remnant carnivores because, although they can eat and digest both animal and plant proteins, their systems are most adapted to processing animal protein. Their teeth are sharp and designed for ripping flesh. Their intestines are relatively short, unlike cattle, sheep, and horses, which have evolved to be strictly vegetarian.

There is a balance that must be reached regarding dietary proteins, carbohydrates, and fats. Dogs must consume enough of the diet to provide them with energy as well as essential amino acids. If the overall energy (calorie) level of the diet is low, dogs will use the proteins for energy rather than as a source of amino acids. Because of this, most commercial diets are formulated so that fats and carbohydrates provide the energy needs and the protein content contributes the essential amino acids.

AMINO ACIDS

You are probably now aware of a fundamental truth regarding protein—the percentage of protein in the diet is largely irrelevant. Whether the diet is 22 percent protein or 62 percent protein, the only important criteria is the content of essential amino acids present in the protein. The energy requirements are best met by carbohydrates and fats anyway. The principal role of protein is to provide the all-important amino acids so that the body can manufacture its own protein. The concept that high protein is better than low protein is a product of pet-food marketing, not nutritional fact.

There are ten known essential amino acids in the dog, but somehow they rarely get mentioned in discussions about nutrition. Recently it also became apparent that L-carnitine may be essential for some breeds.

The Ten Essential Amino Acids

arginine	lysine	threonine
histidine	methionine+cysteine	tryptophan
isoleucine	phenylalanine+tyrosine	valine
leucine		

There may be ten essential amino acids, but if even one is deficient, the body cannot make specific proteins effectively. The reason is that amino acids work in a step-by-step fashion to manufacture protein. If one of the steps is missing, the process stops. The missing amino acid is referred to as the "limiting amino acid," in this case because its absence limits the use of the other amino acids present.

Although all of the essential amino acids are indispensable, there are some that are more specific to canine nutritional concerns than others. Arginine is considered essential for young growing animals, but not adults. However, arginine is also critical as an intermediate in the urea cycle, allowing the ammonia that is generated from eating a high-protein meal to be converted to urea and excreted from the body. Cats are much more sensitive to deficiencies in arginine (and taurine and methionine-

Remember

Amino acids are the building blocks of protein. If even one of the essential amino acids is missing your dog can experience problems regardless of the total protein in the diet.

cysteine) than dogs. For lysine, the amount required appears to increase as the level of protein in the diet increases. This is significant because lysine is often the first limiting amino acid in cereal-based dog foods. In addition, various processing and storing procedures can inactivate the lysine in the diet or bind it, making it less available to the dog.

You probably now understand that the percentage of protein in the diet is a very poor measure of the adequacy of that diet. Similarly, it is misleading when pet-food manufacturers promote their products with marketing slogans such as "contains beef." This is no assurance whatsoever that the diet contains adequate amounts of the all-important essential amino acids.

SOURCES OF PROTEIN

The biggest hoax perpetrated on the pet-owning public is that a dog needs meat. A dog can live a healthy life without consuming any animal protein—meat or otherwise. Animal proteins can be useful in a dog's diet because they are readily usable, yet eggs and milk are much better protein sources than poultry, beef, or pork. In fact, the meats are no better than nuts, seeds, or lentils in their protein content. Fish, soybeans, and cheese contain more protein than meat. Another consideration is that more meat protein also means more saturated fat in the diet. For instance, a T-bone steak may contain 20 percent protein, but the remaining 80 percent of the calories are fat. Imagine the relative percentages for the meat used in dog foods!

Most animal protein contains reasonable amounts of all the essential amino acids and many nonessential ones. One animal protein, gelatin, does not contain adequate levels of tryptophan and lysine. Others are considered only partially complete. For example, the protein from some fish contains small amounts of methionine, and the milk protein casein is weak in arginine. Plant proteins are even more incomplete, but a proper combination of different plant proteins (complementation) corrects any deficits. Another way to optimize the nutritional status of a diet is to use predominantly plant proteins but add a small amount of animal protein.

The richest sources of vegetable protein are legumes, including soybeans, lentils, kidney beans, and black-eyed peas. Although they contain essential amino acids comparable to those found in meat, the amino-acid balance can be further improved by adding rice, corn, or grains. The other advantage to these plant proteins is that they contain no cholesterol and little, if any, saturated fats.

An interesting paradox occurs in the pet-food industry concerning meat-based and cereal-based diets. If meat protein is superior to plant protein in terms of essential amino acids and digestibility, diets based on meat proteins require less total protein to get the job done. Diets that contain beef, poultry, or pork can get away with an overall lower total protein concentration; this form of protein is often better utilized. For example, a dog food with 30 percent total protein based on corn and soy might provide the same amount of essential amino acids as a diet with 20 percent protein based on beef, poultry, eggs, or milk. Why then do the meat-based diets often strive for higher total concentrations of protein than cereal-based diets? Let's consider an example. There are two cars, with car A being more fuel-efficient than car B. The fuel-efficient car A might represent the meat-based diets and car B the cereal-based diets. Because car A is more fuel-efficient, it should require less gas than car B to go the same distance. Similarly, it should take less total meat-based protein to meet a dog's daily requirement. The cereal-based diet should contain a higher total protein concentration to meet those same daily requirements. The pet-food industry, however, often makes meat-based diets higher in protein than cereal-based diets. The result is that most meat-based diets provide significantly more protein than is needed to adequately meet a pet's amino-acid needs.

PROTEIN QUALITY

No discussion of protein is complete without mention of protein quality. Protein quality describes not only the amount of essential amino acids in the diet, but their ability to be digested in the stomach and intestines, absorbed, and then utilized by the body. After all, if a dog can't utilize the protein in his food, what good is it?

There is not one perfect protein source for dogs that provides all of their nutritional needs. Like people, dogs need a combination of food. Protein quality is usually achieved by complementation, combining protein sources to provide an optimal blend of the essential amino-acids. This same principle is used when adding milk to breakfast cereals. The cereals, which are generally low in the amino acids lysine and tryptophan, are augmented by the amino acid content of milk, which is adequate for these nutrients. Most proteins derived from animals (e.g., beef, pork, poultry, lamb) are good sources of lysine and tryptophan, which tend to be less in wheat and corn. Soy products have lower-than-needed levels of the sulfur-containing amino-acids, but are rich in arginine. Dogs need histidine, which is amply supplied in pork and, in lesser amounts, in cereals, chicken and soy.

To add to the confusion, the contents of amino acids in the diet must also reflect the body's ability to digest and absorb the source of the protein. Most cereals and soy products are 70 to 80 percent digested, while meats are 80 to 90 percent digested. Of course, there is tremendous variability in the quality of pet-food ingredients. Good-quality meat or poultry meals may be more digestible than soybean meal, but poor-quality meat or poultry meals are often less digestible than soybean meal. No one can rightly assume that a diet with meat or poultry meal is superior to a

Sources of Proteins

beef	lamb	pork	poultry	corn
soy	eggs	milk	fish	organ meats
		milk by-products		

cereal-based diet. In fact, combinations of corn and soybean meal can provide adequate levels of all of the "known" essential amino acids.

To determine protein quality, you must be able to identify which foods are best digested, absorbed, and utilized by your dog. Some generalizations are helpful, but they are difficult to substantiate by reading pet-food labels. Poultry, meat, and fish meals are considered good-quality proteins along with milk by-products, eggs, and liver, but an ingredient list does not tell how "wholesome" the ingredients really are. When you see "poultry meal" on the label, you may think of a succulent chicken or turkey dinner but is that reality or just good marketing? "Parts is parts"—you decide!

Be aware that dietary ingredients are often selected for you, the consumer, rather than for your dog. Dog food shaped like bones or hamburgers does little to impress dogs. This is a marketing tool. Even the thought of a sirloin steak would not be haute cuisine to a canine palate. They would much prefer intestines, organ meats, and other viscera. The scents that are most appealing to the canine nose are far smellier than most people would want to have in their homes. So, dogs are often fed diets designed to please the human senses.

ADVERSE EFFECTS OF PROTEIN IN DIETS

Dogs are able to tolerate high levels of protein in the diet, but this doesn't mean that those levels are good for them. As long as the need for essential amino acids is met, the protein content makes little difference. In fact, pups that were fed amino-acid supplements only, and no other source of protein, did just fine and grew to be healthy, happy dogs. There have been many claims that high-protein diets are bad for dogs. Although few of these studies have yielded convincing results, they do merit discussion.

Animals with liver, heart, or kidney problems do better on diets containing small amounts of high-quality proteins. That's because small amounts of high-quality protein can be absorbed more easily from the intestine, they do not require extensive processing by the liver, and they are less likely to be lost into the urine as they are filtered by the kidneys. Does this mean that high-protein diets cause liver or kidney disease? No, not really. A potential cause of alarm, however, is that middle-aged dogs might have problems with their kidneys, heart, or liver that in the early stages may not be clinically evident. In this case, the high protein in the diet may be taxing the organs before the problem has even been recognized. Older dogs need even less protein than pups, which means that they should probably not be on high-protein diets unless they are working or competing or are heavily stressed.

You should also consider that a diet high in animal protein is high in animal fat. Fats contain more than twice as many calories as proteins, and your dog could become obese unless he is rigorously exercised on a regular basis. Protein isn't stored, and if it is not used for its amino-acid content, it simply provides additional calories, all of which can eventually turn into fat. These "energy-dense" diets provide many more calories than most dogs need on a daily basis. Whereas they may have some benefit for a working dog, the sedentary house pet is likely to gain weight.

Another potential problem with feeding an "energy dense" diet is that your dog may eat less of the high-protein, high-fat diet than other foods. The concern is whether he then consumes enough of the food to meet his other requirements for vitamins, minerals, and fiber. This concern is legitimate, and there is no information on whether these diets can be completely balanced for all ages, sizes, and breeds of dog. Recently, much attention has been focused on high-protein diets and their role in behavior problems. Many trainers and behavior consultants propose that high-protein diets make dogs less trainable and more excitable. Studies are currently underway that may help support or refute this contention.

Soy, as a specific protein source, has been plagued by bad press over the years, but few scientific studies have shown it to be a real problem. Soybean meal combined with corn actually provides an adequate balance of all the essential amino acids. Soybean oil is also a good source of lecithin and other essential fatty acids.

There are some legitimate concerns with soy, however. Soybeans, like many beans, contain the sugars raffinose and stachyose, which many dogs cannot digest properly. When this happens, the raffinose is broken down in the intestines by bacteria, which then produces gas. Some dogs fed soy-based products therefore have a problem with flatulence. It is important to note that the gas is produced in the intestines rather than in the stomach, so it is unlikely that soy actually contributes to bloating in dogs. Studies have shown that meat-based diets are just as likely as soy-based diets to cause bloat (gastric dilatation/volvulus).

Two other problems that have been linked to dietary soy are zinc deficiency and hypothyroidism. Soy, like other plant proteins, contains phytates, which may interfere with the absorption of zinc from the intestines. But soy is not alone in this regard. In fact, rice bran and sesame-seed meal pose a greater threat than soy, yet receive little attention in this matter. Good-quality soy-based diets, which contain moderate levels of fiber, should not adversely affect dietary levels of zinc. Similarly, just because soy is low in iodine does not mean that it causes hypothyroidism in dogs. True, the risk is increased because there are chemicals in soy that can promote goiter (goitrogens), but most (or all) of these chemicals are destroyed by the heat-processing of the food. The fact is that 95 percent of hypothyroid dogs have either lymphocytic thyroiditis or thyroid atrophy, neither of which result from low iodine levels or goitrogens.

Milk and milk by-products such as whey have a high lactose content and are therefore difficult for dogs to digest. Like many people, dogs do not have much lactase enzyme, which is needed to digest lactose, and so are often called lactose-intolerant. In these animals, feeding milk or whey as a protein source can result in diarrhea, flatulence, or loose stools.

One other concern is that a high-protein diet has an environmental impact that is difficult to ignore. Because the body cannot effectively store protein for long-term use, excess protein fed turns into excess protein excreted. This is extremely wasteful given the global situation of hunger and starvation. And beef is probably the worst offender. Did you realize that you must feed more than seven pounds of grain and soy to cattle to produce one pound of edible beef? Did you know that an acre used to plant leafy vegetables produces fifteen times more protein than using that land to graze cattle? When you also consider that meat meals fed to dogs are often in amounts much higher than needed to meet their dietary needs, the wastefulness of this feeding regimen becomes apparent. The answer is not to discontinue the use of all meat proteins in your dog's diet, but rather to use them in moderation to meet and not exceed his needs.

RECOMMENDATIONS REGARDING PROTEINS

Most dogs in North America consume much more protein than they need. This has resulted more from pet-food marketing than from nutritional research. Dogs have requirements for essential amino acids, and these can be met adequately from vegetable protein combined with moderate amounts of animal protein. Feeding excess animal protein to dogs contributes to obesity and a high intake of saturated fats and is potentially harmful to animals with kidney, liver, or heart disease. Meats with the highest fat content are lamb, beef, and pork. The leanest sources of animal protein are fish, poultry, and wild game.

FATS

Fats are derived from fatty acids, chains of carbon atoms to which are attached hydrogen and oxygen atoms. These fatty acids do more than add pounds to your dog's frame. They are important building blocks for a whole range of important substances and are needed to maintain normal, healthy cells. Therefore, not all fats are the enemy; some are essential for your dog's health.

In any nutritional discussion, it is preferable to use the term "fatty acid" rather than "fat." Fat is the storage depository within the body. Fatty acids are the chemical elements that are present in foods.

Fats are common ingredients in dog foods because they make the food much tastier and because they are "energy dense," providing more than twice as much energy (calories) as either carbohydrates or protein. Just as there is no requirement for protein in a dog's diet, there is also no real requirement for fat. The only true need is for the essential fatty acids, especially linoleic acid. This can be accomplished by feeding 2 percent of the diet as linoleic acid found in vegetable oil. Most dog foods, even dry foods, contain two to ten times the required amount of fatty acid, most of it occurring as the "empty calories" of saturated animal fats. Dogs have absolutely no requirement for saturated fats.

Most commercial dog foods are high in saturated fats and cholesterol because the pet owners want their dogs to eat meat, and lots of it. It should be no surprise that where there's meat, there's fat, and the fat is high in calories. A pound of pure protein may contain 1,800 calories but an equal weight of fat would provide 4,000 calories! Is it any surprise that approximately 25 percent of the dogs in North America are overweight?

Vegetable oils can also contain saturated fats or monounsaturated fats, especially coconut oil and palm oil (which contains palmitic acid and palmitoleic acid). Unfortunately, these are the most common oils added to most fatty-acid supplements and might masquerade under the ingredient title "vegetable oils." These saturated and monounsaturated fatty acids can cause problems, if given in excess, by interfering with the linoleic and alpha-linolenic acids. Olive oil (containing oleic acid) is a little better but still has more than 15 percent saturated fats, with the balance being mainly monounsaturated, not polyunsaturated. Safflower oil (containing the essential linoleic acid) has only about 10 percent saturated fat, the balance being predominantly polyunsaturated. Other acceptable polyunsaturated vegetable oils are flaxseed oil, sesame seed oil, evening-primrose oil, borage oil, sunflower-seed oil, and soybean oil. By contrast, beef fat (containing stearic acid) is more than 50 percent saturated and contains essentially no linoleic acid, the only fatty acid truly required by dogs.

Although most attention is focused on the polyunsaturated fatty acids, the essential fatty acids, and the omega-3 and omega-6 fatty acids, there has been renewed interest in the monounsaturated fatty acids. It has been suggested that in people, monounsaturates lower LDL and VLDL (bad) cholesterol levels without changing HDL (good) cholesterol levels. Medical scientists are investigating the hypothesis that a high ratio of good to bad cholesterol is more important to heart-disease risk than lowering overall cholesterol levels the way polyunsaturates do. High-content monounsaturated oils like olive oil and canola oil are less likely to become rancid than the polyunsaturates. To date, very little research has investigated the merits of monounsaturated oils for dogs.

FATTY ACID QUALITY

The two most important features of a fatty acid that help to determine whether it's good or bad are its length and its degree of "saturation." The length of a fatty acid refers to the number of carbon atoms present in its skeleton. Imagine this skeleton as a train, with individual railway cars linked to one another and creating a chain. Butyric acid, which is found in butter, is short, with only four carbons, while fish oils are usually eighteen to twenty-two carbons long. The length of the chain is more than just a scientific oddity—it determines the fate of the fatty acid within the body.

Fatty acids with less than sixteen carbons can be used as a source of energy (calories), but they are heavily "saturated" with hydrogen atoms making the fats "reactive" within the body. Fatty acids with sixteen to eighteen carbons can become "unsaturated," which is healthier, and can be used as an energy source or be incorporated into fat. This would correspond to the train adding extra links between some of the cars to make sure that they were firmly attached.

Saturation is an important concept regarding fats. Fatty acids are saturated when the carbon atoms in the chain hold as many hydrogen atoms as possible. Using the train example, single links between each of the cars would make it completely saturated. If some of the hydrogens in the fatty acids are stripped away and replaced with stronger "double bonds," they are no longer saturated. They become "unsaturated." When two or more double bonds are present in a particular form of fat, it is described as a polyunsaturated fatty acid, "poly" meaning many. To illustrate, oleic acid in olive oil has one double bond (monounsaturated), linoleic acid in safflower oil has two double bonds, alpha-linolenic acid in flaxseed oil has three double bonds and eicosapentaenoic acid in fish oil has five double bonds. Compounds with one double bond are called monounsaturated fatty acids (MUFAs), and those with two or more are called polyunsaturated fatty acids (PUFAs). In the train analogy, one double link between any two cars would be monounsaturated. Double links between two or more cars would make it polyunsaturated. The more double links between cars, the safer the train; the more double bonds between carbon atoms, the safer the fatty acid.

Sources of Fats

Saturated: milk and milk by-products, meat, coconut or palm oil

Polyunsaturated: safflower oil

Monounsaturated: vegetable oils

Saturated fats with carbon lengths of fourteen or less (e.g., butter) provide calories and little else. Saturated fatty acids with carbon lengths of sixteen to eighteen (e.g., animal fat, palm or coconut oil) tend to cluster together in drops and plugs—a very dangerous situation for people, contributing to atherosclerosis or "clogging" of the arteries. Diets high in beef, mutton, pork, and dairy products contain much saturated fatty acid. The ultimate risk of saturated fats in dogs has been largely unexplored to date.

ESSENTIAL FATTY ACIDS

Some fats are more important than others in the body. Just as protein has its essential amino acids, fat has its essential fatty acids. In the dog, linoleic acid is considered to be an essential fatty acid. Fatty acids form an important part of every cell in the body. The essential fatty acids also act to increase cellular metabolism and help burn fat. The body uses linoleic and alpha-linolenic acid to create other important substances, including prostaglandins, which are important in fighting inflammation.

Essential fatty acids are important to your dog's health but most pet foods contain more fat than needed, and much of it is saturated. This creates a double threat because it provides excess energy (calories), which can contribute to obesity, plus the saturated fats and cholesterol (from meat) can result in medical problems. There is little benefit in using animal fat in your dog's diet other than as a source of calories or as a flavoring. There is no requirement in his diet whatsoever for saturated fats.

Linoleic and alpha-linolenic acid are best provided by vegetable oils and only need to be given in moderation. If only 2 percent of the dietary calories are provided as linoleic acid, all of your dog's daily requirements for fat will be met. Alpha-linolenic acid is discussed as an essential fatty acid, but its absolute requirement in the dog has not been convincingly demonstrated. Because it is present in many of the same vegetable oils as linoleic acid (e.g., soybean oil, flaxseed oil), it is unlikely that your dog will become deficient in it if his requirements for linoleic acid are met.

OMEGA-3 AND OMEGA-6 FATTY ACIDS

Linoleic and alpha-linolenic acids are also the parents of a whole family of fatty acids that are important to your dog. These fatty acids are named for the location of their first double bond, and the method of naming the fatty acids is known as the omega (ω) system. Both linoleic and alpha-linolenic acids have eighteen carbons in each chain. Alpha-linolenic acid has its first double bond after the third carbon (omega-3), while linoleic acid has its first double bond after the sixth carbon (omega-6). This is like putting a double link between railway cars three and four (omega-3) or between cars six and seven (omega-6). Obviously, the names linoleic acid and linolenic acid look similar and can be confused with one another.

They were both originally found in flax (*Linum* in Latin), hence the similarity in their names.

Both the omega-3 and omega-6 fatty acids are important because they have natural anti-inflammatory properties once they have been converted to their active forms in the body. To be functional, linoleic acid must be converted in the body to gamma-linolenic acid (GLA). Alpha-linolenic acid must be converted to eicosapentaenoic acid (EPA). Sometimes dogs (and people) do not have enough enzymes to make this conversion complete. When this happens, the alpha-linolenic and linoleic acids in the diet can provide energy but cannot fight inflammation. This problem can be remedied by supplementing directly with oils that contain EPA and GLA.

The parent compounds, linoleic and alpha-linolenic acid, are plentiful in many plant and seed oils. Products with a relatively high percentage of linoleic acid include the oils of safflower, sunflower, soybean, sesame seed, and flax. Products with a relatively high percentage of alpha-linolenic acid include flax, pumpkin seed, and soybean. These substances are found in many dietary supplements designed to add gloss to the coat. If a dog has a normal enzyme system for converting fatty acids, these fatty acids can be elongated (carbons added) and can help battle inflammation.

The omega-3 (n-3) fatty acids are all derived from alpha-linolenic acid. By adding carbons and double bonds, eicosapentaenoic acid (EPA) and docosahexaenoic acid (DHA) can be created. These fatty acids tend to be anti-inflammatory because they produce products that are less inflammatory than would normally be produced. These products compete for enzymes with the more inflammatory components, thus reducing inflammation by a process known as competitive inhibition. Since alpha-linolenic acid itself has little anti-inflammatory potential, supplementation with eicosapentaenoic acid (EPA) in marine oils is the best option.

The omega-6 (n-6) fatty acids are all derived from cis-linoleic acid which is found in safflower, sunflower and corn oils. By adding a double bond, gamma-linolenic acid (GLA) is created (found in borage and evening primrose oils) and adding another carbon results in dihomogamma-linolenic acid. Supplementing with GLA also has anti-inflammatory effects but by slightly different mechanisms than the omega-3 fatty acids.

At present, it seems best to supplement with both omega-3 and omega-6 fatty acids. Although the optimal ratios of the two are currently being hotly debated, at least one group of researchers suggests that an optimal ratio for omega-6 to omega-3 fatty acids in the diet should be between 5:1 and 10:1. Not surprisingly, these researchers have formulated a canine commercial diet with just those ratios (Eukanuba Veterinary Diets™ Response Formula FP™).

In the omega-3 series, important compounds include eicosapentaenoic acid (EPA) and docosahexaenoic acid (DHA). These compounds are found in high concentrations in the muscles of coldwater fish (salmon, trout, mackerel, and sardines), krill, and marine mammals. The most important

Use Eukanuba Veterinary Diets Response Formula FP for Dogs only as directed by your veterinarian.
Your veterinarian may ask you to follow custom feeding instructions special for your dog, or ask you to follow the standard portions shown below:

Weight of Dog (lbs)	Canned Only	Canned Mixed with Dry Response Formula FP
3	1/3 can	1/8 can + 3/8 cup dry
10	3/4 can	1/5 can + 1 cup dry
20	1 1/4 cans	1/4 can + 1 1/2 cups dry
30	1 2/3 cans	1/3 can + 2 cups dry
40	2 cans	1/2 can + 2 1/2 cups dry
60	2 2/3 cans	2/3 can + 3 1/4 cups dry
80	3 1/4 cans	3/4 can + 4 cups dry
100	3 2/3 cans	1 can + 4 1/2 cups dry

Calorie Content Statement:
Metabolizable Energy (ME) = 1,263 kcal/kg or 505 kcal/can.

Ask your veterinarian.
If you have questions about your dog's health or about any Eukanuba Veterinary Diets product, talk to your veterinarian or call one of The Iams Company pet health professionals at 1-800-535-8387.

Eukanuba Veterinary Diets Response Formula FP Ingredients
Water, Catfish, Herring Meal, Modified Potato Starch, Mackerel, Dried Beet Pulp, Calcium Carbonate, Corn Oil, Monosodium Phosphate, Choline Chloride, Zinc Oxide, Ferrous Sulfate, Vitamin E Supplement, Ascorbic Acid (Vitamin C), Copper Sulfate, Manganese Sulfate, Manganous Oxide, Vitamin A Acetate, Biotin, Calcium Pantothenate, Vitamin B12 Supplement, Niacin, Thiamine Mononitrate, Riboflavin Supplement, Inositol, Pyridoxine Hydrochloride (Vitamin B6), Vitamin D3 Supplement, Potassium Iodide, Folic Acid, Cobalt Carbonate, Sodium Selenite.

110% Satisfaction Guaranteed
If you are not satisfied with the quality of a Eukanuba Veterinary Diets dog food product, we will replace the product or refund the purchase price plus 10%. Simply save the unused portion, together with the proof of purchase, and return it to your veterinarian.

Guaranteed Analysis

Crude Protein not less than	9.0%
Crude Fat not less than	6.0%
Omega-6 Fatty Acids not less than	0.95%
Omega-3 Fatty Acids not less than	0.19%
Crude Fiber not more than	1.0%
Moisture not more than	78.0%

functional omega-6 fatty acid is gamma-linolenic acid, which can be found in the seed oils of evening primrose, black currant and borage. For people, omega-3 fatty acids have been shown to lower triglyceride levels, while omega-6 fatty acids lower cholesterol. Exercise also lowers triglyceride levels by burning up the excess for energy.

Be careful when you choose supplements of omega-3 and omega-6 fatty acids. They are temperamental and can be destroyed easily by exposure to heat, light, and air. It is advisable that you keep these supplements in opaque containers, protected from heat. You may wish to refrigerate them. Tightly cap the product so that it is not exposed to air. Unfortunately, this care may not have been taken during the production and processing stages.

CHOLESTEROL

Cholesterol has both its good and bad points, but because of the diets consumed in North America, most attention focuses on the bad points. Cholesterol is present in all cells and helps keep the contours of cells pliable and accommodating, rather than loose or rigid. It is also an important component of the steroid hormones, which include the steroids produced by the sex and adrenal organs, as well as vitamin D and the bile acids.

In people, cholesterol deposits narrow the blood vessels, leading to cardiovascular disease. The reasons for the laydown of cholesterol in these sites is not entirely known, but the causes are probably related to diet as well as to damage of the vessels (e.g., by free radicals). When arteries harden (arteriosclerosis), the vessels become narrower and less pliable, increasing the blood pressure and making the heart work harder to move blood around the body.

Cholesterol can be made by the body or be ingested in foods. Highly refined carbohydrates and nonessential fatty acids "drive" the body to make cholesterol. Eating processed foods, even if they themselves are not high in cholesterol, can result in elevated cholesterol levels in the body. Animal-derived foods (meat, poultry, eggs) contain cholesterol, but plants do not.

RECOMMENDATIONS REGARDING FATS

North American dogs ingest much more fat than they can possibly use productively. When meat is used in the diet to create a high-protein density, the fat content is also increased, often with saturated fats. If dogs are at all like people, they may have less energy, they may exercise less, and they may become progressively fatter if they eat a diet high in saturated fat. In the process, they also will increase their risk of developing degenerative diseases such as arthritis, cancer, and heart disease. *Dogs do not require saturated fats in their diet.* Their only requirement is for linoleic acid, which is best provided by vegetable oils. Beef contains little linoleic acid. Fats make diets tastier, but they provide empty calories that promote obesity in your dog. The entire daily fat requirement for your dog can be met by ensuring that his diet includes 2 percent of its calories as linoleic acid.

CARBOHYDRATES

Carbohydrates can be simple (sugars) or complex (starches) and are added to a dog's diet as a source of energy (calories) and to provide bulk. Dogs, however, have no specific nutritional requirement for carbohydrates. There are no "essential" carbohydrates for the dog as there are essential amino acids or essential fatty acids. And yet carbohydrates are an important nutrient in dog foods.

Carbohydrates get a lot of bad press about being fattening, but this is just not true. Carbohydrates contain the same number of calories, by weight, as do proteins. The complex carbohydrates, all derived from plants, contain no cholesterol either. The complex carbohydrates also provide fiber or "roughage," which helps keep the digestive system running efficiently and regularly.

Most of the concerns about carbohydrates focus on sugar. Sugar means different things to different people. Most doctors concentrate on glucose, the body's form of sugar. Consumers are more concerned with sucrose (table sugar), lactose (milk sugar), and fructose (levulose). Syrup, honey, and dextrins also fall into this category. Because sugars are so quickly absorbed by the body, the calories are available instantly and are more likely to be stored as fat. Sugars are therefore not the preferred source of carbohydrate unless an instantaneous source of calories is desired.

The simple sugars reach their highest levels in semimoist dog foods. These diets contain large amounts of simple sugars like sucrose and syrup and comparatively less starch than dry foods. In fact, 20 percent or more of these diets may be made up of sugar. Because these sugars are absorbed quickly, dogs eating semimoist diets may produce less stool but frequently produce much more urine. These diets may also promote obesity because of their high caloric content.

Starches are composed of sugar chains. Starch is the plant's way of storing energy, just as animals store energy as fat. The simpler the formation (such as in rice, white flour, and cornstarch), the more easily the body can convert these carbohydrates to sugar and thence to fat. The more complex carbohydrates (such as in grains, bananas, potatoes, and cornmeal) are digested more slowly, are less likely to convert to fat, and contain important enzymes. In general, cooked starch in commercial dog foods is well digested—most of it comes from corn, rice and wheat. Soy flour, corn-gluten meal, wheat gluten, and wheat middlings are not completely digested by dogs and are therefore poor sources of usable starch. Most sources of fiber are tomato pumice, beet pulp, corn bran, oat bran, and wheat bran.

Complex carbohydrates are digested slowly, principally because of their fiber content, and are only slowly converted into sugars within the body. If a dog is active, these carbohydrates provide a ready energy supply in addition to vitamins and minerals. A dog can "burn off" these calories easily and stay fit if given even moderate amounts of exercise. Even for a dog that doesn't exercise much, the complex carbohydrates provide a safer form of energy than do sugars or fats.

A major concern about carbohydrates is that dogs digest them differently than people do. Dogs possess enzymes that can break down different forms of carbohydrate, such as sucrose, lactose, dextrin, and maltose, but the efficiency of this process changes as dogs age. Newborn puppies have almost no ability to digest starch. As they get older, however, and are exposed to highly digestible starches, the levels of the enzyme amylase increase significantly. This allows older dogs to digest starches very well after a few weeks of adapting to the new diet. Poorly digestible starches (such as raw potato starch) added to the diet do not result in the same increase in enzyme activity. When dogs are exposed to highly digestible starches, they also increase their ability to digest simple sugars.

As dogs age, however, they do worse with milk sugar (lactose). Obviously, puppies that are still nursing have the ability to digest lactose. As they get older, they have more trouble digesting the lactose. Few adult

Carbohydrates provide a ready energy supply in addition to vitamins and minerals. A dog will burn off these calories with even a moderate amount of exercise. Photo by Judith Strom.

dogs are capable of digesting it at all. Most adult dogs that have been fed milk routinely without problem probably still are lactase deficient. They tolerate the milk, in most cases, because their intestinal microbes have adapted to the milk in the diet. In these cases, bacteria that can use the milk (bacteria such as lactobacillus-acidophilus) occupy a more prominent niche in the intestines.

There are many practical applications of this information. Because pups lack the enzyme amylase, do not give nursing puppies milk substitutes containing starch unless it has been decomposed (boiled or baked). Likewise, do not give sucrose (table sugar) in milk-replacement products, and never let it exceed 5 percent in other products. Puppies can, however, digest lactose (milk sugar), and so milk replacers can include skim milk. Older dogs cannot usually tolerate milk sugar (lactose) in amounts constituting more than 5 percent of their diet.

Products like raw potato starch are often tasty for dogs but don't get digested. For this reason, they are often added to weight-reducing diets. In this way, dogs feel full but don't absorb the raw starch, or the calories that it contains. Decomposed (cooked) starch is digested by dogs and may be added to diets to replace other items that need to be restricted. As an example, for dogs on protein-restricted diets, cooked starches may be used to provide more of the bulk and calories in place of the protein content.

FIBER

Fiber is that part of the plant that resists digestion. Most dog foods have fiber levels between 2 and 4 percent. There are different kinds of fiber. Some are very absorbent and soak up excess water in the intestinal tract. Some can be broken down to a variable extent by intestinal bacteria while others pass through the system largely unchanged. The most common sources of fiber are whole grains, fruits, and vegetables, and the actual types of fiber include cellulose, hemicellulose, lignin, pectin, gum, and mucilage.

Fiber increases the "bulk" of the food and gives your dog a full feeling. Fiber can also be used as a laxative for constipation because it absorbs intestinal fluid, making the stool softer yet bulkier and stimulating the intestinal rhythm that pushes the stool through the system. Because the stool passes through the digestive tract with less effort, diets fortified with fiber are frequently used in dogs with bowel disorders. Whole grains are the preferred source of fiber for a "sluggish gut." Also, because fiber gives dogs a "full" feeling, they consume fewer calories with their meal and are apt to lose weight. That's why fiber is increased in the new "Lite" diets that are appearing in the marketplace. For this purpose, most any type of fiber will do.

Other benefits of fiber are only now being explored. Some types of fiber, notably pectins, guar gum, and the fibers in rolled oats and carrots, can help lower cholesterol levels in the blood. These same fiber sources may also be beneficial in regulating blood-sugar and insulin levels in diabetic animals. But not all fibers are equal in this regard. Bran, which contains predominantly cellulose, will not help regulate cholesterol or blood-sugar levels.

Although the fiber content of dog foods is important, there are some risks to feeding high-fiber, "Lite" diets. Although a dog will lose weight with these diets, it has been shown that they reduce the digestibilities of protein, carbohydrate, and fat. There is also some evidence that high-fiber diets might interfere with the absorption of several minerals (e.g., calcium, copper, iron, magnesium, phosphorus, and zinc) and possibly vitamin B_{12}. Thus, they should not be fed indefinitely, and not to young growing animals or any dog that is stressed or sick. High-fiber diets do have their place, but they should only be fed to dogs under strict veterinary supervision.

FRUCTOOLIGOSACCHARIDES (FOS)

Fructooligosaccharides (FOS) are sugars found in a variety of foods (e.g., onions, garlic, bananas, wheat, etc.) and they can also be manufactured by altering sucrose with enzymes. Why might this type of sugar hold interest for nutritionists and internists? Well, it appears that some species of intestinal bacteria can utilize FOS instead of glucose, while others can't. Thus, studies are underway to see if substituting FOS for other carbohydrates in the diet may be effective in the management of intestinal infections, including small intestinal bacterial overgrowth (SIBO). See Chapter 10 for more information.

CARBOHYDRATE QUALITY

How do carbohydrates end up being fat? Well, in the body, all carbohydrates eventually become the simple sugar glucose. Refined sugars and starches make this conversion quickly while complex carbohydrates are broken down more slowly, giving the body time to respond. When refined and processed sugars are prominent in the diet, they quickly convert in the body to glucose. This causes a sugar "high" in the bloodstream, which then signals the pancreas to produce more insulin. When the insulin level climbs, it acts to remove the excess sugar from the bloodstream by converting glucose to fatty acids (glycerides), binding three together to form triglycerides and storing them as fat. These triglycerides are not only weak in nutritional value, but they are saturated fats that can cause potential problems in the body. Making fat from sugar is not only dangerous, it is a one-way street. Although excess carbohydrates in the diet can end up as fat, fat cannot be converted back to carbohydrates. The only way to get rid of this fat once it forms is by burning it off with exercise.

Some pets, as mentioned, can be lactose-intolerant. This means that they lack the enzymes to properly break down the lactose. In this case, the lactose is broken down by the microbes in the colon and can result in diarrhea and flatulence. It is best that these dogs not be fed appreciable (greater than 5 percent of calories) milk proteins, including whey.

The best sources of carbohydrates for dogs are potatoes, legumes, grains, vegetables, and fruit. Natural sugars can be found in vegetables

Canine High Fiber Diet - Typical Analysis

	Dry
Approximate Calories ME[1]	226 kcal/cup (302 kcal/100 g)
Palatability[2] vs Hill's® Prescription Diet® Canine w/d®[3]	84:16
Digestibility	
Dry Matter, %	77%
Protein, %	75%
Fat, %	85%
Energy, %	84%

and fruits to provide a quick source of energy (calories), while the potatoes and grains provide starch and fiber. Unfortunately, processed and refined sugars and starches are robbed of most of their nutritional value. Natural starches are an excellent source of vitamins, minerals, and other essential nutrients.

Carbohydrates harbor many nutrients, but modern refining and processing techniques have done much to remove the goodness from the natural ingredients. Refined white flour has been stripped of bran and wheat germ, removing up to 80 percent of the nutrients found in whole wheat, including most of the fiber and vitamin E. Whole-grain brown rice is an excellent source of energy, minerals, and vitamins (especially B vitamins), but polished rice has most of the riboflavin, pyridoxine, niacin, thiamin, and protein removed. Although instant or "minute" rices contain fewer calories than brown rice, they have the lowest nutrient content.

Legumes such as soybeans, lentils, and kidney beans contain high-quality protein in addition to carbohydrate and have no cholesterol or saturated fat. They are also rich in many essential minerals, including potassium and phosphorus. Soybean meal is a common ingredient in dog foods because it provides cheap protein, complex carbohydrate, and texture. Two sugars found in soy products, namely, raffinose and stachyose, are poorly digested by dogs. When diets high in soy are fed to dogs, bacteria in the colon will take on the job of digesting these sugars, producing gas in the colon. This is one of the main reasons why flatulence is common in dogs fed diets high in soy content.

Corn also contains natural carbohydrate and is commonly found in dog foods as a cheap form of energy. Cornmeal is an excellent source of starch and contains much less sugar than sweet corn. Cornstarch, on the other hand, is purified starch and has none of the nutrients found in the corn kernel. This is often one of the more common ingredients in pet foods.

Whole-grain or bran cereals are very nutritious for dogs and are an excellent source of fiber. Oats contain the most protein. When they are prepared by "rolling," most of the nutrients are conserved.

Potatoes are an excellent carbohydrate source in the dog but are rarely found in commercial pet foods. They also contain appreciable levels of vitamin C, protein, minerals, and trace nutrients. Do not skin potatoes prior to feeding because most of the nutrients are located in and just beneath the skin. Even without their skin, potatoes rival rice and pasta in nutritional value.

Fruits and vegetables provide natural sugars and starches but are not commonly found in commercial dog foods. This is just as well, because their nutrient load is largely lost during processing. Fresh fruits and vegetables, by contrast, are loaded with vitamins, minerals, trace nutrients, and fiber. For home-prepared meals, many dogs enjoy fresh apples, carrots, green peppers, and celery and sometimes even broccoli and cauliflower. Remember that for your dog to digest the sugars and starches in fresh fruits and vegetables you must gradually introduce these foods into his diet over a two-week period. For dogs that have been fed highly digestible starches such as boiled or baked cornstarch or cereal starch, there is increased digestibility of the simple sugars.

RECOMMENDATIONS FOR CARBOHYDRATES

Carbohydrates are probably the most underrated nutrient for dogs. They are inexpensive and are a great source of fiber, protein, vitamins, minerals, and other nutrients. Ideally, most of the carbohydrate provided to your dog should be starches found in potatoes and whole grains. This allows a sustained source of energy and a wealth of vitamins, minerals, and fiber. Unfortunately, the processing of feeds for commercial dog foods removes much of the nutritional value from the natural ingredients, and as a result, nutrients must be re-added to the finished "enriched" product. Cheaper forms of fiber (such as beet pulp) are often used for this process.

Excellent sources of carbohydrates for use in commercial dog foods include cornmeal (not cornstarch), soybean meal, whole-grain rice, whole wheat, oats, and bran. For homemade diets, potatoes provide a wealth of nutrients in addition to their content of complex carbohydrates. Fresh fruits and vegetables added to a homemade diet provide natural sugars, high-quality starches, and an excellent source of fiber.

Although fiber is an important ingredient in dog foods, not all fibers are created equal. Therefore, it is best for your dog to acquire fiber by eating a variety of foods such as whole grains, fruits, and vegetables rather than relying on any one source. Raw fruits and vegetables are better than those that have been peeled, cooked, or processed. Consider adding some carrots, apple slices, and whole-grain cereals to your dog's meals rather than bran.

WATER

Water is critical for life and provides the medium for chemical reactions, lubrication, and temperature regulation within the body. Water is the major component of blood, joint fluid, cerebrospinal fluid, digestive fluids, and the fluid within the eye. In fact, 60 to 70 percent of the entire body is made up of water. Body organs contain the most water and bones and cartilage the least. But most of the water is not loose in tissues, like a sponge. About 40 percent of the total water weight of a body is found inside the cells, about 15 percent is outside the cells, and 45 percent is found in the bloodstream as the fluid portion of the blood.

It may be difficult to think of water as a nutrient, but clearly, all life on earth would cease without water. What better definition of an essential nutrient is there? Water not only provides the fluids that make up body tissues but it is a vehicle for animals and people to ingest other important nutrients as well. Water is an excellent source of essential and trace minerals. The water-soluble vitamins, vitamin C and the B vitamins, depend on water as a vehicle for their ingestion and absorption.

Fresh, clean water must always be available to your dog. Never restrict access to fresh water even if you feel your pet is drinking more than he needs. In this instance, contact your veterinarian and have your dog evaluated. Dehydration is serious and can occur in a very short time if your dog is losing fluids and not replacing them adequately. Dogs will not drink too much water if given free access. Water does not accumulate normally in the body and will be excreted as urine to keep the system in optimal water balance.

Make sure that the water is always fresh and clean and that it is changed at least daily, if not more frequently. Ensure also that the bowl is clean and disinfected regularly. Stale water that has been sitting for days is no more attractive to dogs than it would be to you.

Surprisingly, the life-enhancing properties of water are often taken for granted. It's just something that comes out of a tap. It's not an essential nutrient. Nothing could be farther from the truth. The water that comes out of the tap has many characteristics. In addition to the water itself, you might find other ingredients, including chlorine, fluoride, minerals, toxic chemicals, microbes, and other organic substances. And you may have added other devices that change the quality of the water you drink and that you provide to your pet.

Hard water has high concentrations of calcium and magnesium and can leave deposits in sinks, bowls, and other containers. Water softeners remove the calcium and magnesium and replace these minerals with sodium. This can be significant if your dog has heart disease or high blood pressure. Why put him on a low-sodium diet if you're providing him with high-sodium water? It is also known that potentially toxic trace minerals such as lead and cadmium reach higher levels in soft water than they do in hard water. One way to solve the problem is to connect a water softener only to hot-water pipes. In this way, soft water can be used for cleaning and bathing, and hard water is available for drinking and preparing meals.

In some polluted environments, metals such as mercury, cadmium, and lead may reach alarming proportions in the drinking water. These metals inflict considerable damage on a body, including altering enzyme functions, causing cancer and birth defects, and even altering the genetic material (DNA) that contributes to future generations. Obviously, contaminated water such as this is not suitable for your pet or yourself.

Although most people worry about contamination of drinking water from sewage, this is usually closely monitored by public-health officials. There is more likelihood of contamination from a shallow well than from a municipal water supply. Unfortunately, if microbial contamination is found, it is likely that caustic substances such as chlorine have been added to the water to kill whatever microbes are present.

A more pervasive but less-understood concern is the pollution of drinking water by organic compounds from sewage, insecticides, petrochemicals, and other sources, that are difficult to detect and even more difficult to remove from the water supply. Chemicals such as organophosphates, dioxin, PCBs, and organochlorines pose risks to people and animals, and public-health standards are still a matter of debate.

The answer is not to buy bottled water to escape the risks we all share. There is no certainty that water from "springs" or "spas" is any healthier than the water that comes out of your tap. Providing your dog with distilled water is also not preferable, because regular water is an excellent source of essential and trace minerals. These are removed when water is distilled. Probably the safest water to provide for your pet is water that has been carbon filtered and passed through a reverse-osmosis unit. This tends to remove organic contaminants but leave the mineral composition of the water intact. Of course, the ideal option is to ensure that the drinking water for the entire population is clean and fresh to begin with. In this regard, it is indeed unfortunate that the purity of a water supply is often a political issue.

*All dogs are individuals, thus they have individual
requirements when it comes to their diets as well.
Photo by Tammy Geiger.*

IN SUMMARY

Energy, as calories, is provided to the body by carbohydrates, fats, and to a lesser extent, proteins.

Essential amino acids are those proteins which must be supplied in the diet. These proteins make it possible for the dog to manufacture other proteins needed for good health.

A balanced diet will provide enough carbohydrates and fats as energy sources, so that the dog does not have to use protein for energy. Most common diets allow for this.

Animals with liver, heart, and kidney problems should be fed diets with smaller amounts of higher quality proteins. Too much protein puts an extra burden on these organs to excrete them.

Fats contain twice as many calories as proteins and carbohydrates, and most dog foods have 2-10 times the required amount of fatty acids.

Essential fatty acids (EFAs) are those needed by the body for cellular function, including metabolism, and are indirectly important in fighting inflammation.

Linoleic acid is the only true essential fatty acid utilized by dogs.

Simple carbohydrates are sugars that provide instant energy but also store quickly as fat.

Complex carbohydrates are starches that are digested more slowly and are less likely to store as fat. Dogs make better energy uses of complex carbohydrates.

Different enzymes break down different carbohydrates. Newborn puppies cannot digest starch and older dogs cannot digest lactose (milk sugar).

Fiber is used for weight loss, control of bowel disorders, and to maintain a healthy gut.

Never restrict access to fresh water, even if a dog seems to be drinking excessive amounts of water.

ADDITIONAL READING

Ackerman, L., "Fatty Acid Supplements—Practical Applications." *Advances in Nutrition,* 1993; 1 (2): 9-11.

Ackerman, L., "Reviewing the Biochemical Properties of Fatty Acids." *Veterinary Medicine,* 1995; (12): 1138-1148.

Brown, R.G., "Protein in Dog Foods." *Canadian Veterinary Journal.,* 1989, 30: 528-531.

Eastwood, M.A., "The Physiological Effect of Dietary Fiber: An Update." *Annual Review of Nutrition,* 1992; 12: 19-35.

Fernstrom, J. D., "Dietary Amino Acids and Brain Function." *Journal of the American Dietetic Association,* 1994; 94(1): 71-77.

Hilton, J., "Carbohydrates in the Nutrition of the Dog." *Canadian Veterinary Journal,* 1990; 31: 128-129.

Hilton, J.W. and Atkinson, J.L., "High Lipid and High Protein Dog Foods." *Canadian Veterinary Journal,* 1988; 29: 76-77.

Huber, T. L., Laflamme, D., Comer, K.M., and Anderson, W. H., "Nutrient Digestion of Dry Dog Foods Containing Plant and Animal Proteins." *Canine Practice,* 1994; 19(2): 11-13.

Hudson, B.J.F., "Oilseeds as Sources of Essential Fatty Acids." *Human Nutrition: Food Sciences and Nutrition,* 1987; 41F: 1-13.

Lyle, B.J. McMahon, K.E., and Kreutler, P.A., "Assessing the Potential Dietary Impact of Replacing Dietary Fat with Other Macronutrients." *Journal of Nutrition,* 1992; 122: 211-216.

Messina, M. J., Persky, V., Setchell, K.D.R., and Barnes, S., "Soy Intake and Cancer Risk—A Review of the Invitro and Invivo Data." *Nutrition and Cancer—An International Journal,* 1994; 21(2): 113-131

Miles, C.W., "The Metabolizable Energy of Diets Differing in Dietary Fat and Fiber Measured in Humans." *Journal of Nutrition,* 1992, 122: 306-311.

Schmidt, E.B. and Dyerberg, J., "Omega-3 Fatty Acids—Current Status in Cardiovascular Medicine." *Drugs,* 1994; 47(3): 405-424.

Watson, P., Simpson, K.W., and Bedford, P.G.C., "Hypercholesterolemia in Briards in the United Kingdom." *Research in Veterinary Science,* 1993; 54(1): 80-85.

White, P.D., "Essential Fatty Acids: Use in Management of Canine Atropy." *Compendium on Continuing Education for the Practicing Veterinarian,* 1993; 15(3): 451-457.

Good nutrition is essential for working dogs and dogs that are under constant stress on the show circuit. Photo by Judith Strom.

Questions to Ponder . . .

What is beta-carotene and why is it safer than vitamin A? Why should vitamin A supplementation be supervised by a veterinarian? What is a major drawback to beta-carotene?

What is the most common use for vitamin E in foods?

What age of dog requires increased amounts of thiamin (vitamin B_1) in the diet?

Should B vitamins be supplemented to your older dog?

Can deficiencies in certain vitamins cause skin and haircoat problems in your dog?

Are certain vitamin supplementations effective in treating diseases?

Which vitamins in excessive amounts can cause toxicities?

What are some sources for vitamin D, other than the sun's conversion in your skin?

Although vitamin C is not required, why might supplementation be recommended?

**Learn the answers to these
and many other nutrition questions
in Chapter 4.**

4

VITAMINS

Vitamins are organic substances required in a dog's diet. They are derived entirely from plants or animals. One of the main differences between vitamins and other nutrients is that they are critical to life but are only required in very small amounts. The need for vitamins is expressed in milligrams (thousandths of a gram) or even micrograms (millionths of a gram). All of the vitamins needed by your dog on a daily basis could be provided in a fraction of a teaspoon. Vitamins are one of the family of nutrients that does not contribute calories (energy) to the diet. Many, however, are important in the conversion of calories to usable energy.

Vitamins are critical to any discussion on nutrition. If vitamins are not provided adequately in the diet, deficiencies can result. This is one of the definitions of vitamins—they cannot be made by the body in sufficient amounts to maintain life and need to be provided in the diet. If a substance does not cause deficiency symptoms when limited in the diet, it is not considered a true vitamin. Deficiencies are actually rare in dogs fed commercial diets.

Vitamins often have at least two names, a vitamin name and a chemical name. The vitamin name is usually just one of convenience and doesn't imply a specific compound. Most of the vitamins actually belong to "families" of compounds, and the terminology can become confusing. Take, for instance, vitamin A. It is also called retinol, retinal, and retinoic acid. Many synthetic products on the market, such as Retin-A and Accutane (isotretinoin), are derivatives of vitamin A (retinoids). To truly appreciate

Guide to Vitamins and Vitamin Look-Alikes

Vitamin	AKA	Solubility	Active In
A	Retinol	Fat-soluble	Skin, eyes, mouth, intestines, reproductive tract
B_1	Thiamin	Water-soluble	Carbohydrate metabolism
B_2	Riboflavin	Water-soluble	Enzyme formation; protein, fat and carbohydrate metabolism
B_3	Niacin	Water-soluble	Nutrient utilization; cholesterol regulation
B_5	Pantothenic acid	Water-soluble	Reactions involving carbohydrates, fats, and amino acids
B_6	Pyridoxine	Water-soluble	Amino acid metabolism
B_{12}	Cobalamin	Water-soluble	Carbon-mover; carbohydrate and fat metabolism; nerve transmission
B_{15}	Dimethylglycine	Water-soluble	Immune function; tissue repair
B_{17}	Laetrile	Water-soluble	Unknown
C	Ascorbate	Water-soluble	Antioxidant; collagen formation
D	Calcitriol	Fat-soluble	Calcium and phosphorus regulation
E	Tocopherol	Fat-soluble	Antioxidant; prostaglandin regulation
K	Menadione	Fat-soluble	Blood clotting
Folic acid	Folate	Water-soluble	Carbon-mover; genetic transfer
Biotin	Biotin	Water-soluble	Protein construction
Choline	Choline	Water-soluble	Nerve transmission; liver function
Inositol	Inositol	Water-soluble	Fat metabolism

the practical aspects of nutrition, it is necessary to leave behind old prejudices toward long and confusing chemical names and try to understand why the vitamins do what they do.

Vitamins function with other nutrients and enzymes to help the body function optimally, to help create blood cells, hormones, genetic material, and special chemicals, and to promote normal function of the eyes, skin, reproductive system, heart, and internal organs. Because vitamins assist in all of these other processes, most are regarded as coenzymes—substances that help get things done.

There are many substances that have been designated as vitamins. Four of these will dissolve in fat (vitamins A, D, E, and K), and nine are soluble in water (vitamin C and eight B vitamins). These two families of vitamins are referred to as fat-soluble and water-soluble, respectively. A vitamin to people, however, may simply be a nutrient to dogs. For example, vitamin C is essential in people, but because dogs can make their own, it really doesn't fit the definition of a vitamin. In dogs, vitamin C should really be referred to as ascorbic acid. Similarly, inositol and choline share many similarities with the B vitamins, but because deficiency syndromes haven't been described for either, they are not considered true vitamins. For the purpose of discussion, just assume that there are many vitamins as well as nutrients that have vitamin-like effects on dogs.

FAT-SOLUBLE VITAMINS

Fat-soluble vitamins are those that can be dissolved in fats. Those that can't are said to be water-soluble. It's sort of like an oil-and-vinegar salad dressing. Some ingredients dissolve in the oil and others dissolve in the vinegar. The combination provides a balance of the two. Most fat-soluble vitamins are no more related to one another than the B vitamins are to vitamin C. This is an old distinction used from the days when vitamins were still being explored and characterized. It doesn't imply that they are better, stronger, or more necessary than the water-soluble vitamins.

When dogs eat their food, the fat-soluble vitamins are present in the fat content of the meal and can be stored in fat. This is one advantage that they have over the water-soluble vitamins. Because they can be stored in the body, to some degree it is not essential that they be consumed on a daily basis. These vitamins are eaten and then combine with other fats in the diet, or with bile, to be later absorbed through the intestines. The fat-soluble vitamins include A, D, E, and K.

VITAMIN A

Vitamin A is not a single chemical but rather a series of compounds that include retinol, retinal, and retinoic acid. All are derived from animals (primarily in the liver, eggs, milk, and kidneys), and all are fat-soluble. One form of vitamin A, retinyl palmitate, can be absorbed without dietary fat and may be useful in dogs with chronic digestive diseases. A compound related to vitamin A, beta-carotene, is found in vegetation and can be converted to vitamin A in the body. The process of how vitamin A functions in the body is a wonder to behold.

Foods Rich in Vitamin A

Liver	Kidney	Egg yolk	Whole milk

In many ways, vitamin A functions more like a hormone than a vitamin. What does this mean? Well, vitamin A is regulated by the body, just like insulin or any of the other hormones. When a dog eats his meal, vitamin A may exist in several different chemical forms. If vegetables are eaten, vitamin A may even start as beta-carotene, but the liver converts this to one of the forms of vitamin A. In the body, the predominant form of the vitamin (retinol) is transported throughout the bloodstream attached to a carrier protein (retinol-binding protein). The body uses specific carrier proteins to ferry important substances around to different organs. When vitamin A reaches the bloodstream, therefore, it doesn't just float around aimlessly. The carrier protein picks it up and delivers it to where it needs to go. This carrier protein is manufactured in the liver as needed. The more vitamin A there is in the diet, the more carrier protein is produced and the more vitamin A is delivered to tissues. In many ways, this is similar to how hormones function. Their production is closely regulated, they travel in the bloodstream tightly bound to protein, and they exert their effects throughout the body.

While vitamin A is being shuttled around the body attached to its carrier protein, each individual tissue determines which form of the vitamin it prefers to perform its unique function. Although retinol is the main form of vitamin A, it is converted within the cells of the body tissues to other products that perform specific actions. For instance, within the eyes, retinol is converted to retinal (retinaldehyde) before it can function in vision. Other vitamin A derivatives (retinoids) have specific actions in the skin, intestines, mouth, respiratory tract, and other epithelial tissues. Synthetic chemical derivatives of vitamin A are used to treat acne (isotretinoin) and psoriasis (etretinate), and topical products (Retin-A) are also available.

Vitamin-A deficiency is rare in dogs, but conditions that are vitamin A-responsive are more common. This is an important distinction. Because vitamin A has so many actions in the body, and because it often acts like a hormone, conditions may respond to supplementation even if the dog isn't deficient in the vitamin. This is also how antibiotics work, although people and animals never have actual antibiotic deficiency. The uses of supplemental vitamin A are covered more completely in Chapter 9.

Never use vitamin A indiscriminately, because toxicity is a possible complication. Vitamin A is stored in the liver, which means that oversupplementation can result in extremely high levels of accumulaton in the body. Vitamin A toxicity can even occur *without* supplementation if the diet contains a high percentage of ingredients rich in vitamin A, such as liver or fatty acids (cod-liver oil). Side effects can be widespread, including dry skin and mucous membranes, bone pain, weight loss, and dry eyes. Only consider vitamin A supplementation if your dog is directly under veterinary supervision.

Beta-carotene is sometimes referred to as a precursor or provitamin, because it is converted to vitamin A within the body. For this reason it is mentioned here, even though it is not a vitamin by the strict definition. Beta-carotene is also an important antioxidant that scavenges dangerous free radicals within the body. It is found in highest concentration in green, yellow, or orange produce, including carrots, spinach, sweet potatoes, and cantaloupes. Beta-carotene is safer than vitamin A because it doesn't result in a buildup of vitamin A in the body; vitamin A is created from beta-carotene only as the body needs it. This makes it impossible to overdose on beta-carotene.

Foods Rich in Beta-Carotene

Spinach	Broccoli	Carrots	Sweet potatoes

Scientists speculate that beta-carotene, acting as an antioxidant, may prevent oxygen-derived free radicals from converting LDL cholesterol ("bad cholesterol") into more harmful derivatives that clog arteries. Combining beta-carotene with aspirin appears to lessen even more the risk of heart attack in people. A diet rich in beta-carotene is related to a lowered incidence of lung, colon, prostate, cervical, and breast cancer in people. Almost no research has been done concerning the merits of beta-carotene in the diets of dogs. Before you consider supplementation, it is important to realize that a beta-carotene capsule may lack some of the goodness of natural vegetables. Other ingredients found in these foods, such as canthaxanthin and lycopene, are not converted to vitamin A but are thought to have beneficial effects.

Beta-carotene can be converted to vitamin A in the body, and for this reason, most current nutrient labels talk about retinol equivalents (RE) rather than specific amounts of both nutrients. One RE is equivalent to 3.33 IU of vitamin A or 10 IU of beta-carotene.

The one drawback to beta-carotene is that it can't be used for vitamin A–responsive diseases because it doesn't cause marked elevations of vitamin A in the blood following supplementation. But it is still an important antioxidant that might be helpful in preventing various heart ailments and cancers.

VITAMIN D

Vitamin D is another fat-soluble vitamin that functions much like a hormone. There are several different forms of vitamin D. One form, vitamin D_2, is absorbed from the intestines, a process that requires adequate bile acids and pancreatic enzymes. A different form, vitamin D_3 is activated in the skin (cholecalciferol) and then converted by enzymes in the liver to another form (calcifediol). It is finally converted by the kidney to its final, biologically active form—calcitriol.

Why is it important for you to understand vitamin D metabolism in your dog's body? There are several good reasons, but the most important is that if you understand the process, you are less likely to bring harm to your dog by giving him an inappropriate diet.

Foods Rich in Vitamin D

Fortified milk	Yogurt	Cottage cheese	Cheese

The perceived need for vitamin D has changed dramatically since it was originally used to prevent rickets in children. During the past twenty years, extensive research has shown that vitamin D does much more than regulate calcium in the small intestine, bones, and kidneys. For many years, vitamin D was considered a safe and effective vitamin that prevented rickets by helping the body correctly utilize calcium. Only recently has it become known that other tissues, including the mammary glands, the thymus, the brain, the ovaries, the pituitary gland, the stomach, the pancreas, the skin, and white blood cells also have "receptor sites" for vitamin D. For example, extracts of the cancer malignant melanoma have been suppressed in laboratory situations by calcitriol, the active form of vitamin D. That's the good part. The bad part is that vitamin D can also cause toxic reactions in dogs.

Vitamin D is a powerful force in regulating calcium and phosphorus in the body. The principal players in this drama are vitamin D, calcium, phosphorus, the hormones of the parathyroid gland (located in the neck beside the thyroid gland), the kidneys, the intestines, and the bones.

Vitamin D levels are kept very constant in the body and are regulated by blood levels of calcium. When the body perceives a need for calcium, it causes the parathyroid gland to produce a hormone called parathormone or parathyroid hormone (PTH). This, then, causes the kidney to produce the active form of vitamin D, called calcitriol. The "feedback loop" works this way: when calcium levels are low, PTH is released from the parathyroid gland, which then signals the kidney to release activated vitamin D. The vitamin D then exerts itself on many organs of the body. First, it increases the absorption rate for both calcium and phosphorus from the intestines. In this way, it maximizes the amount of calcium that can be utilized from the foods eaten. With a similar purpose, it lessens the amount of calcium and phosphorus that are lost by the kidneys into the urine. In a somewhat counterproductive move, vitamin D also causes a loss of calcium from bones to increase the amount of calcium in the blood. As a result, vitamin D causes increased levels of calcium in the bloodstream by increasing use of dietary calcium, preventing loss of calcium into the urine, and borrowing calcium from its storehouse in the bones.

Obviously, vitamin D, calcium, phosphorus, and hormones act in a very complicated way to regulate the levels of calcium in the blood. Supplementating your dog's diet with these nutrients can be potentially dev-

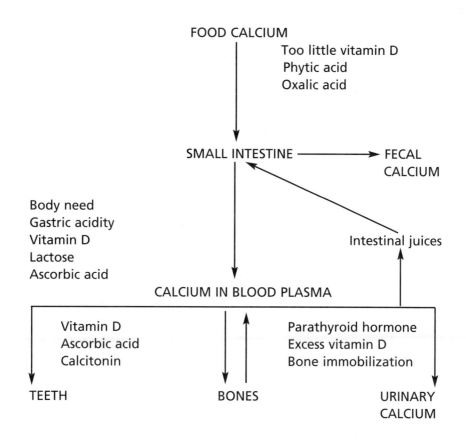

astating. There is also much evidence to suggest that vitamin D is not even needed in the diet. There is sufficient vitamin D activated in the skin to meet the body's needs, even in rapidly growing puppies.

A deficiency of vitamin D is referred to as rickets in the young and as osteomalacia in adults. Do not confuse osteomalacia with osteoporosis. Vitamin D deficiency is very rare in dogs, so there is little reason to consider supplementation. Almost all dog foods are well fortified with vitamin D, which means that there is a very real risk that toxicity could result from supplementation. Unfortunately, many owners and breeders supplement their dog's diets with vitamin D, especially growing pups. These owners are trying to be helpful, because they know that vitamin D will provide more calcium to their dogs. They believe that these dogs need calcium because they are growing, or they're pregnant, or they've just whelped puppies and are nursing. After all, children are encouraged to drink milk to get vitamin D and avoid rickets!

Although the amounts present in supplements may not seem excessive, they can generate blood levels of vitamin D hundreds of times higher than recommended. The result of the vitamin D overload is that calcium levels climb in the blood, causing stiffness, joint pain, and weakness. With prolonged use (months), mineralized calcium deposits can occur in a variety of tissues, including the kidneys, lungs, intestines, blood vessels, and joints. Because vitamin D is fat-soluble and is stored in the liver, even immediate discontinuation of supplementation can cause problems that last for weeks or months.

Another source of vitamin-D toxicity that you may want to be aware of is rat poison. Many of the newer rodent poisons contain cholecalciferol and kill rats by vitamin-D overload. The poison increases blood levels of calcium to excessive amounts that in turn lodge in the kidneys, causing kidney failure and electrolyte disturbances. A package that contains only 0.75 percent cholecalciferol may seem safe enough, but it provides about 10,000 times the daily recommended dosage of vitamin D—easily enough to kill a dog. If your dog is exposed to one of these rodenticides, seek immediate veterinary attention care or your dog may suffer permanent kidney damage. Most animals that are poisoned experience weakness, vomiting, and constipation. With kidney failure, animals have increased thirst and urination. Exposed dogs should be kept indoors at the veterinary hospital, avoiding sun exposure that stimulates vitamin D production by the skin. Most animals will require fluid therapy, and even hormones (calcitonin) may be necessary to promote calcium excretion by the kidneys.

VITAMIN E

Vitamin E is not a single chemical, but rather a family of compounds called tocopherols. The tocopherols are all fat-soluble and require effective digestion and absorption of fat to become usable. Alpha tocopherol is the most common and most potent form of the vitamin. Vitamin E is found in most vegetable oils, seeds, and soy but is not plentiful in most foods derived from animals. And not all forms of vitamin E are equally active. For example, safflower oil is not only a good source of linoleic acid, but 90 percent of the vitamin E contained in it is alpha tocopherol, the most potent form. Compare this with corn oil, in which only 10 percent of the vitamin E is present as alpha tocopherol. The vitamin E in soybean oil is mainly gamma tocopherol, which has very little potency. Therefore, soybean oil may be listed as a good source of vitamin E, but the form present is not likely to be very beneficial. The vitamin E present in vegetable oils is nature's way of preventing those oils from going rancid (oxidation)

Foods Rich in Vitamin E

Wheat-germ oil	Safflower oil	Sunflower oil	Spinach

Vitamin E is particularly efficient as an antioxidant, halting the damage done to body tissues by free radicals. It stabilizes cell membranes and protects tissues. It is also thought that vitamin E affects the production of the prostaglandins, hormonelike substances that regulate a variety of body functions, including inflammation, blood pressure, muscle contraction, and reproduction.

There are many myths surrounding vitamin E. What *is* known is that vitamin E is an effective antioxidant, and this alone makes supplementation worth considering. In this regard, its function is often associated with the mineral selenium, with which it works in concert. More information on vitamin E supplementation can be found in Chapter 9.

Vitamin-E deficiency is very rare in dogs, and most information has been gleaned from experimental studies. In dogs that have been fed vitamin E–deficient diets, reproduction and muscle activity are affected. A disorder of the eyes, similar to retinal atrophy, also results. Vitamin E, more than any other vitamin, is an important regulator of the immune system.

The body's requirement for vitamin E actually depends on the amount of polyunsaturated fatty acids (PUFAs) in the diet. Although polyunsaturates are considered to be "good fats," they do increase the body's requirement for vitamin E. When foods are cooked and processed, their vitamin-E content is reduced. In fact, most of the vitamin E used in supplements is derived from the by-products of flour and oil processing. Cold-pressed, unbleached vegetable oils, such as safflower oil, are the best natural sources of vitamin E. Unfortunately, the term "cold-pressed" is often emphasized without being clarified. An oil that is cold-pressed will not have exceeded 110 °F at any stage of processing. Refined oils are often degummed, separated, bleached, and deodorized at temperatures that deactivate most of the vitamin E present.

When it comes to supplementation, vitamin E is much safer than the other fat-soluble vitamins. Although complications with blood clotting or thyroid activity are associated with excessive supplementation in people, this does not appear to be a problem in dogs.

VITAMIN K

Vitamin K is also a group of substances (quinone derivatives) that are important in blood clotting. This vitamin is involved in the production of prothrombin, a specific protein necessary for coagulation of blood. Deficiencies of vitamin K can lead to bleeding disorders.

Most of the vitamin K that is needed for clotting comes from the diet, but an adequate amount is also produced in the intestines from bacteria in the small bowel. Important food sources of vitamin K include broccoli, turnips, lettuce, liver, and cereals.

Theoretically, a vitamin-K deficiency should be very rare in dogs because they produce most of their daily requirements through bacterial action in the small intestines. It is only under abnormal conditions, such as interference of intestinal bacteria or impaired absorption or utilization of vitamin K, that supplementation would be required.

Foods Rich in Vitamin K

| Broccoli | Turnip greens | Lettuce | Spinach |

There are two circumstances that warrant vitamin-K supplementation. Both are preventable. Many rodent poisons contain coumarins (e.g., warfarin) that exert an anti-vitamin K effect. If dogs are accidentally or maliciously exposed to these rodent poisons, they can bleed to death. The other potential risk is that vitamin-K levels can be hampered in dogs maintained on long-term antibiotic therapy. The antibiotics may attack the problem-causing microbes but may also destroy beneficial intestinal bacteria, including those that manufacture vitamin K.

Vitamin-K supplementation is only warranted when prescribed by a veterinarian for a specific purpose. There is absolutely no benefit from providing vitamin K to an otherwise healthy dog.

WATER-SOLUBLE VITAMINS

The water-soluble vitamins include the series of B vitamins as well as vitamin C. In contrast to the fat-soluble vitamins, the water-soluble vitamins can be dissolved in the blood and are not stored to any appreciable extent, although there are exceptions. The water-soluble vitamins are readily excreted into the urine and are lost from the body, meaning that they need to be provided on a regular basis.

B VITAMINS

The B vitamins share some similarities, but for the most part they are distinct nutrients. They are all water-soluble and are often found in the same foods, but other than that, marked differences occur between the compounds referred to as B vitamins.

Thiamin (Vitamin B_1)

Thiamin was one of the first vitamins to be recognized when the consumption of polished or refined rice in the Far East was found to cause beri-beri (extreme weakness). That's because the rice bran contained most of the thiamin and it was lost in processing.

Thiamin deficiency has been reported in dogs, but it is rare. Because thiamin is progressively destroyed by the cooking of foods, a deficiency could become a problem in commercially processed foods. Most dog-food manufacturers, however, add plenty of thiamin to the ration before processing so that the final product meets or exceeds requirements.

Foods Rich in Thiamin

| Pork | Organ meats | Green peas | Dried beans |

The actual requirement for thiamin varies depending on the amount of carbohydrate in the diet. Because the vitamin is important in carbohydrate metabolism, dogs consuming diets low in carbohydrates require less thiamin than those on high-carbohydrate diets. Supplementation is rarely necessary but may be considered in dogs on high-carbohydrate or high-fiber diets. The semimoist dog foods contain much processed or "refined" carbohydrate and might potentially increase thiamin requirements.

Thiamin deficiency can also occur when dogs consume foods that contain large quantities of thiaminase, an enzyme that destroys thiamin. This is most common in dogs fed uncooked fish. Thiaminase (and thiamin) are progressively destroyed by cooking, so most processed dog foods do not contain this enzyme. A diet high in fats, sugar, or other nutrient-poor foods is likely to be low in thiamin.

Thiamin is widely distributed in foods, and good sources include whole grains, beef, beans, lentils, brewer's yeast, and brown rice. Refined foods lose most of their thiamin content. The absorption of thiamin from the diet requires the presence of folic acid. Therefore, anything that interferes with body stores of folic acid can potentially result in lowered levels of thiamin. Also, if home-cooked meals are being prepared, much of the

Older dogs often benefit from supplementation with all the B vitamins. Photo by Judith Strom.

thiamin can be lost if the cooking water is discarded.

The body has no real mechanism to store thiamin, and daily intake is necessary. Within the body, most of the vitamin is found in the muscle, heart, brain, kidney, and liver. Because thiamin is excreted by the kidneys into the urine, diseases that cause an increase in urine production can result in lowered levels of this vitamin. Dogs with kidney disease, diabetes, or heart disease or dogs being treated with diuretics (water pills) or digitalis might benefit from thiamin supplementation. Puppies, working dogs, pregnant bitches, and geriatric dogs require increased amounts of thiamin in the diet.

Riboflavin (Vitamin B$_2$)

Riboflavin plays a crucial role in the formation of several enzymes and is found mainly in the liver. This vitamin plays a major role in the metabolism of proteins, fats, and carbohydrates and enhances the utilization of pyridoxine (vitamin B$_6$). Riboflavin is also needed to help convert tryptophan to niacin. Unlike most of the B vitamins, riboflavin maintains some stores in the liver and therefore is not depleted as rapidly

---

Foods Rich in Riboflavin

Dairy products	Liver	Lean meat	Mushrooms

Riboflavin is found in milk, other dairy products, cereals, meats, and some vegetables. In dogs, a small amount is also manufactured by bacteria in the intestines. Unlike thiamin, riboflavin is not readily destroyed by cooking, but it does deteriorate on exposure to light. This means that milk should not be stored in clear glass bottles and that fruits and vegetables should be kept in a crisper, covered from exposure to light.

Riboflavin deficiency occurs in dogs, but it is rare because riboflavin is liberally added to commercial dog foods. It has been implicated in eye and skin problems and in small-testicle development. Supplementation is sometimes used as general supplements in breeding males and females and in dogs with specific eye or skin diseases. Elderly dogs often benefit from supplementation with all of the B vitamins.

Niacin (Vitamin B$_3$)

Vitamin B$_3$ comes in several forms, and niacin is one of them. The others are called nicotinic acid and niacinamide. The classic deficiency in people is referred to as pellagra, a condition characterized by skin problems, diarrhea, and dementia. In dogs it is sometimes referred to as "black-tongue," in which the mouth is affected.

In the body, niacin is converted to niacinamide (also called nicotinamide), which functions as part of an enzyme system essential for the proper utilization of nutrients. In dogs, the requirement for niacin is not static. The actual requirement depends on the levels of the amino acid tryptophan, which can be converted to the vitamin inside the body. This conversion can be accomplished by dogs but not by cats. Therefore, in some nutritional tables, requirements may be expressed as "niacin equivalents," including the preformed niacin ingested as well as that converted in the body from tryptophan. This can be calculated reliably because tryptophan usually constitutes 1 percent of the total protein intake, and it takes 60 mg of tryptophan to produce 1 mg of niacin.

Foods Rich in Niacin

Chicken	Fish	Beans	Brewer's yeast

Niacin is found in many foods including meat, milk, fish, soybeans, Brewer's yeast, and whole grains. Corn is a poor source of niacin and tryptophan, which means that diets high in corn content and low in other protein sources might require supplementation. This is commonly done by pet-food manufacturers to ensure that their products are not deficient in any of the B vitamins. Wheat and other grains are also weak in niacin but usually contain enough tryptophan to prevent deficiencies. Supplementation with niacin itself is usually not necessary. Excessive amounts can cause a flushing reaction in both dogs and people.

Nicotinic acid, one of the metabolites of niacin, is used to treat people with high cholesterol and triglyceride levels. The nicotinic acid lowers blood cholesterol, LDL-cholesterol (bad cholesterol), and triglycerides and increases HDL-cholesterol (good cholesterol) levels. Niacin is also a possible aid in treating schizophrenia. This was investigated because some of the symptoms of pellagra are similar to those of schizophrenia. Niacinamide (nicotinamide) has been used successfully in the treatment of some immune-mediated diseases in the dog, especially lupus erythematosus. Ultimate success rates are not yet available.

Pantothenic Acid (Vitamin B_5)

Pantothenic acid plays a crucial role in many of the reactions involving carbohydrates, fats, and amino acids, but receives less press than the other B vitamins. Deficiencies are highly unlikely in dogs because pantothenic acid is widespread in animal and plant tissues. Good dietary sources include liver, fish, poultry, grains, and potatoes. Significant amounts of pantothenic acid are lost in the milling and refining of grains, however, and as much as 50 percent of the pantothenic acid is lost in the thawing and cooking of meat. The ubiquitous nature of vitamin B_5 explains its name, derived from the Greek "Pantothen," meaning "from all sides" or "from everywhere."

Foods Rich in Pantothenic Acid

| Liver | Fish | Chicken | Cereals |

In the body, pantothenic acid is converted to coenzyme A, an important contributor in breaking down proteins, fats, and carbohydrates for energy. It accomplishes this by acting in concert with thiamin, riboflavin, niacin, pyridoxine, and biotin. It also aids in the production of vitamin D, cholesterol, and some hormones and neurotransmitters.

Deficiencies of pantothenic acid have been recognized in dogs but only when the dogs have been fed semipurified diets. The clinical signs of deficiency include hair loss, depression, indigestion, fatty liver, and poor growth. Once again, properly prepared diets are exceedingly unlikely to result in pantothenic-acid deficiency.

Pyridoxine (Vitamin B_6)

Vitamin B_6, like many of the other vitamins examined, is not a single chemical substance. It consists of three closely related cousins, namely pyridoxine, pyridoxal, and pyridoxamine. Although pyridoxine is the most common form taken in supplements, all dietary sources are eventually converted to pyridoxal in the body. This process relies heavily on the presence of riboflavin and magnesium.

Vitamin B_6 is an essential nutrient in the dog, and is important in amino-acid metabolism. Pyridoxal is involved in the conversion of tryptophan to niacin. Vitamin B_6 is also required in the formation of prostaglandins. High-protein diets increase the requirements for vitamin B_6, just as high-carbohydrate diets increase the need for thiamin. The higher the protein content of the diet, the greater amount of pyridoxal needed. In dogs, a vitamin-B_6 deficiency causes weight loss and anemia; in some cases, hair loss and itchiness have been reported.

Foods Rich in Pyridoxine

| Lean meat | Wheat germ | Brewer's yeast | Soybeans |

Good dietary sources of vitamin B_6 are protein-rich foods such as meats, fish, egg yolks, seeds, nuts, and whole-grain cereals. As much as 70 percent of the vitamin is lost when foods are frozen or when cooking water is discarded. Because cottage cheese is low in vitamin B_6, animals on restricted protein diets based on this protein source may require supplementation. Supplementation with high levels of vitamin B_6 can cause side effects, so a general-purpose B-vitamin preparation is more desirable.

Much research has been done on the use of vitamin-B_6 supplementation in people-related health problems. It has been recommended as an aid in treating asthma and is sometimes suggested for people with insomnia, depression, irritability, and nervousness. It is occasionally recommended for patients with carpal tunnel syndrome, heart disease, and even premenstrual syndrome. Little research has been done in dogs regarding supplementation, but vitamin B_6 might help with allergies, chronic infections, heart disease, and calcium oxalate urolithiasis (urinary-tract stones).

Cobalamin (Vitamin B_{12})

Cobalamin was one of the last vitamins to be studied and was not isolated until the 1950s. It is effective in treating pernicious anemia in people. It is the only vitamin that contains a trace element and the first nutrient found to contain cobalt. In its common form, the active ingredient, cobalamin, is combined with cyanide to form cyanocobalamin. The cyanide group is not found on the vitamin naturally but is a consequence of processing. It is not present in toxic amounts.

Vitamin B_{12} is responsible for several important functions within the body. It helps "move carbons" but is also involved in carbohydrate and fat metabolism. Myelin, the coating of nerves, is also synthesized with the help of cobalamin. This myelin sheath allows the nerve transmissions to proceed at top speed. Cobalamin has another critical role in the process of replicating genetic material in each cell of the body.

Foods Rich in Cobalamin

Poultry	Fish	Milk	Organ meats

Vitamin B_{12} is found only in animal-based foods so animals (and people) on vegetarian rations are prone to deficiency. The best sources are liver, organ meats, and meats. Lesser quantities are found in eggs, dairy products, yogurt, fish, and brewer's yeast. For animals on vegetarian diets, deficiency is still unlikely if the ration contains eggs, yogurt or other dairy products. This vitamin is not produced in plants, only microbes. Therefore, any product that has been allowed to ferment (e.g., yogurt) or otherwise includes bacteria or yeast (e.g., brewer's yeast, algae, kelp, some forms of aloe) will likely provide at least some of the requirements for cobalamin. At least some of the vitamin will be lost if the foods are cooked above the boiling point. Because cobalamin is stored in the liver, deficiencies do not occur until after being on a poor or deficient diet for many years.

Deficiencies of vitamin B_{12} are uncommon in the dog but, when they do occur, often reflect neurological disturbances because of the effect on myelin. The vitamin B_{12} in the diet is absorbed from the small intestines with the help of a compound known as intrinsic factor, which is produced in the stomach. Therefore, diseases of the stomach or small intestine could result in B_{12} deficiency. The same is true for processes that result in the overgrowth of bacteria in the intestines. A vitamin-B_{12} deficiency is often not seen during an acute crisis, because stores of cobalamin are present in the liver.

Supplementation with vitamin B_{12} is sometimes necessary for dogs with anemia or those with chronic digestive diseases. Because in these cases it might be poorly absorbed, supplementation is usually accomplished by injections. To minimize any risk of toxicity, hydroxycobalamin is often used for supplementation to avoid the cyanide component of the parent compound.

FOLIC ACID

Folic acid, folacin, and their parent group, the folates, were named because they are found in green, leafy vegetables (i.e., foliage). Other important sources include liver, kidneys, eggs, brewer's yeast, and whole-grain cereals. In dogs, it is likely that most of the required folic acid is contributed by bacteria in the intestines. In nature, folic acid is commonly associated with the amino acid, glutamic acid. When ingested, the folic acid is converted to its active form with the help of vitamin B_{12}, niacin, and vitamin C.

The folates perform a vital function in the body by transferring single carbon groups. This may not sound essential, but the process is necessary for the synthesis of thymidine, an integral component of DNA. This allows folacin to maintain the genetic code of each cell and to transfer genetic material from one cell to another. A deficiency limits cell function and affects the growth and repair of all cells in the body. Those affected most are the ones with the highest growth rates. Therefore, with folic-acid deficiency, anemia can result as the lack of adequate amounts of DNA affect red blood cell production.

Foods Rich in Folic Acid

Brewer's yeast	Liver	Dark-green, leafy vegetables

Supplementation of folic acid is often used in dogs with anemia or those given chronic antibiotic therapy. It is used in conjunction with antibiotics because these medications may kill intestinal bacteria important in the manufacture of folic acid. In people, this B vitamin appears to guard against two of the most common neurological defects afflicting newborns: spina bifida and anencephaly. Controlled experiments in mice, however, show that folic-acid deficiency is only part of the problem. Other research has purported a link between folic-acid deficiency and cervical cancer. Studies have shown that the folic-acid content of the American diet is only half that recommended. These human applications of folic acid supplementation have not yet been evaluated in dogs. However, dogs are not as prone to deficiencies because they can produce their own unless we hamper them with chronic antibiotic use.

BIOTIN

Biotin is important in the transfer of carbon dioxide (carboxyl) groups and a deficiency in this B vitamin results in a reduction of amino acids being incorporated into proteins. This also impairs fatty acid synthesis and the proper utilization of glucose. Biotin works intimately with folic acid, pantothenic acid, and cobalamin in the processing of fats, amino acids, and carbohydrates.

Foods Rich in Biotin

Kidney	Liver	Oatmeal	Egg yolk

Biotin deficiency is unlikely in dogs because it is found in many sources and because intestinal bacteria can manufacture all the biotin needed on a daily basis. Biotin is widely distributed in meats, soybeans, Brewer's yeast, dairy products, and wholegrain cereals. The feeding of eggs to dogs has often been discouraged because of the fear that biotin deficiency would result. This fear is based on the fact that raw egg whites contain avidin, which can bind biotin, making it unavailable for use. This is true, but avidin is very heat sensitive, and cooking the eggs before feeding (which is common anyway) removes the risk. Also, if the whole egg is fed, egg yolks are a very rich source of biotin.

A biotin deficiency results in scaly skin but actual deficiencies are extremely unlikely. The easiest way to create a deficiency, however, would be to give antibiotics long term (which destroys intestinal bacteria that could make biotin) and feeding large quantities of raw egg whites. Tetracyclines and sulfa drugs are the worst offenders in reducing the growth of intestinal bacteria that produce biotin. Although biotin has been recommended for scaling skin diseases, it rarely contributes to an effective treatment.

B-VITAMIN LOOK-ALIKES

CHOLINE

Choline is recognized as an essential nutrient but, because deficiencies have not been reported, it is not considered a true vitamin. However, its actions are related to that of the B vitamins. It is a part of acetylcholine, the important neurotransmitter involved in the electrical conduction of nerve impulses. Choline is also one of the essential components of cell membranes that surround every cell in the body. Another important function of choline is that it can serve to transfer carbon (methyl) groups, like the folates and vitamin B_{12}.

A deficiency of choline in the dog can result in impairment of liver and kidney function. The main cause for this is fatty infiltration of the liver, presumably because fat transport is impaired. Choline functions in the production and transportation of fats from the liver, thus having a sparing effect. Despite this vital role, an actual deficiency is highly unlikely if there is adequate methionine (an amino acid) in the diet, which can also act as a carbon donor. Methionine, together with the help of cobalamin and folic acid, help to prevent deficiencies of choline. Because choline is common in the diet and due to the sparing effect of methionine, a deficiency in the dog is highly unlikely.

Choline is used frequently as a supplement for dogs, especially those with liver disease. It can be supplemented individually, or as lecithin, which combines choline with glycerol and certin fatty acids. Other important dietary sources include brewer's yeast, eggs, liver, other organ meats, wheat-germ, lean meats, and soybeans.

INOSITOL

Inositol, like choline, is involved in fat metabolism, especially as it relates to the liver. Also, like choline, it is not considered a true vitamin although it is frequently grouped with the B vitamins. The body and intestinal bacteria can make inositol but whether these levels are optimal or not has yet to be determined. To avoid confusion throughout this book, choline and inositol will be discussed along with the vitamins.

DIMETHYLGLYCINE (DMG)

Dimethylglycine is sometimes referred to as vitamin B_{15} or pangamic acid, but it is not really a vitamin at all; it is a tertiary amino acid. Most of the research on this important nutrient has been conducted within the former Soviet Union. North American studies have been slow to materialize. The benefits of using this nutrient as a supplement are covered in more detail in Chapter 9.

LAETRILE (VITAMIN B_{17})

Laetrile is not a "true" B vitamin and has been shrouded in controversy since it was touted as a cancer cure many years ago. It is actually composed of two sugar molecules, called an amygdalin. Small amounts of laetrile are found in the pits of apricots, apples, peaches, plums, cherries, and nectarines. It is one of the few members of the B-vitamin family not found in brewer's yeast. Clinical trials in dogs have not been published, so any potential benefit is anecdotal at best. Fear of toxicity is based on the realization that cyanide is included in the molecular formula for laetrile.

VITAMIN C

No vitamin draws more attention from the press than vitamin C, and yet dogs have no specific requirement for it in their diets. Dogs, unlike people, are not prone to scurvy because they can manufacture ascorbic acid internally from glucose. Although dogs are not prone to scurvy, we use the term "ascorbic" anyway, which means "without scurvy."

The best sources of dietary ascorbic acid are fresh fruits and vegetables. Most meats, fish, poultry, milk, eggs, and cereals are poor sources of this vitamin. Remember, ascorbic acid is a water-soluble vitamin and the benefits of canned fruits and vegetables might be lost if the canning water is discarded. Excessive slicing or chopping of fruits and vegetables also results in increased loss of vitamin C, so minimal processing is preferred.

Foods Rich in Ascorbic Acid

Fresh fruits and vegetables

Ascorbic acid has an important role in the formation and maintenance of collagen, the foundation for the connective tissues of the body. Collagen is the supporting system for the skin, bones, tendons, ligaments, joints, blood vessels, and other tissues of the body. With the assistance of ascorbic acid, collagen is needed for the healing of wounds and the restructuring of healthy tissues.

Vitamin-C supplementation is useful in dogs, but not to correct any deficiency syndromes. Ascorbic acid is a potent antioxidant that helps tame free radicals within the body. In people, it has also been used to help postpone the onset of cataracts and to lower the incidence of cancer and heart disease. In relation to heart disease, it appears that ascorbic acid decreases the amount of a specific protein, lipoprotein (A), which has a special role in causing "clogging of the arteries." Although studies often appear to be shrouded in some degree of controversy, certain patterns of benefit have been demonstrated. In dogs, supplementation has been recommended by some breeders and researchers for hip dysplasia, osteodystrophy, and osteochondrosis. The subject of supplementation is discussed more fully in Chapter 9.

IN SUMMARY

Vitamins function as coenzymes to help convert calories to energy and create blood cells and other substances to help assure normal function of the body.

Fat soluble vitamins (A, D, E and K) are stored in fat and therefore do not have to be consumed daily.

Two of the fat soluble vitamins, A and D, could become toxic if over-supplied in the diet. Side effects from vitamin A include bone pain, dry skin and eyes, and weight loss. Too much vitamin D can cause leaching of calcium from bones, resulting in weakness, joint pain and stiffness.

Rat and mouse poisons affect vitamins D or K. Poisons with cholecalciferol cause a vitamin D overload and result in kidney failure. Poisons with coumarins (warfarin) inactivate vitamin K so that blood will not clot.

Vitamin E is an effective antioxidant and, more than any other vitamin, is an important regulator for the immune system.

Vitamins B_1, B_5, B_6, and B_{12} are all destroyed or lost by either cooking or discarding the cooking water. Vitamin B_2 is sensitive to light.

Vegetarian diets are somewhat deficient in B_{12}. To remedy this, add eggs, dairy, yogurt, fish or brewer's yeast.

Vitamin-B_6 (pyridoxine) deficiencies can cause weight loss, anemia, hair loss and itchiness.

A deficiency in folic acid affects growth, repair and function of cells. Also, it inhibits proper synthesis of DNA, which can cause anemia.

Dogs have no specific requirement for vitamin C (ascorbic acid), although it is important as an antioxidant and as an aid to collagen in wound healing.

Biotin deficiencies can cause a decrease in amino acids being synthesized into proteins, which in turn affects fatty acids and glucose.

ADDITIONAL READING:

Baker, H., et. al., "Blood Vitamin and Choline Concentrations in Healthy Domestic Cats, Dogs, and Horses." *American Journal of Veterinary Research,* 1986; 47(7): 1468-1471.

Bendich, A., "Vitamins and Immunity." *Journal of Nutrition,* 1992; 122: 601-603.

Bell, N.H., "Vitamin D—Endocrine System." *Journal of Clinical Investigation,* 1985; 76: 1-6.

Blomhoff, R., Green, M.H., and Norum, K.R., "Vitamin A: Physiological and Biochemical Processing." *Annual Review of Nutrition,* 1992; 12: 37-57.

Folkers, K., "A Renaissance in Biomedical and Clinical Research on Vitamins and Coenzymes." *Journal of Optimal Nutrition,* 1992; 1(1): 11-15.

Heid, M.K., Bills, N.D., et. al., "Folate Deficiency Alone Does Not Produce Neural Tube Defects in Mice." *Journal of Nutrition,* 1992; 122: 888-894.

Houston, D.M. and Hulland, T.J., "Thiamin Deficiency in a Team of Sled Dogs." *Canadian Veterinary Journal,* 1988; 29: 383-385.

Kolb, E., Kramer, T., and Kuba, M., et al., "Concentration of Ascorbic Acid in Blood Plasma of Lambs and Dogs Before and After Oral Application of Ascorbic Acid and Ascorbylphosphate-compounds and Excretion in the Urine of Dogs Eight Hours After." *Monatshefte fur Veterinarmedizin,* 1993; 48(8): 395.

Rath, M. and Pauling, L., "Vitamin C and Lipoprotein (A) in Relation to Cardiovascular Disease and Other Diseases." *Journal of Optimal Nutrition,* 1992; 1(1): 61-64.

Rumore, M.M., "Vitamin A as an Immunomodulating Agent." *Clinical Pharmacy,* 1993; 12: 506-514.

Scriver, C.R., "Vitamins: An Evolutionary Perspective." *Journal of Inherited and Metabolic Diseases,* 1985; 8 Suppl. 1: 2-7.

Somer, E., "The Essential Guide to Vitamins and Minerals." *Health Media of America,* 1992; 403 pp.

Steiner, M., "Vitamin E: More Than an Antioxidant." *Clinical Cardiology,* 1993; 16 (Suppl. 1): 116-118.

Toufexis, A., "The New Scoop on Vitamins." *Time,* 1992; April 6: 54-59.

White, S.D., Rosychuk, R.A.W., Reinke, S.I., and Paradis, M., "Use of Tetracycline and Niacinamide for Treatment of Autoimmune Skin Disease in 31 Dogs." *Journal of the American Veterinary Medical Association,* 1992; 200(10): 1497-1500.

White, S.D., Rosychuk, R.A.W., and Scott, K.V., et. al., "Use of Isotretinoin and Etretinate for the Treatment of Benign Cutaneous Neoplasia and Cutaneous Lymphoma in Dogs." *Journal of the American Veterinary Medical Association,* 1993; 202(3): 387-391.

Ziegler, R.G. and Byers, T., "Health Claims about Vitamin C and Cancer.", *Journal of the National Cancer Institute,* 1994; 86(11): 871-872.

Questions to Ponder . . .

Are all minerals required in the same amounts?

Should I supplement my growing puppy with calcium?

Do minerals have an effect on the immune system?

What is the function of silicon in the body?

What mineral could potentially control diabetes in dogs?

What foods are rich in zinc?

**Learn the answers to these
and many other nutrition questions
in Chapter 5.**

5
MINERALS

Minerals, also known as elements, are inorganic nutrients that perform many important functions within the body. They contribute significantly to the strength of bones and teeth and are intimately involved with many enzyme functions.

Just as the discussions of amino acids and fatty acids covered essential varieties, the same is true for minerals. For convenience, the minerals are subdivided into the macrominerals (macroelements) and the microminerals (trace elements). The division is somewhat arbitrary, but the macrominerals are needed in (relatively) large amounts while the microminerals are needed only in minute or "trace" amounts.

MACROMINERALS

CALCIUM

Calcium is the most abundant mineral in the body, and still it makes up only 2 percent of the body weight. Even before the interest in osteoporosis, pet owners and breeders seemed very concerned with the calcium intake of their dogs, especially with their rapidly growing puppies and with their bitches that were pregnant or had just whelped and were nursing their pups. After all, it was appreciated that these animals would have a higher requirement for calcium than other dogs. Right?

More than 95 percent of the body's calcium is tied up in bones, while only a percentage or two is in the teeth. Still, remember that the calcium content of the body amounts to only about 2 percent of body weight. Also, calcium is not static within the bones and teeth; it can still move around. In fact, there is a constant exchange of calcium from the blood to the tissues, and about 20 percent of the calcium in bone is replaced annually.

Foods Rich in Calcium

Dairy products	Cooked dried beans	Canned fish with bones

The calcium in the body is maintained in normal balance by a series of hormones that work together with vitamin D. These regulating agents keep track of where the calcium is in the body and make fine adjustments frequently to keep the level of calcium within a predictable normal range. In many ways, calcium in the body is regulated much like the thermostat in a house keeps the temperature in a normal range. If the blood-calcium level gets too low, vitamin D and parathyroid hormone (PTH) cause the levels to rise by increasing absorption of calcium from the intestines so that the body can maximize the use of calcium in the diet. They also cause the kidneys to conserve as much calcium as possible and make sure that little is lost into the urine. Finally, if necessary, calcium can be removed temporarily from the bones to meet immediate needs. On the other hand, when calcium levels get too high in the blood, another hormone (calcitonin) is responsible for bringing them back into normal range.

This is an intricate balance, and supplementation with calcium is not recommended for dogs. Most commercial dog foods contain many times the amount of calcium needed on a daily basis. Supplementation with vitamin D is also not necessary, because dogs can produce their own vitamin D internally even though they receive adequate amounts in their diet. The fact is that dogs are at risk of exposure to too much calcium (hypercalcemia) more often than they are at risk for calcium deficiency.

Calcium deficiency *does* occur in dogs, but almost always when owners feed their own formulations that have not been balanced nutritionally. These diets are often comprised predominantly of meat (hamburger, beef, pork, chicken), which is a very poor source of calcium. This can result in a serious medical condition called nutritional secondary hyperparathyroidism, in which the parathyroid gland must secrete excessive amounts of parathyroid hormone (PTH) because there is insufficient calcium in the diet. This, then, causes calcium to be withdrawn from the bones, and they become weaker and more brittle. The result is bone and joint pain, and bones may even break on their own (pathological fractures). One of the first areas to lose bone is the jaw and loss of teeth can occur when their supporting tissue is disturbed. Remember—the body is designed to regulate calcium and keep blood levels normal. It will do this in any way it can, including removing the calcium from the bones.

Not only is it difficult for you to formulate your own diets for your dog regarding calcium content, but you also must consider the ratio of calcium in the diet to that of phosphorus. The ideal balance is approximately 1.3 parts calcium to 1 part phosphorus. If the ratio is much higher or lower than this, problems can result. An optimal calcium:phosphorus ratio also minimizes the vitamin-D requirement. Of course, the ratio of calcium and phosphorus is only valid if the total dietary intake of these minerals is in the normal range.

PHOSPHORUS

Phosphorus is the next most abundant mineral in the body. About 80 percent of the body's phosphorus is found in the bones and teeth. The remainder is scattered amongst all of the cells in the body, where it is critical for metabolic processes.

It is impossible to describe all of the roles of phosphorus within a single book chapter. It is essential for converting proteins, carbohydrates, and fats into energy. It is a critical component for growth, maintenance, and repair of body tissues. It helps maintain the proper pH balance of the blood. It is an important component of many different proteins and helps activate the B vitamins.

Foods Rich in Phosphorus

Fish	Poultry	Milk	Eggs

Phosphorus deficiency is very rare in dogs, because foods rich in protein are also rich in phosphorus. Therefore, meat, fish, poultry, eggs, and organ tissues provide more than adequate amounts of phosphorus. Unfortunately, when these ingredients form the basis of a dog's diet, too much phosphorus is more likely than too little. This, then, interferes with calcium levels and can cause a variety of medical problems.

MAGNESIUM

More than half of the body's stores of magnesium are found in the bones. The balance is found in muscle, the heart, the kidneys, and body fluids. Magnesium helps convert fats, carbohydrates, and proteins into energy. It is also involved in assembling proteins, removing toxins from the body, and aiding in muscle and nerve function.

Like most of the minerals, magnesium does not function on its own. It is part of a very complex interrelationship among the other nutrients. For example, too much magnesium inhibits the proper formation of bone. Too much calcium can cause clinical signs suggestive of magnesium deficiency by impairing absorption from the intestines. Calcium and magnesium also have an important give-and-take relationship when it comes to muscle and heart function. Calcium stimulates muscles, and magnesium causes relaxation of muscles. The proper balance is critical. If magnesium levels in the heart muscle are too low compared to those of calcium, the risk of heart attack increases. There is also a higher incidence of heart attack in people who drink soft water. In part, this may result from lowered levels of magnesium in addition to increased sodium content.

Foods Rich in Magnesium

Nuts	Beans	Grains	Seafood

Magnesium deficiency is probably rare in dogs fed commercial diets. Dogs fed unbalanced homemade diets or dogs that experience chronic vomiting, diarrhea, diabetes, or kidney disease are more likely to have deficiencies. Magnesium deficiency can cause stunted growth, poor appetite, seizures, abnormalities in potassium and sodium transport, skin and haircoat changes, and general weakness. Abnormalities in potassium and sodium transport are also reported. And, of course, heart attack and arterial damage can result from chronic deficiency as calcium and phosphorus mineral deposits form in the aorta and other vessels. In addition, *too much* magnesium can cause problems, including interference with calcium in the body.

Good dietary sources of magnesium include nuts, whole-grain cereals, soybeans, fish, and dark-green, leafy vegetables. The vegetables high in magnesium are also usually rich in the important antioxidant, beta-carotene.

POTASSIUM, SODIUM, AND CHLORIDE

Potassium, together with sodium and chloride, helps maintain the normal balance of fluids within the body and within each cell. The relationship of these minerals also permits muscles to contract, nerves to relay transmissions, and the body to maintain a normal pH balance. These minerals are so interrelated that there is no benefit to discussing each one individually.

Sodium excess obviously results in increased blood pressure (hypertension), yet other studies have shown that increased dietary intake of *potassium* may actually prevent hypertension. In this way, the relationship between sodium and potassium is much like that of calcium and phosphorus, suggesting that the ratio of sodium to potassium is more important than either level alone. Achieving the proper ratio will optimally regulate blood pressure and help prevent hypertension. The same appears to be true in dogs.

Sodium deficiency probably does not occur on its own, although it might be associated with starvation or chronic vomiting and diarrhea. In fact, most commercial dog foods contain many times the amount of sodium needed by dogs.

Similarly, potassium deficiency is not common but can become a problem in dogs with chronic diarrhea, vomiting, diabetes, or kidney disease, or those that have been treated with certain diuretics (water pills). These dogs are prone to weakness, kidney damage, and heart failure.

Foods Rich in Potassium

Fruits	Vegetables	Milk	Grains

Chloride deficiency removes acid from the body, increasing the pH and resulting in a condition called alkalosis. This occurs most frequently in dogs with chronic vomiting, which removes stomach acid from the system. Eventually, as more and more acid is removed, the blood actually becomes more alkaline than normal. Hence the term "alkalosis." A dietary cause of chloride deficiency is very unlikely, because chloride is found in salt, together with sodium, and is very common in the diet of most dogs.

Both sodium and chloride are provided in the diet in the form of salt. Salt is frequently added to dog food in large amounts to increase its palatability. Also, most processed diets as well as numerous food additives contain large amounts of sodium. Potassium is found in a variety of foods, including potatoes, fruits, vegetables, meat, milk, and grains.

Supplementation of the diet with sodium, chloride, or potassium is not needed. Do so only on the recommendation of your veterinarian. Occasionally, chloride is recommended for animals that have been vomiting for a long time. In these cases, the chloride is usually added to intravenous fluids, and is not given orally. Potassium may be given to dogs being treated with certain diuretics but is used cautiously, because toxicity can result from indiscriminate supplementation.

TRACE MINERALS

ZINC

Zinc is found in many different enzymes in the body and is essential for a normal functioning immune system. It also aids in normal growth and development and in the production of hormonelike prostaglandins and other proteins. Zinc is necessary for the production of DNA, RNA, and proteins. As if this is not enough, zinc also helps the body use vitamin A properly and assists insulin in regulating blood-sugar levels.

The best dietary sources of zinc are lean meat, poultry, fish, and organ meats. Lesser amounts are found in whole-grain cereals. Even if zinc is adequately provided in the diet, it has been shown that other nutrients such as calcium, phytates (fiber), copper, iron, and tin can interfere with the absorption of zinc from the intestines.

Foods Rich in Zinc

Lean meat	Poultry	Fish	Organ meats

A relative zinc imbalance has been implicated in several different syndromes in dogs. One appears to be a genetic disorder involving intestinal absorption, and Siberian Huskies, Samoyeds, and Malamutes are mostly affected. Another syndrome is reported in rapidly growing pups such as Great Danes and Doberman Pinschers, some of which were receiving calcium supplements that interfered with the utilization of zinc in the diet. Finally, a number of dogs fed generic dog foods developed a similar condition called "generic dog-food disease." Although zinc levels in these diets were adequate, it is presumed that other ingredients, such as fiber, might have created a relative zinc imbalance in affected dogs.

Zinc is also commonly used as a dietary supplement, especially for dogs with less than optimal immune function. The use of zinc in treating a variety of diseases is covered in more detail in Chapter 9.

SULFUR

Sulfur is present in all body tissues, especially those that contain large amounts of protein. These include the hair, muscles, claws (nails), and skin. These tissues contain amino acids that have large amounts of sulfur, such as methionine, cysteine, and cystine. Sulfur is also prevalent in thiamin, biotin, pantothenic acid, and insulin.

Sulfur fulfills many roles in the body. It is part of collagen, which is the framework for connective tissues (the dermis of the skin, muscles, tendons, etc.), and helps determine shape, such as the curliness of the hair. To a limited degree, sulfur is also found in bones. Because of its association with certain amino acids, sulfur becomes important in activating certain enzymes, in regulating blood clotting, and in mediating blood-sugar levels.

Foods Rich in Sulfur

Meat	Organ meats	Eggs	Beans

Sulfur deficiency probably does not occur on its own but may be seen in dogs that are severely protein-deficient. Most dogs receive more than enough sulfur to meet their needs because sulfur is present in meat, poultry, fish, eggs, milk, and organ meats. Arsenic poisoning can cause inactivation of the sulfur-containing amino acids, accounting for its toxicity.

There are few indications for sulfur supplementation in dogs. Occasionally, however, sulfur-containing amino acids will be used in dogs experiencing claw (nail) abnormalities, hair loss, or other skin problems.

COPPER

Copper is found in all tissues of the body but reaches its highest concentration in the brain, the heart, the kidney, and the liver. It is found in many unprocessed foods, including whole grains and cereals, organ meats, poultry, and dark-green leafy vegetables. Copper is essential to health but is also potentially toxic.

Copper is a component of several key enzymes, including superoxide dismutase, the important scavenger of dangerous free radicals in the body, and tyrosinase, the compound that helps impart color to hair and skin. Copper is also important in the maintenance of red blood cells. Like most other trace minerals, the ultimate availability of copper depends on competition from other nutrients in the body, including fiber, phytates, zinc, and molybdenum. In some respects, resistance to infection is related to the ratio of zinc and copper levels. If copper is high and zinc is low, patients are more susceptible to infections.

Foods Rich in Copper

| Cereals | Organ meats | Poultry | Beans |

Copper deficiency is rare in dogs although it is suspected that dogs consuming generic diets or diets high in fiber could develop a marginal deficiency. These dogs often manifest reddening or bronzing of their hair color. An association with copper has been suspected but not confirmed. A genetic form of copper deficiency, somewhat similar to Menke's syndrome in people, has been demonstrated in the Alaskan Malamute and perhaps the Samoyed. The Alaskan Malamutes described were dwarfed and had bowing of the legs with enlarged joints.

Clearly, copper toxicity poses a greater risk than copper deficiency. Copper is stored in the liver and, under normal conditions, excesses are excreted in the bile. In chronic liver and gall-bladder disease, copper excretion may be reduced and toxicity could result. More troublesome is that a genetic disease exists in dogs, similar to Wilson's disease in people, in which excessive amounts of copper are deposited in the liver. Breeds at risk include Bedlington Terriers, Skye Terriers, West Highland White Terriers, and perhaps Doberman Pinschers. The condition is inherited as an autosomal recessive trait in the Bedlington terrier; the mode of inheritance in the other breeds has not yet been determined. The diagnosis is typically confirmed by measuring copper levels on liver biopsy specimens. In addition, a new DNA-linkage test for suspected carriers in the Bedlington Terrier breed has recently been introduced.

One of the most effective non-drug forms of therapy for copper storage disease is zinc supplementation. Dogs are typically dosed with 100 mg of zinc (as zinc acetate) twice daily for three months and then the dosage is halved if the desired effect is reached. Since zinc can also be toxic, it is important that veterinarians regularly assess blood samples to maintain the blood zinc levels between 200 and 500 micrograms per deciliter.

The treatment of dogs with copper toxicity may require some degree of chelation therapy that relies on drugs to "bind" to the mineral and help remove it from the body. Penicillamine, a nonantibiotic derivative of penicillin, is the most commonly used chelator, but unfortunately it also removes zinc and has an adverse effect on the immune system. Dogs being treated with penicillamine should probably be supplemented with zinc and vitamin B_6 because pyridoxine is also adversely affected. Alternative chelator drugs include trientine and tetramine. A more impressive and safe option is to use zinc acetate, which helps block the absorption of copper from the intestines. A similar but less profound benefit has been seen with ascorbic acid (vitamin C).

IRON

Iron is an important constituent of hemoglobin, the oxygen-carrying part of the red blood cell. It is also found in several different enzymes, and a percentage of the daily intake is stored for future use. Adequate levels of iron are needed to strengthen the immune system and to increase resistance to disease. Excellent dietary sources include organ meats, beef, poultry, fish, and dark-green, leafy vegetables. Red iron oxide, a pet-food additive, is used to make these foods look "meaty." It provides little, if any, dietary iron useful to dogs.

You have probably heard of the term "iron-poor blood," and this refers to the condition that results when there is not enough iron in the body to provide much-needed oxygen to the tissues. In dogs, this can happen with blood loss that robs the body of iron before it can be adequately replaced by the diet. Bleeding is only one way that iron-deficiency anemia can occur. A more innocuous way for anemia to occur is when pups have worms, especially hookworms. These parasites latch on to the intestinal wall to suck blood. If many parasites are present, a pup might even die. With copper deficiency, iron is absorbed, but hemoglobin does not form properly and anemia will still result.

Foods Rich in Iron

| Organ meats | Beans | Fish | Poultry |

Most dogs' diets are heavily fortified with iron (up to twenty-five times the recommended amounts) because there are many other nutrients (e.g., fiber) that interfere with iron absorption. Iron toxicity has been studied extensively in dogs and results in poor appetite, vomiting, diarrhea, intestinal upset, and weight loss. Do not add iron to your dog's diet unless recommended by your veterinarian for medical reasons.

SELENIUM

Selenium is considered a minor element, but it is an important component of the immune system. It forms part of the enzyme glutathione peroxidase, an important antioxidant. As such, it protects the cells of the body, especially red blood cells, from the ravages of oxygen-derived free radicals. Selenium also acts in a supporting capacity for vitamin E.

Recent research has shown that adequate selenium in the diet decreases the damage caused by some cancers, arthritis, and heart disease. These benefits are often enhanced by providing adequate levels of vitamin E. Studies have shown that diseases such as cardiomyopathy (a heart ailment), leukemia, and cancers of the colon, rectum, breast, ovaries, and lungs are less likely to develop in people consuming a selenium-rich diet

---

Foods Rich in Selenium

| Brown rice | Oatmeal | Poultry | Organ meats |

The best sources of selenium are found in whole wheat, brown rice, legumes, vegetable oils, and oatmeal, but much of the benefit is lost by processing. The ultimate content of any food depends on the concentration of selenium in the soil in which it is grown. Selenium-deficient areas of the United States include the southeastern, northeastern, midwestern, and far northwestern portions of the country. A form of selenium deficiency (white muscle disease) has been reported in dogs that have been fed mutton raised on selenium-deficient soil. Oversupplementation is not recommended, because toxicities do result and can be severe. Recent research has shown that optimal absorption of dietary selenium can be achieved with cellulase-containing enzyme supplements.

MINOR TRACE ELEMENTS

CHROMIUM

The main use of chromium in the body is as glucose tolerance factor (GTF), which helps regulate blood sugar levels by driving glucose into the body cells. GTF also contains niacin and several amino acids. Studies have shown that chromium salts (especially chromium picolinate) potentiate the effects of insulin in people and can overcome the insulin resistance seen in some diabetics. By so doing, it also reduces the risk of associated heart disease. Limited research has been done on dogs, but chromium picolinate supplementation will likely be an important aspect of diabetes control in dogs.

Foods Rich in Chromium

Brewer's yeast	Cereals	Wheat germ	Lean meat

COBALT

Cobalt is an important component of vitamin B_{12}, also known as cobalamin (see Chapter 4). As such, it is important in the formation of red blood cells and helps maintain nerve tissue and normal cell function. Cobalt is found in meats and organ meats, and dogs on strictly vegetarian diets are at risk of vitamin B_{12} deficiency (and hence cobalt deficiency). Although cobalt can be found in vegetables and fruits, it is the combined vitamin-mineral that is needed to prevent anemia. Small but significant amounts of cobalamin can be found in Brewer's yeast, aloe, kelp, and algae, which should help prevent deficiencies, even in die-hard vegans.

Foods Rich in Cobalt

Liver	Kidney	Fruit	Vegetables

FLUORINE

You are probably familiar with the role of fluorine as an aid in protecting teeth. Present in only one part per million, fluoride can significantly lower the incidence of cavities in people. Most dogs receive more than adequate fluoride in their drinking water, and deficiencies are not a problem. Normal levels of fluorine in the diet help protect the arteries from mineral deposition in dogs that may be receiving a diet deficient in magnesium.

Like most minerals, oversupplementation is to be discouraged because toxicities can result. With mild overdoses, your dog's teeth can become mottled; with significant overdoses, he may experience damage to his bones and teeth.

IODINE

Most of the iodine consumed in the diet makes its way to the thyroid gland, where it is incorporated into glandular hormones. Adequate amounts of dietary iodine are found in saltwater fish and iodized salt and in plants grown in iodine-rich soils. Inadequate iodine in the diet is one of the causes of hypothyroidism (endemic goiter) in dogs, although this accounts for only a very small percentage of cases. Goitrogens (goiter-causing agents) are present in soybeans, and it is possible that dogs on soy-based diets could develop goiter. Most hypothyroid dogs have adequate intakes of iodine, and their disease is most often caused by a defective immunologic mechanism, not diet. Dogs on commercial diets are very unlikely to have iodine deficiency, because iodized salt is usually added to these rations. Additional supplementation is unnecessary and unlikely to provide any benefits. Toxic reactions (iodism) are possible, however, if supplementation is overdone.

Foods Rich in Iodine

Iodized salt	Fresh seafood and shellfish

MANGANESE

Manganese is important in the formation of connective tissues, bones, and proteins. Under some circumstances, it even functions like an antioxidant. Manganese also works with vitamin K to form blood-clotting factors.

Little attention has been paid to manganese, and the first report of deficiency in a person was as recent as 1972. Deficiencies in people can result in birth defects, poor fertility, stunted growth, and general weakness. Manganese deficiency has not been well described in the dog, and requirements are often based on research conducted in other species.

Excellent dietary sources include spinach and whole-grain cereals. Oversupplementation is not recommended, because excessive levels interfere with the absorption of calcium, iron, copper and zinc.

Foods Rich in Manganese

Spinach	Cereals	Raisins	Wheat bran

MOLYBDENUM

Most of the molybdenum in the body is found in the liver, the kidneys, bone, and skin. It is necessary for normal growth and development and helps mobilize iron from its storage sites. It also works with riboflavin in converting food to energy. The molybdenum content of most plants depends on the levels of this mineral in the soils in which they are grown. Too much molybdenum in the diet interferes with the absorption of copper and vice versa.

Foods Rich in Molybdenum

Lean meat	Cereals	Beans	Organ meats

SILICON

Silicon is found is more places than just computer chips. Dietary sources include whole-grain cereals, horsetail grass (a medicinal herb), and vegetables. Most of the silicon in the body develops and maintains bone structure, and deficiencies can result in weakened bones. In dogs, it is sometimes used as a nutritional supplement for dogs with weakened or cracked claws (nails).

Foods Rich in Silicon

Cereals	Vegetables	Beans and peas

Providing the proper ratios of vitamins, minerals and amino acids will help keep your dog's bones, muscles and coat in a healthy condition. English Setter on point. Photo by Judith Strom.

IN SUMMARY

Minerals are classified into macrominerals (macroelements) and microminerals (trace elements).

Minerals account for many important functions in the body. They contribute significantly to strength of bones and teeth and are involved in enzyme functions.

Calcium is the most abundant mineral in the body.

Calcium needs a series of hormones (parathyroid hormone and calcitonin) and vitamin D to be regulated accurately in the body.

Calcium and vitamin D should not be supplemented to your dog. More than adequate levels are found in foods. The risk of your dog becoming hypercalcemic (too much calcium) is much higher than becoming hypocalcemic (not enough calcium).

Sodium and potassium work closely together to maintain normal fluid balance in the body, muscle contractions, nerve transmissions, and a normal pH balance.

A deficiency in copper can cause a reddening or a bronzing of the hair.

Puppies grow rapidly, so it is important to select a high-quality commercial diet for them.
Photo by Judith Strom.

ADDITIONAL READING

Banta, C.A., "The Role of Zinc in Canine and Feline Nutrition." *Nutrition of the Dog and Cat*, edited by I. H. Burger and J. P. W. Rivers. Cambridge University Press, 1989; 317-327.

Barrette, D.C., "Calcium and Phosphorus for Cats and Dogs." *Canadian Veterinary Journal*, 1988; 29: 751-752.

Brewer, N.R. "Comparative Metabolism of Copper." *Journal of the American Veterinary Medical Association*, 1987; 190(6): 654-658.

Greger, J.L., "Using Animals to Assess Bioavailability of Minerals: Implications for Human Nutrition." *Journal of Nutrition*, 1992; 122: 2047-2052.

Hazewinkel, H.A.W, et al., "Influences of Chronic Calcium Excess on the Skeletal Development of Growing Great Danes." *Journal of the American Animal Hospital Association*, 1985; 21: 377-391.

Luecke, R.W., "Domestic Animals in the Elucidation of Zinc's Role in Nutrition." *Federation Proceedings*, 43: 2823-2828.

McCarty, M.F., "The Case for Supplemental Chromium and A Survey of Clinical Studies with Chromium Picolinate." *Journal of Applied Nutrition*, 1991; 43(1): 58-66.

Michell, A.R., "Sodium in Health and Disease—What Can We Learn From Animals?" *Advancement of Veterinary Science: the Bicentenary Symposium Series*, 4: 171-183.

Norris, D., "Zinc and Cutaneous Inflammation." *Archives of Dermatology*, 1985; 121: 985-989.

Olson, W.G., et al, "Iodine: A Review of Dietary Requirements, Therapeutic Properties and Assessment of Potential Toxicity." *Compendium on Continuing Education for the Practicing Veterinarian*, 1980; 2(10): S164-S167.

Sherman, A.R., "Zinc, Copper, and Iron Nutriture and Immunity." *Journal of Nutrition*, 1992; 122: 604-609.

Somer, E., "The Essential Guide to Vitamins and Minerals." *Health Media of America*, 1992, 403 pp.

Sternlieb, I., "Copper and the Liver: Comparative Aspects in Man and Animals." *Proc. 10th ACVIM Forum*, May 1992; 49-52.

Van Vleet, J.F., "Current Knowledge of Selenium-Vitamin E Deficiency in Domestic Animals." *Journal of the American Veterinary Medical Association*, 1980; 176(4): 321-325.

Questions to Ponder . . .

How do I know which brand of dog food is adequate for my dog and will meet all of his nutritional requirements?

Why is there so much fat in dog foods?

How many treats are too much in one day?

The word "offal" appears on dog food labels. What is offal and what nutrients does it provide?

What are good protein products, and what kind of proteins are poorly utilized by my dog?

What are sources of fiber on the nutrition labels?

Should I worry about preservatives in my dog's food?

**Learn the answers to these
and many other nutrition questions
in Chapter 6.**

6
COMMERCIAL
DIETS

Choosing a commercial dog food has to be one of the toughest decisions you have to make for your dog. In human nutrition, you merely need to select from the four food groups, minimize cholesterol and saturated fats, and make sure you get enough fresh fruits and vegetables. But when it comes to your dog, you want a food that meets all of his needs, is economical, is wholesome, and tastes good. You also want the food to be stable for many weeks or months without refrigeration, yet not contain harmful preservatives.

It is unrealistic to ask, "What is the best commercial food to feed my dog?" There is not one brand name or type of food that is best for all dogs. Some dogs don't tolerate soy, while others manage fine on it as a protein source. Some dogs don't need high-fiber diets, while others do for medical reasons. Some dogs do better on dry foods, while others favor canned diets. Some dogs are couch potatoes and get fat even on maintenance rations, while others benefit from calorie-dense, super-premium diets and remain lean.

The best approach to intelligently selecting a commercial dog food is to understand the facts *as they relate to your dog*. Asking other people for an opinion about what they feed their dog is irrelevant in most cases. Dogs are individuals. That doesn't mean you need a Ph.D. in nutrition to understand the issues. You can go a long way by learning to read dog-food labels so that you can effectively compare products based on ingredients, nutrients, and price, although remember—it is difficult to determine the *quality* of a dog food by reading the label. You may wish to obtain additional information that most ethical manufacturers will send upon request.

GENERAL GUIDELINES FOR SELECTING A DOG FOOD

Any dog food that you choose should be deemed adequate on the basis of feeding trials for your dog's stage of life. The criteria have been proposed by AAFCO in the United States and by the CVMA in Canada. These are not foolproof criteria but are the best options available.

The feeding trials proposed by AAFCO are not ideal for many reasons. Typically, they include only a few animals and don't take into consideration large breeds or very small breeds. There is also some concern that the trials don't run long enough. For example, a growth feeding trial for puppies may end by four to five months of age, yet the pups continue to grow after this time. Also, the growth-related nutritional disturbances will probably not be detectable by this time. How is a puppy's growth assured by PFI testing? Six pups are used (same breed), representing at least three litters that are at least eight weeks of age. The test runs for ten weeks and is a success if the average weight of the dogs falls within the normal ranges for the breed tested. This, of course, does not assure that the diet is really optimal for pups. Also, most orthopedic diseases are not evident at this age, which means that no associations can be made with the short-term diet.

These trials are also relatively lax in their expectations. They consider a gestation/lactation trial successful if two-thirds of the bitches evaluated lose no more than 15 percent of their body weight by weaning. How about the one-third that lose even more? Ideally, bitches should return to their optimal weight by weaning if their nutritional status has been well maintained.

Even with these shortcomings, the AAFCO feeding trials are better than nothing and are far superior to relying on NRC requirements alone. For more information on AAFCO and CVMA, see Chapter 1.

Don't try to compare dog foods on the basis of protein content. The percentage of protein in the diet is only a reflection of what is needed to supply essential amino acids. Additional protein only turns to fat or gets excreted in the urine. Don't be fooled! It is the quality of the protein provided, not the quantity, that makes the real difference in a dog food.

Pay attention to the ingredient list, even though it is hard to predict quality based on the terms used. For a canned product, there should be at least one animal-based protein source in the first two ingredients listed. For dry foods, an animal-based protein source should be one of the first three ingredients. This is a good clue as to how appropriately the diet has been formulated, because animal-based protein sources contain a better balance of essential amino acids. If meat or poultry meal is listed first on the label but the grains have been sub-categorized (e.g., cornmeal, kibbled corn, flaked corn), it is safe to assume that the manufacturer is trying to sell you a cereal-based diet but wants you to pay the price of a meat-based diet.

Too much meat in the diet is not desirable, either. In dry dog foods, it is impossible to overload on meat because of the technological process involved. For canned foods, however, high meat content means low calcium. It also means that meat is providing most of the calories when a digestible carbohydrate would do a better and safer job. When canned foods contain a high percentage of meat, the companies must add a calcium supplement to guard against calcium/phosphorus imbalance. Too high of a mineral concentration (ash) is also not good and probably implies that the ration contains a lot of bonemeal and poor-quality protein sources.

Buy commercial dog foods manufactured by a well-respected company that has contributed substantially to nutritional research in pets. These companies have the most to lose by distributing an inferior product because they have a reputation to protect. Fad diets and manufacturers will come and go, but the dog-food companies that intend to be around will be the ones most concerned with adequate nutrition.

How to Select a Good Quality Dog Food

Don't compare foods on the basis of protein content. It is the quality, not the quantity, of protein that counts.

In a canned food, at least one of the first two products listed should be animal-based protein; one of the first three ingredients in a dry food.

Select a food by a major company that has conducted substantial research into pet nutrition.

Select foods that use higher quality ingredients.

Select the correct formulated diet for your pet's age.

Learn how to read ingredient labels and guaranteed analysis labels.

TYPES OF DOG FOODS

There are three main types of dog foods that are determined by the manufacturing process: canned, dry, and semimoist. To a certain extent, the type of dog food determines which ingredients can be included in the ration, as well as the ultimate cost. Let's look at each of the choices individually.

CANNED DIETS

Canned diets are sometimes referred to as "wet" or "moist." There's a good reason for this—they contain about 75 percent water. These are the common varieties of dog food that line the shelves in grocery stores and pet-supply outlets. The percentage of water may seem excessive, but this is not significantly different than the amount of water present in fresh meat or in living animals. It may seem that the water content is designed to provide more filling than the nutrients, but there is a reason for this. All canned foods are sterilized by high-pressure steam. The high water content is needed to ensure adequate and uniform heat penetration without burning some areas while inadequately cooking others.

Most meats used in canned foods are ground while they are still frozen. This helps reduce bacterial contamination of the product while promoting efficient grinding. The meat is then mixed with ground cereal, chopped vegetables, and micronutrients. It is interesting to note that, for the most part, manufacturers discount the nutritional value of the ingredients and add vitamin and mineral "premixes" to the ration to meet the actual nutritional requirements of dogs. So, despite all the advertising hype of the nutritional value of the ingredients used in a dog food, most manufacturers concede that the processing removes much of the wholesomeness and goodness of the ingredients.

The "maintenance" diets are formulated with one-third meat and two-thirds cereal, while the "luxury" or "gourmet" diets usually mix two-thirds meat with one-third cereal. Even the so-called "all-meat" rations usually have about 10 percent carbohydrates. At this stage, some ingredients are "cold processed" by loading the ingredients directly into the can. Other manufacturers first heat the mixture to about 180°F., which may produce colors and flavors, inactivate enzymes, and cause controlled swelling of starches. The canned ingredients are then sealed and loaded into a pressure cooker and processed.

DRY FOODS

Dry foods, often referred to as "kibble," were the first dog foods available commercially. Although they were originally baked on sheets and broken into pieces by a kibbling roller, this process has been replaced by extrusion. Extrusion uses pressure heating and steam cooking to treat the cereal-based product. The usual ingredients for these extruded dry foods include a source of protein (soybean meal, meat, fish, or poultry meal), carbohydrate (corn, wheat, barley), fat, and vitamins and minerals.

To make dry foods, the ingredients are mixed together and steam heat is added to begin the cooking process. Later, the ingredients are removed to a pressure cooker and the finished product gets extruded and cut into appropriate pieces. At the final stages, the "kibble" can be sprayed with hot fats to increase its palatability. The moisture content of these foods is reduced to about 10 percent by the use of hot air drying. Most extruders have a limitation in the fat content of the ration (8 to 10 percent) for mechanical reasons, but newer, twin-screw extruders can actually create a high-fat, dry dog food (30 to 40 percent fat). Even with the old extruders, the fat content can be increased by overspraying the dry food once it is removed from the barrel of the extruder.

SEMIMOIST FOODS

Semimoist dog foods are intermediate between the dry and canned foods in their moisture content. These are the products that often look like hamburgers made for dogs, containing 25 to 35 percent water. It is hard to get much reliable information about semimoist processing, because pet-food companies still regard this as a closely guarded trade secret. The trick to making a semimoist dog food is to create a ration that isn't canned, that contains appreciable moisture, that has a long shelf life, and that is not subject to mold growth. To accomplish this, "humectants" are added to the ration that allow the food to be "moist," yet bind the water so it is inaccessible to microbes. The most common humectants are glycols, sucrose (table sugar), and phosphoric acid.

NUTRIENTS IN DOG FOOD

Dogs need nutrients, not ingredients, so the first concern is meeting the nutritional needs of your dog on a daily basis. Then you can worry about the ingredients needed to provide those nutrients. Because pet-food manufacturers add a vitamin-and-mineral "premix" to their foods, the real requirements that are left are for energy (calories), essential amino acids, and essential fatty acids.

When manufacturers process dog food, they assume that most or all of the essential vitamins or minerals in the original ingredients are destroyed. To compensate for this loss, the pet-food industry adds standard vitamin-mineral premixes to rations. There is therefore very little difference between commercial pet foods when it comes to meeting these requirements. There is, however, a potentially big difference when it comes to *availability* of these nutrients. For example, your dog may not be able to digest many of the nutrients in a food with a high fiber content, regardless of what the label says. If the food contains a lot of bone meal (a source of calcium), there may be an adverse effect on the absorption of zinc, even though the ration shows adequate zinc on laboratory analysis.

Dog-food manufacturers are quick to say how much protein their foods contain, but it is the amino-acid content of the protein that is important, not the quantity of protein in the ration. The quality of a protein is determined by how well the protein is digested and how well it provides the essential amino acids required by your dog. The quality of a protein in the diet must therefore be determined by how it relates to your dog. A source of high-quality protein for a dog is not the same as for a rat, a cow, or a human. Each of these species digests proteins slightly differently and has different "essential" amino acids. Although dogs are omnivores and can digest meats as well as vegetation, they manage meat more efficiently. This is different than people, who have evolved to accommodate a more vegetarian-based diet. In dogs, more of the essential amino acids can be supplied by meat. Plant proteins require combination (such as soy with corn), because each has deficiencies in certain amino acids. Yet blends can provide a complete spectrum of needed nutrients.

Pet-food companies honestly try to provide the essential amino acids in their dog foods, but, to a certain extent, they are also dealing with unknowns. It is relatively easy to measure the amino-acid content of a food but often difficult to determine how much will be digested and absorbed by dogs. If a dog food is overcooked during processing and there is a fair amount of cereal in it, certain amino acids (especially lysine) will become less available. The amino acids tryptophan, methionine, and arginine are most likely to be "limiting" in commercial dog foods. The risk is often higher for dry foods, which usually contain more cereal than the canned foods.

There is little or no information that can help you equate protein quality with cost. A cereal-based dog food will need to contain a higher percentage of crude protein than a meat-based diet just to provide an equivalent amount of usable amino acids. This doesn't mean that the food with the higher protein composition is better for the dog or more expensive to produce. Many high-protein, cereal-based dog foods are much cheaper to manufacture than high-quality but low-protein, meat-based diets. That's why you can't base dog-food cost on the percentage of protein. The quantity of protein needed depends on the protein quality. Any additional protein in the diet serves only as a source of calories or gets excreted in the urine. Nutritionists use formulas such as the "egg equivalent" or "Essential Amino Acid Index," but this information is not readily available. One thing is certain, however—dry dog foods that are properly formulated provide a much more cost-effective form of protein than either canned or semimoist foods.

When it comes to fats, dogs require linoleic acid and perhaps alpha-linolenic acid. If the diet contains 2 percent linoleic acid, all of the body's requirements for fat are met. Of course, most dog foods, especially canned foods, contain much more fat than this. The best sources for the essential fatty acids are vegetable oils, especially safflower oil and flaxseed oil. These, however, are not the predominant fats found in dog foods. Fat is added to the diet for taste and to provide energy. The large amounts of fat in dog foods are not there for their nutritional value.

Why is there so much fat in dog foods? Fat provides an efficient and cheap form of calories. Dogs need to eat enough food to satisfy their energy (caloric) requirements. The daily energy requirement is usually determined as kilocalories per day for a given weight of dog. For example, a sedentary, thirty-pound dog requires about 900 calories a day to meet his energy requirements, or roughly thirty kilocalories per pound per day. Smaller dogs need more energy on a per-pound basis, and large dogs need relatively less. For instance, a ten-pound Lhasa Apso may need 420 kilocalories/per day (42 Kcal/lb/day) while a 100-pound German Shepherd would require about 2,200 Kcal/per day (22 Kcal/lb/day). The German Shepherd would eat about five times as much as the Lhasa Apso, not ten times as much as you might first expect. This energy can be provided as protein, carbohydrate, or fat; vitamins and minerals add no calories to the diet.

The energy needs of a dog, as well as his size, determine which ration you should feed. The Frisbee-catching Whippet will need nearly double the Kcal per pound than the Cocker whose only exercise is an outing to the back yard, even though both breeds are medium size.
Photos by Judith Strom.

Most dog foods are formulated so that a dog consumes his calorie requirements and in the process ingests his needed amino acids, vitamins, and minerals. This is important, because high-calorie, "energy-dense" foods must also provide the other essential nutrients in higher concentrations. Let's take a hypothetical situation. Say you feed your dog a pound of maintenance dog food a day to provide adequate energy and nutrients. At this amount, your dog's weight remains constant, neither increasing nor decreasing significantly. Now double the number of calories provided to your dog. You can do this in several ways. First, you might buy a "premium" diet that is high in fat and that meets your dog's energy requirements while feeding only a half-pound of food each day. This means that your dog must also receive his essential amino acids, fatty acids, vitamins, and minerals in more concentrated form, because if he doesn't, he will receive only half as many nutrients as he did when eating the full pound of maintenance food.

You can also unbalance a ration by adding energy-dense supplements to your dog's food. This happens every day in most households in the United States and Canada. The three biggest offenders are fat supplements, table scraps, and biscuit treats. Adding just one tablespoon of fat or vegetable oil per cup of dog food can increase the caloric count of the ration by 30 percent. Each biscuit treat adds about 100 calories. And the typical table scraps are not lean meat and vegetables. Your dog usually gets pieces of fat that contain the most calories and the fewest nutrients. If a maintenance dog food is designed for your dog to eat a pound a day, this amount likely needs to be consumed to meet his nutrient requirements. If he eats only half a pound per day because of fat supplements and "cookies," can you be sure he is really receiving adequate non-energy nutrients like vitamins and minerals?

In general, supplements, treats, and table scraps should not make up more than 10 percent of your dog's diet, or it may become unbalanced. This is most critical for small dogs. A small, ten-pound dog needs only about 420 Kcal per day to meet his energy requirements. One tablespoon of vegetable oil added to the food each day contributes about 125 Kcal. Two cookies a day (not unreasonable) provide almost 200 Kcal. But, although more than half of the day's caloric requirements are met with these supplements, how are you doing for essential amino acids, vitamins, and minerals? If you feed this dog a maintenance dog food, he probably will eat only half as much as the manufacturer intended and therefore may not meet his nutritional requirements. If a "superpremium" dog food is fed, you've given this little dog even more calories.

Although it is not critical that you count calories for your dog, you do need to realize that commercial dog foods provide for nutritional needs based on your dog consuming adequate amounts of the ration each day. There must be a balance between providing your dog with needed calories as well as with noncaloric nutrients like vitamins and minerals. Some cereal-biscuit manufacturers have anticipated this problem and fortified their treats with vitamins and minerals. They've capitalized on the notion that if a dog eats nothing but treats all day, he could still meet most or all of his nutritional requirements.

There are some situations in which the question still exists as to whether supplementation may be necessary to meet requirements. We now know that if dogs eat the recommended portions described by manufacturers, they should ingest all the important nutrients they need on a daily basis. But, do dogs always eat as much as the manufacturers recommend? The answer appears to be "no!"—especially for the larger breeds of dog. Although a dog food company may recommend that you feed your 120 pound dog 12 cups of dry food daily, most large breeds do not consume nearly that much. Are they still getting all their needed vitamins and minerals? It's not always easy to tell. Therefore, there are still times when a vitamin-mineral supplement may be beneficial, regardless of what pet food manufacturers might recommend.

INGREDIENTS IN DOG FOODS

The pet-food industry has a language all its own when it comes to dog-food ingredients. This can be confusing if you don't learn some basic rules about terminology. "Meat" implies the muscle of animals and the associated fat. Lean meat, devoid of fat, contains about 75 percent water and 25 percent protein whether it comes from cattle, sheep, pigs, or poultry. The real difference is the fat content. Lean cuts of poultry, veal, beef, and rabbit tend to have less fat (two to five percent) than lamb or pork (seven to nine percent fat). Lean beef has about 5 percent fat, steak about 20 percent fat, and brisket up to 36 percent fat. Leg of lamb may contain 18 percent fat, whereas lamb chops may have up to 36 percent fat. Is the meat in dog foods lean or fatty? Unfortunately, that information is not given, but it is fair to assume that fatty meats are probably used most often. Fat from poultry and pigs is likely to be more unsaturated than fat from beef and sheep.

The term "meat by-products" or "offal" is commonly seen on dog-food labels, but there is little other explanation offered as to what this means. By-products are items like udders, lungs, stomachs, livers, hearts, spleens, and tripe but also includes heads, feet, blood, bone, and carcasses. The organ meats are usually rich in water-soluble vitamins but, like meat, are low in calcium. The carcass ingredients are usually rich in calcium and phosphorus but are poor nutrient sources otherwise. Can you tell what you're getting when it says "meat by-products" on the label?

The original method of getting meat by-products (offal) was to collect from slaughterhouses material that would not be used for human consumption. Animals that were 4-D (dead, dying, diseased, or disabled) or that had died before reaching market were also likely candidates for dog food. The material was ground up, cooked (rendered), and prepared as a ration. Most of the nutritional goodness was lacking, but once the food was fortified with vitamins and minerals, it provided a dog with his daily requirements.

Today, most prominent pet-food manufacturers select higher-quality meat by-products and combine them with cereal grains and cereal by-products. In a multibillion-dollar industry, few of the big players want to be associated with serving questionable ingredients to today's pampered dogs.

Animal proteins are an important part of a dog's diet, but not all are equal in terms of nutritional goodness. When individual items such as beef, eggs, or liver are present, the nutrient quality is usually good or excellent. Meat, fish, or poultry meals are also of high quality. On the other hand, ingredients such as feather meal or meat and bone meal likely contain more bone, feathers, and connective tissue than usable protein.

The use of cereal grains has allowed the cost of dog foods to remain competitive while still supplying dogs with a good source of usable energy. Dogs don't typically digest most raw cereals well, but the cooked ingredients are highly digestible. These carbohydrates are usually the by-products of the breakfast-cereal, bread, and beer industries. Some whole grains (soybeans, corn, wheat, oats, and barley) are grown specifically for use in pet foods. The highest-quality starch sources are corn (cornmeal, ground corn), rice (brewer's rice, rice flour), oats (oatmeal, oat flour), and wheat (wheat flour, whole-ground wheat). On the other hand, certain starches are not digested well by dogs, even with processing, and are thus considered low-quality ingredients. These include whey, soy flour, soybean meal, corn-gluten meal, wheat gluten, and wheat middlings. It is important to appreciate that high-quality carbohydrate sources are not necessarily high-quality protein sources. Corn is a great source of energy, but as a protein source, it leaves a lot to be desired.

The sources of fiber in a commercial diet are usually bran, beet pulp, and tomato pumice. Because they are not meant to be digested anyway, all are acceptable dietary additives. It is important, however, that the fiber content of the diet not be too high or you may run the risk of decreasing the overall digestibility of the ration. This could cause imbalances of protein, fatty acids, vitamins, and minerals.

Fat is added to commercial diets because it is loaded with energy (calories) and because it increases the palatability of the ration. Favorite sources of fat include turkey, chicken, and pork because they are highly digestible by dogs. Unfortunately, these fats are saturated and provide very little of the "fat nutrient" that dogs need—linoleic acid. This polyunsaturated fatty acid is more commonly found in vegetable oils, especially safflower oil and flaxseed oil. The most common vegetable oils used in dog food are corn oil, soy oil, sesame-seed oil, and linseed oil.

Vitamins and minerals in commercial dog foods are mostly unusable by the time the pet food has been "processed." As discussed earlier in the chapter, all of the premium pet-food companies add a vitamin-mineral premix to their foods to replace the nutrients lost in manufacturing. This is the way they ensure that the pet food meets daily requirements.

WHAT THE LABEL TELLS YOU ABOUT INGREDIENTS

You have a right to be concerned about the quality and wholesomeness of ingredients found in dog foods, but it is difficult to completely appreciate the contents of a dog food from information provided on the label. There are just too many tricks of the trade that make you believe whatever image the manufacturer wants to project.

For example, the manufacturer must list ingredients in descending order by weight. This seems simple enough. The ingredient that appears first should be the predominant ingredient in the food. This makes sense, but there are many ways around it. First, ingredients are listed on an "as is" basis, and second, ingredients can be arranged creatively to show almost anything.

Saying the ingredients are listed "as is" means that the manufacturer has not taken the water content of the ingredient into consideration. The ingredients are weighed "as is" before processing. This is the same way that a fast-food restaurant may advertise a quarter-pound hamburger. The hamburger ingredients weigh a quarter pound "before cooking." After cooking, they frequently weigh substantially less than a quarter pound. Most meat is 60 to 75 percent water by weight, while cereal grains contain only about 10 percent water by weight. If a pound of meat were dehydrated, it would weigh only about a quarter pound. If a pound of cornmeal were dehydrated, it would still weigh about nine-tenths of a pound. In this way, a dog food that is predominantly plant-based (once water content is considered) could still list meat first on the label and be technically correct. To be ethically correct, however, it would be more appropriate to list ingredients on a dry-matter basis.

There is another way of looking at dry matter (DM) and why it is important in pet-food labeling. Suppose you went to the supermarket to buy sponges and found that they were only available in packages. In some of the packages, the sponges had absorbed their weight in water. Other packages contain sponges that were completely dry. You're smart enough to realize that the water-soaked sponges contain more water than sponge, but you still find the pricing confusing. The sponges packed in water cost only twenty-five cents per pound, while the dry sponges cost two dollars per pound. Which is the better deal? You now have the same dilemma as you do looking at dog foods. Why can't the packages just tell you how many dry sponges you're getting for your money? After all, why should

GUARANTEED ANALYSIS

	Canned	Dry
Crude Protein, % Min.	8	25
Crude Fat, % Min.	6	11
Crude Fiber, % Max.	1	3
Moisture, % Max.	78	12
Calcium, % Min.	0.20	0.70
Phosphorus, % Min.	0.15	0.50

INGREDIENTS (CANNED) – CHICKEN & RICE DINNER:
Chicken by-products, chicken, water sufficient for processing, brewers rice, vegetable gums, natural flavors, sodium tripolyphosphate, potassium chloride, zinc sulfate, vitamin A, D_3, and E supplements, calcium pantothenate, thiamine mononitrate (vitamin B,).

GUARANTEED ANALYSIS: CRUDE PROTEIN, MIN 8.0%; CRUDE FAT, MIN 6.0%; CRUDE FIBER, MAX. 1.5%; MOISTURE, MAX 78.0%.

INGREDIENTS: SUFFICIENT WATER FOR PROCESSING, POULTRY BY-PRODUCTS, MEAT BY-PRODUCTS, CHICKEN, BEEF, LIVER, FISH, VEGETABLE GUMS, CALCIUM SULFATE, SODIUM TRIPOLYPHOSPHATE, POTASSIUM CHLORIDE, ONION POWDER, GARLIC POWDER, TETRAPOTASSIUM PYROPHOSPHATE, CARAMEL COLORING, SODIUM NITRITE (FOR COLOR RETENTION), ZINC SULFATE, VITAMIN A, D3 & E SUPPLEMENTS, CALCIUM PANTOTHENATE, THIAMINE MONONITRATE (VITAMIN B1).

COMPARISON OF TWO CANNED FOOD LABELS

The label above may be a better quality food than the label to the left. The upper label contains the ingredients which are more bioavailable (chicken by-products, chicken, and brewer's rice) than the left label which contains ingredients of less quality (poultry by-products and meat by-products). However, without providing information on bioavailability, it's still hard to tell.

you be paying for the water absorbed into the sponges? If the prices of both packages reflected the value on a dry-matter basis, the decision would be easy. If the pet-food label listed the ingredients on a dry-matter basis, comparisons would also be much easier.

The situation with pet foods is still more complicated than the sponge comparison, because there are several different ingredients in dog foods and all have different water contents. Meat shrinks about 75 percent when it is converted to dry matter, whereas many grains shrink only 10 percent. If you formulate ten pounds of dog food with six pounds of beef (as is) and four pounds of cereal (as is), it sure seems like beef is the predominant ingredient, accounting for 60 percent of the ration. If, however, you consider the water content of your ration, the facts seem to change. If the beef is 75 percent water, you really have one and one-half pounds of beef and four and one-half pounds of water. If the grains are 10 percent water, you really have about three and one-half pounds of grain and about one-half pound of water. Now your formulation looks more like five pounds of water, three and one-half pounds of grain, and one and one-half pounds of beef. What started out looking like a meat-based diet of 60 percent beef managed to change to a ration of only 15 percent beef and more than twice that amount in grain. Would you say this diet is cereal-based or meat-based?

The second way that dog-food labels can be misleading is by creatively arranging ingredients to make them look the most favorable. If lungs, intestines, blood, and kidneys are added to the diet, they can all be listed under the comprehensive term "meat by-products." This increases the overall proportion of meat by-products even though some ingredients are more desirable than others. At the same time, the cereals can be subdivided into terms like meal, middlings, starch, and flour. In this way, a diet that is predominantly wheat can still list meat by-products first, followed in variable order by its composite products (wheat-germ meal, kibbled wheat, ground wheat, flaked wheat) and other ingredients. If you're not aware, you really don't know what you're paying for.

Most of the information on the ingredient list reflects legal terms and doesn't allow for valid comparisons between different foods. Meat by-products, cereal grain products, and other terms can mean many things, from high-quality organ meats and whole-grain cereals to cow udders and oat hulls. How can you possibly tell from the term "by-products"?

Even dog food labeling and advertising can be confusing if you don't understand the current laws, and they do change from time to time. Do you know the difference between beef dog food, beef dinner, dog food with beef and beef flavor dog food? For example, do you understand the subtle distinctions between Doc Ackerman's Beef Dog Food (which will contain at least 95 percent beef plus sufficient water for procesing), and Doc Ackerman's Premium Dog Food WITH BEEF (which need only contain 3 percent beef). What a difference a name makes! Beef dog food implies that the meal is 95 percent beef, allowing for sufficient water for processing. The term beef dinner means that a food contains 25-95 percent beef. Any dog food labeled "with beef", no matter how prominent, need only contain 3 percent beef to meet label claims. A food with "beef flavor" implies that there is less than 3 percent beef in the ration.

PRESERVATIVES IN DOG FOOD

The chemical preservatives used in most dog foods include ethoxyquin, butylated hydroxyanisole (BHA), butylated hydroxytoluene (BHT), proprionic acid, and ascorbic acid (vitamin C). They are added to prevent the fats in the food from going rancid. These preservatives are what allow dry dog foods to have such a long shelf life. How long would you leave a mixture of hamburger and cooked corn sit on your pantry shelf without being refrigerated and without using preservatives?

If a commercial dry dog food claims "no preservatives added," take it with a grain of salt unless it provides valid laboratory analysis of the finished product. Even if no preservatives are added by the manufacturer, there is no assurance that they are not in the ration, because many suppliers add the preservatives before the product is received by the manufacturer. The manufacturer must list only those preservatives that it puts into the food, not those that were added by the supplier. Preservatives added as "preprocessed" ingredients do not need to appear on the label. Therefore, antioxidants added to source ingredients, such as animal fat or by-products, currently do not have to be reported by the manufacturer. Hopefully, this policy will change to allow consumers to make more intelligent decisions regarding the purchase of pet foods.

Are preservatives harmful for dogs? There is little doubt that preservatives and other additives may have undesirable effects in some dogs. It is also obvious that you want to buy dog foods that don't go rancid. The only way to avoid preservatives altogether is for you to make your own dog food (see next chapter). The other option is to feed only canned foods. Canned dog foods are heat-sterilized in the can, and no preservatives are needed to keep out bacteria and yeast. Dry dog foods contain the most preservatives because they stand the highest risk of becoming rancid. Semimoist dog foods use humectants as preservatives.

Ethoxyquin, an antioxidant present in many dog foods, has been incriminated in several vague and poorly documented health concerns. The fact is that ethoxyquin appears to be safer than many of the antioxidants that have been used in human food preparations for more than twenty-five years. Probably some animals will react adversely to it, but it would be surprising if there were *any* ingredient that would be completely safe. For most animals, the lack of an antioxidant in pet foods poses many more risks than the presence of ethoxyquin.

To be fair, dog-food preservatives present the same concerns as other food additives, such as MSG (monosodium glutamate) or sulfites. Some people react adversely when they ingest MSG, and others, especially asthmatics, react adversely when they consume sulfites. These individuals are often cautioned to avoid eating these substances. Similarly, dogs that react adversely when fed a commercial diet containing ethoxyquin or other preservatives should avoid the substances. This is a relatively simple task with appropriate pet-food labeling. No preservative should be regarded as completely safe. Preservatives are often designated "generally regarded as safe" or "GRAS" by regulatory agencies, which is hardly an endorsement of wholesomeness. It is best to regard preservatives as a necessary evil as long as you want the convenience of buying commercial dog foods.

NEW APPROACH TO DOG FOODS

The need for synthetic antioxidants can be minimized if dog foods can be preserved with natural ingredients (e.g., vitamins C and E) and don't have to sit on store shelves for very long. Although buying large bags of dog food is more cost-effective, having that food sit around for months encourages nutrient losses. It is therefore best to buy food that can be fed within four weeks once it's opened.

Several pet-food companies propose to do just that by using home delivery and natural antioxidants. The diets are freshly prepared without synthetic antioxidants and are heavily fortified with important nutrients, including vitamin C, vitamin E, and beta-carotene. The home-delivery system ensures that a supply of food is delivered directly to consumers without spending time on a store shelf. In this way, the food fed is always fresh. Natural antioxidants are sufficient, and chemical preservatives such as ethoxyquin, BHA, and BHT are not needed or used. This represents a major advance in pet nutrition.

FROZEN PET FOODS

Frozen pet foods are usually similar in consistency to canned diets, except that they are frozen rather than being heat-processed. Most frozen pet foods are marketed in a regional fashion. There are both advantages and disadvantages to frozen diets. These diets often retain subtle flavors that may be lost in heat-processing so they tend to be tastier for dogs. If the foods have been fresh frozen, they will have less need for chemical preservatives than dry foods. Most canned foods, however, don't use preservtives because of their heat-processing in the can. The biggest disadvantage of frozen diets is the special handling required. Pet-supply shops must not allow thawing and refreezing of the product, and must have proper facilities to ensure this. Similarly, owners must have freezer space at home to accommodate their dog's food needs as well as their own. Finally, there is the extra time needed to thaw the food at mealtime, although microwave thawing can be used.

NATURAL DOG FOODS

What could be better than feeding your dog an all-natural food? Probably the only way to really do this is to make it yourself at home. Unfortunately, "natural" is one of those terms, like "gourmet" or "premium," that has no legal definition when it comes to dog foods. "Natural" can mean anything the manufacturer would like it to mean. The definition of "natural" and "organic" can be vastly different, depending on who's doing the interpreting. In many ways, all dog foods are natural. They are made of combinations of plant and animal ingredients. What could be more natural than that? At the other extreme, no commercial dog foods are natural. When ingredients are processed and packaged for retail sale, they bear little resemblance to the original "natural" ingredients. Using ascorbic acid (vitamin C) as a preservative rather than a chemical does not make a dog food natural.

INGREDIENTS

Ground Whole Brown Rice, Soy Flour, Barley Flour, Vegetable Oil, Carrots, Garlic Powder, Salt, Choline Chloride, Ferrous Sulfate, Zinc Oxide, Vitamin A Supplement, Calciferol (Source of Vitamin D_2), Vitamin E Supplement, Niacin, Calcium Pantothenate, Riboflavin (Vitamin B_2), Manganous Oxide, Copper Sulfate, Thiamine Mononitrate, Pyridoxine Hydrochloride, Folic Acid, Biotin, Vitamin B_{12} Supplement, Calcium Iodate, Cobalt Carbonate and Sodium Selenite.

GUARANTEED ANALYSIS

CRUDE PROTEIN . . . . 18.0% MINIMUM
CRUDE FAT . . . . 8.0% MINIMUM
CRUDE FIBER . . . . 4.4% MAXIMUM
MOISTURE . . . . 10.0% MAXIMUM

AMOUNTS TO FEED

Weight of Dog	Amount of Food
3 – 10 Lbs.	½–1 CUP *
10 – 20 Lbs.	1–1½ CUPS*
20 – 50 Lbs.	1½–3 CUPS*
50 –100 Lbs.	3–7 CUPS*
100 + Lbs.	Add ⅔ Cup for each 10 Lbs. body weight over 100 lbs.

*Measures are based on standard 8 oz. cup.

NATURE'S RECIPE VEGETARIAN CANINE DIET provides all the nutritional needs for all stages of a dog's life, as substantiated by feeding tests performed in accordance with the procedures established by the Association of American Feed Control Officials (AAFCO).

A label from a vegetarian canine diet that claims no artificial preservatives, colors, or flavors.

WHAT'S ON THE LABEL

Ideally, it would be nice to pick up a package or can of dog food and see on the label what the ingredients are, the level of nutrients provided, the number of calories per serving, and what artificial chemicals and preservatives are included. Unfortunately, that is not what you see when you examine the label.

All commercial dog foods are required to provide a "guaranteed analysis" of what's in the ration. This is a laboratory evaluation of the relative (crude) amounts of protein, carbohydrate, fat, water, fiber, and minerals (ash) included in the dog food. They use the term "crude," because the laboratory tests rarely measure actual nutrients. The "crude" protein is approximated by measuring the amount of nitrogen in the ration. The fat content is approximated by measuring the percentage of the ration that dissolves in ether, and so on. Of course, dogs don't have a protein requirement. They need specific amino acids, and this information is not provided. Nor do dogs have a fat requirement. They need specific fatty acids, yet this information is not provided. The label may give feeding recommendations, but it is unlikely that you'll see any information on calorie content. In fact, the guaranteed analysis provides you with very little useful information.

It is hard to compare dry, canned, and semimoist foods, because the values don't even seem close. The protein content of dry food may be 22 percent but a high-quality canned food may contain only 9 percent protein. How can that be if canned foods often contain so much more meat than dry foods? As if things weren't complicated enough, valid comparisons can be made only when the moisture content has been taken into

CANNED SENIOR DIET
Beef & Liver Dinner for Dogs

Nutrient	Per 100 g "as is"	Requirements per 1000 kcal M.E.[1]	Typical Nutrient Analysis per 1000 kcal[1]	Typical Nutrient Analysis per 100 g dry matter
PROXIMATE ANALYSIS				
Protein, g	7.91	23.23	66.76	33.72
Fat, g	8.66	13.6	73.09	36.91
Crude fiber, g	0.24	—	2.03	1.02
Ash, g	1.74	—	14.69	7.42
AMINO ACIDS				
Arginine, g	0.49	0.28	4.14	2.09
Histidine, g	0.39	0.30	3.29	1.66
Isoleucine, g	0.18	0.65	1.52	0.77
Leucine, g	0.46	1.13	3.88	1.96
Lysine, g	0.41	0.67	3.46	1.75
Methionine + cystine, g	0.23	0.40	1.94	.98
Methionine, g	0.14	0.20	1.18	0.60
Phenylalanine + tyrosine, g	0.53	1.16	4.47	2.26
Phenylalanine, g	0.33	0.58	2.79	1.41
Threonine, g	0.27	0.59	2.28	1.15
Tryptophan, g	0.09	0.18	0.76	0.38
Valine, g	0.28	0.81	2.36	1.19
Dispensable amino acids, g	3.49	17.07	29.46	14.88
MINERALS				
Calcium, g	0.3	1.6	2.4	1.2
Phosphorus, g	0.3	1.2	2.2	1.1
Potassium, g	0.2	1.2	1.3	0.6
Sodium, g	0.06	0.15	0.51	0.26
Magnesium, g	0.02	0.11	0.17	0.09
Iron, mg	5	10	39	20
Copper, mg	0.1	0.8	0.8	0.4
Manganese, mg	0.2	1.4	1.4	0.7
Zinc, mg	1.5	12.5	12.7	6.4
Iodine, mg	0.03	0.16	0.25	0.13
VITAMINS				
Vitamin A, IU	1146	1011	9676	4887
Vitamin E, IU	1.8	6.7	14.9	7.5
Thiamine, mg	0.15	0.27	1.27	0.64
Riboflavin, g	0.16	0.68	1.35	0.68
Pantothenic acid, mg	1.0	2.7	8.4	4.3
Niacin, mg	2	3	19	9
Pyridoxine, mg	0.1	0.3	0.8	0.4
Folic acid, mg	0.060	0.054	0.506	0.256
Vitamin B$_{12}$, mcg	4	7	36	18
Choline, mg	66	340	557	281
ESSENTIAL FATTY ACIDS				
Linoleic acid, g	0.6	2.7	5.3	2.7

DRY SENIOR DIET
for Dogs

Nutrient	Per 100 g "as is"	Requirements per 1000 kcal M.E.[1]	Typical Nutrient Analysis per 1000 kcal[1]	Typical Nutrient Analysis per 100 g dry matter
PROXIMATE ANALYSIS				
Protein, g	17.7	23.23	53.1	19.7
Fat, g	9.5	13.6	28.5	10.6
Crude fiber, g	2.65	—	7.96	2.95
Ash, g	5.16	—	15.49	5.74
AMINO ACIDS				
Arginine, g	0.60	0.28	1.80	0.67
Histidine, g	0.59	0.30	1.77	0.66
Isoleucine, g	0.42	0.65	1.26	0.47
Leucine, g	1.39	1.13	4.17	1.55
Lysine, g	0.84	0.67	2.52	0.93
Methionine + cystine, g	0.61	0.40	1.83	0.68
Methionine, g	0.31	0.20	0.93	0.34
Phenylalanine + tyrosine, g	1.22	1.16	3.66	1.36
Phenylalanine, g	0.78	0.58	2.34	0.87
Threonine, g	0.65	0.59	1.95	0.72
Tryptophan, g	0.22	0.18	0.66	0.24
Valine, g	0.76	0.81	2.28	0.85
Dispensable amino acids, g	9.71	17.07	29.15	10.80
MINERALS				
Calcium, g	0.81	1.6	2.4	0.9
Phosphorus, g	0.78	1.2	2.3	0.9
Potassium, g	0.5	1.2	1.6	0.6
Sodium, g	0.35	0.15	1.05	0.39
Magnesium, g	0.15	0.11	0.45	0.17
Iron, mg	12	10	37	14
Copper, mg	0.6	0.8	1.9	0.7
Manganese, mg	4.2	1.4	12.6	4.7
Zinc, mg	18.3	12.5	54.9	20.3
Iodine, mg	0.18	0.16	0.54	0.20
VITAMINS				
Vitamin A, IU	7163	1011	21506	7965
Vitamin E, IU	27.7	6.7	83.1	30.8
Thiamine, mg	0.40	0.27	1.20	0.44
Riboflavin, mg	0.41	0.68	1.23	0.46
Pantothenic acid, mg	2.6	2.7	7.7	2.9
Niacin, mg	6.1	3	18.2	6.8
Pyridoxine, mg	0.3	0.3	1.0	0.4
Folic acid, mg	0.070	0.054	0.210	0.078
Vitamin B$_{12}$, mcg	6	7	19	7
Choline, mg	239	340	717	266
ESSENTIAL FATTY ACIDS				
Linoleic acid, g	2.2	2.7	6.5	2.4

GUARANTEED ANALYSIS

	Canned	Dry
Crude Protein, % Min.	6	16
Crude Fat, % Min.	6	8
Crude Fiber, % Max.	1.5	5
Moisture, % Max.	78	12
Calcium, % Min.	0.20	0.50
Phosphorus, % Min.	0.15	0.40

INGREDIENTS (CANNED) – BEEF & LIVER DINNER:
Water sufficient for processing, beef, meat by-products, chicken, brewers rice, liver, vegetable gums, caramel color potassium chloride, natural flavors, vitamin A, D$_3$, and E supplements, zinc sulfate, calcium pantothenate, thiamine mononitrate (vitamin B$_1$), sodium nitrite (for color retention).

INGREDIENTS (DRY):
Ground corn, rice, chicken by-product meal, ground wheat, wheat mill run, digest of poultry by-products, animal fat (preserved with BHA), brewers yeast, dried whole egg, iodized salt, vegetable oil, calcium carbonate, potassium sorbate (a preservative), potassium chloride, choline chloride, zinc oxide, vitamin E supplement, vitamin A supplement calcium pantothenate, vitamin D$_3$ supplement, calcium iodate, riboflavin (vitamin B$_2$) supplement, copper sulfate, vitamin B$_{12}$ supplement.

consideration. After all, the protein is found in the dry-matter portion of the food, not the water content. Remember the lesson with sponges? Dry dog foods contain only 10 percent moisture, while canned foods contain about 75 percent water. It's only fair to compare the two on a dry-matter basis, because the water does not contribute to the protein, fat, fiber, or ash levels. Whereas the values may not change much for dry foods, they will climb appreciably for canned foods once the moisture content has been considered.

If you really want to make valid comparisons, you can calculate the dry-matter (DM) amount of any nutrient as follows:

$$\frac{\% \text{ nutrient from label}}{100 - \% \text{ moisture}} \times 100 = \% \text{ dry matter}$$

For the dry-food (10 percent moisture) example above, 22 percent protein translates to be:

$$\frac{22}{(100-10)} \times 100, \quad \text{or} \quad \text{just over 24 percent protein.}$$

For the canned-food (75 percent moisture) example, 9 percent protein translates to be:

$$\frac{9}{(100-75)} \times 100, \quad \text{or} \quad 36 \text{ percent protein.}$$

Using this formula and the information from the guaranteed analysis, you can make valid comparisons of protein, fiber, fat, and ash. You still can't determine if the diet provides the actual essential nutrients that your dog needs. You also don't know if the levels listed are actually digestible by your dog. You have to take it on faith that the manufacturer has actually taken all of these variables into account. This is why it is so important to look on the label and confirm that feeding trials have been performed for that ration. The diet should be shown to be sufficient for the stage of life of your dog (i.e., growth, maintenance, senior). It is not enough for the food to contain nutrient levels recommended by the National Research Council (NRC). This would be no assurance of the suitability of a dog food for any stage of life.

WHAT'S WRONG WITH THIS PICTURE?

By now, you probably realize that you have to be diligent to evaluate any commercial dog food. It's not easy to compare products with the information on a label and you often need to do calculations to compare canned, semimoist, and dry foods. It's hard to even know how many calories you are providing your dog when you feed a commercial diet. And it's almost impossible to determine the levels of essential amino acids, essential fatty acids, vitamins, and minerals included in the ration.

Even if all pet-food manufacturers make the best-quality products they can, there is still a lot of incomplete nutritional information if you keep your dog on this prepared ration for his entire life. In 1975 it was discovered that taurine was an essential nutrient for cats and that most commercial cat foods did not provide adequate levels. It is now being discovered that L-carnitine may be more important in dogs than was originally thought. And for many of the nutrients that *are* appreciated, their "bioavailability" in different forms in dog foods is not understood. For example, it's relatively easy to create a zinc imbalance in a dog food if you don't take bioavailability into consideration.

Stability and potential loss of nutrients in commercial rations are other concerns. Exposure to heat and moisture can result in a significant loss in vitamin potency. Although a particular food formulation may be designed to be nutritionally complete, the vitamin levels could be dramatically reduced due to processing and storage losses. After a bag of dry dog food has been sitting in a storage room for four months before it's purchased, there is really no assurance about nutrient content. It is also known that 20 to 35 percent of Vitamin A can be lost in dry food, whereas little is lost in canned and semimoist dog foods. On the other hand, thiamin loss is greater in canned food than in dry food.

WOULDN'T IT BE NICE?

It sure would be nice if a standardized "nutrient profile" could be available on request. This would allow you to determine how well the commercial dog food measures up to your expectations. It would give information on the levels of all the vitamins, minerals, essential amino acids, and essential fatty acids found in the diet. This material would be expressed in terms of the metabolizable energy content of the diet, which is a more reliable figure than numbers alone. The pet-food companies could keep their information about protein, fat, and fiber, because that doesn't tell you anything anyway. These new labels would also tell you how many usable calories (Kcal) are in each serving and what percentage of those calories are supplied as fat, protein, and carbohydrate.

Another request would be for manufacturers to list all ingredients on a dry-matter basis so that you could really know whether meat by-products were the main ingredient or whether you were paying meat prices for a predominantly cereal-based diet. It would help if they would volunteer the dry-matter percentage of plant and animal ingredients and specify the relative proportions of all individual ingredients used.

Finally, it would be nice if there was a responsible "third party" that would regulate the pet-food industry. In Canada, this is partially accomplished by the certification program of the Canadian Veterinary Medical Association. In the United States, the pet-food industry is still regulated entirely by the industry itself.

IN SUMMARY

Before you even consider a pet food make sure that a nutritional feeding trial has been done on the food. These trials should be approved by the AAFCO in the U.S. or the CVMA in Canada.

There is little difference between foods when comparing nutrient content (e.g., vitamins and minerals). The difference is the availability of the nutrients to your pet.

It is very easy to unbalance your dog's ration by giving treats and table scraps. Supplements and treats should not exceed 10 percent of your dog's diet.

It is very important to read and understand the ingredient labels. Some ingredients that have good bioavailability for your dog are: beef, meat, fish, poultry, eggs, liver, cornmeal, ground corn, brewer's rice, rice flour, oatmeal, oat flour, wheat flour and whole-ground wheat. Some ingredients that are of lower quality are: feather meal, meat or bone meal, whey, soy flour, soybean meal, corn-gluten meal, and wheat middlings.

Preservatives such as ethoxyquin, butylated hydroxyanisole (BHA), butylated hydroxytoluene (BHT), proprionic acid and ascorbic acid (vitamin C), are used to keep the fats in the ration from going rancid.

It is best to not keep food for more than four weeks once it has been opened. Food that sits around too long loses nutrients.

Dogs need certain amino acids, not a certain protein content; likewise with fats, they need specific fatty acids. This information is not on the label. Consumers must learn how to evaluate labels by looking at the quality of the ingredients and comparing ingredients on a dry matter basis, and the diet should be formulated for the proper stage of your dog's life (i.e., growth, maintenance, or senior).

ADDITIONAL READING:

Allard, C., "Labelling and Advertising Pet Foods." *Canadian Veterinary Journal,* 1988; 29: 403-405.

Brown, R.G., "Making Pet Foods." *Canadian Veterinary Journal,* 1988; 29: 465-466.

Brown, R.G., "Gastrointestinal Upsets with High Performance Diets." *Canadian Veterinary Journal,* 1987; 28: 419-420.

Cargill, J.C., "A Look at the Ethoxyquin Controversy: It's Still the Consumer's Choice." *Dog World,* 1991; February: 14-15, 111-113.

Dzanis, D.A., "Safety of ethoxyquin in dog foods." *Journal of Nutrition,* 1991; 121: S163-S164.

Friedman, M., "Dietary Impact of Food Processing." *Annual Review of Nutrition,* 1992; 12: 119-137.

Hilton, J.W., "Potential Nutrient Deficiencies in Pet Foods." *Canadian Veterinary Journal,* 1989; 30: 599-601.

Hilton, J.W., "Feed Energy (Caloric Density): Determination and Significance in Pet Foods." *Canadian Veterinary Journal,* 1989; 30: 183-184.

Huber, T.L., Laflamme, D., Comer, K.M., Anderson, W.H., "Nutrient digestion of dry dog foods containing plant and animal proteins." *Canine Practice,* 1994; 19(2): 11-13.

Huber, T.L., Wilson, R.C., and McGarity, S.A., "Variations in Digestibility of Dry Dog Foods with Identical Label Guaranteed Analysis." *Journal of the American Animal Hospital Association,* 1986; 22(5): 571-575.

Kallfelz, F.A., "Evaluation and Use of Pet Foods: General Considerations in Using Pet Foods for Adult Maintenance." *Veterinary Clinics of North America Small Animal Practice* 1989; 19(3): 387-402.

Kronfeld, D.S., "Protein Quality and Amino Acid Profiles of Commercial Dog Foods." *Journal of the American Animal Hospital Association,* 1982; 18(4): 679-683.

Kronfeld, D.S., "Health Claims for Pet Foods: Principles." *Journal of the American Veterinary Medical Association,* 1994; 205(1): 34-37.

Kronfeld, D.S., "Health Claims for Pet Foods: Particulars." *Journal of the American Veterinary Medical Association,* 1994; 205(2): 174-177.

Lonsdale, T,. "Feeding vs. Nutrition- have we lost the plot in small animal dietetics." *Australian Veterinary Practitioner,* 1993; 23(1): 16-19.

Lynn, R.C., "Pet Food Labels—Read the Fine Print to Determine Which Foods are Best." *Pet Age,* 1989; July: 28-31.

Phillips, T., "Meet the NRC: The National Research Council: What It Is and Isn't." *Pet Veterinarian,* 1992; March-April: 10-12.

Phillips, T., "Ethoxyquin: Scrutinizing Rumors about This Petfood Antioxidant." *Pet Veterinarian,* 1989; Nov.-Dec.: 13-14.

Remillard, R.L., "Providing Dietary Evaluations as a Nutritional Service in Your Clinic." *Veterinary Medicine,* 1991; July: 734-742.

Shojai, A.D., "Reading the Dog Food Label." *Dog World,* 1992; September: 14-18.

Sousa, C.A., et al., "Dermatosis Associated with Feeding Generic Dog Food: 13 Cases (1981-1982)." *Journal of the American Veterinary Medical Association,* 1988; 192(5): 676-680.

Questions to Ponder . . .

For home-made diets to be healthy and adequate, what two conditions must be verified?

What are some of the preferred methods of cooking homemade foods?

Maintenance diets are for dogs at what ages?

What types of dogs will benefit from performance diets?

What is a food trial, and what information will it provide in determining a diet?

When feeding diabetic animals, how important is it to establish a routine and why?

Why must a diagnosis of struvite crystals be made before treating with a special diet?

**Learn the answers to these
and many other nutrition questions
in Chapter 7.**

7
HOMEMADE
DIETS

$\mathbb{P}$reparing a homemade diet can be rewarding for you and healthy for your dog, but it isn't without problems. Although a homemade diet can be prepared with wholesome ingredients and doesn't contain preservatives, additives, or colorings, you run a greater risk of improperly nourishing your dog. Whenever a diet is prepared at home, there is a danger that the ingredients will not be balanced properly. You can manage this effectively by being aware of the problem.

Balancing a homemade diet takes more than just combining a protein and a carbohydrate in the proper ratios. This is enough to cover the protein, carbohydrate, and fat needs but does little to balance the vitamins and minerals. It is difficult to account for nutrients like calcium, vitamin A (beta-carotene), vitamin E, and some of the B vitamins (folic acid, cobalamin) because you typically don't feed your dog dairy products, green, leafy vegetables, and fruit. In the wild, hunting dogs would get these nutrients by eating the intestines, bones, and organs of their prey. Our job is to provide them with a limited number of food items to which pet owners have access. Commercial diets don't have these restraints. That's why you'll see ingredients such as ferrous sulfate (iron and sulfur), D-calcium pantothenate (calcium and panthothenic acid), and choline chloride (choline and chloride) on the label.

Vitamin and mineral supplements are important to all homemade rations. Calcium supplements are available in several forms, including oyster shell, bonemeal, calcium carbonate, calcium phosphate, and dicalcium phosphate. Each contains a different form of calcium and varies in the ratios of calcium to other minerals, especially phosphorus. It is not enough to meet the calcium requirement of your dog. It is also important to *balance* the amount of calcium with the amount of phosphorus. An ideal ratio is about 1.3 parts calcium to each part phosphorus. A dietary supplement that meets *all* of the vitamin and mineral needs of your dog on a daily basis is essential for all homemade diets.

The diets in this chapter are balanced by today's nutritional standards. As the science of canine nutrition grows (and it does so on a daily basis), you may need to modify the formulas. If you want to go it alone with your own ingredient list, do so intelligently. Either contact a nutritionist or purchase a nutritional-formulation computer program such as "Small Animal Nutritionist" by N-squared Computing of Salem, Oregon. Do not accept the recommendations of anybody, including the recipes listed here, unless the diet has been verified to be balanced and includes all needed nutrients.

Whenever you introduce a new diet, whether commercial or homemade, do so gradually. A sudden change of diet is likely to result in diarrhea or other digestive upsets. Start by adding a small amount of the new food to your dog's usual diet, and gradually increase the proportion of homemade diet over one to two weeks. This is especially important with the low-protein and low-salt diets, because they may not be as tasty as their high-protein and high-salt predecessors. Regardless, the change can be made effectively and with a minimum of fuss if the process is gradual.

Do not assume that dinnertime for your dog means meat. Whole grains, vegetables, and starches are important parts of any nutritious meal for your dog. Meat may provide a source of essential amino acids, but the grains and vegetables provide most of the vitamins, minerals, and fiber. Whole grains are low in fat, cholesterol, sugar, and salt and have many important nutrients. And the selections are not limited to rice and oatmeal. Dogs can eat whole wheat, rye and raisin breads, buns, bagels, and even tortillas. Most of the whole-grain breakfast cereals are acceptable, but if you cook them they will be more digestible for your dog. Avoid granola and commercially made biscuits and muffins, which are typically high in fat. The more grains and starches are processed, the higher the fat and sugar content and the lower the content of vitamins, minerals, and fiber. Most fruits and vegetables (except avocadoes and olives) are low in fat and packed with nutrients. Only use products that are fresh or frozen in water. Foods frozen in sauces usually contain fat or salt. Use small portions of fruit, because fruit is not well digested by dogs. Small amounts, however, provide useful nutrients, fiber, and taste.

It is worth repeating here that *all* of these diets should be supplemented with a vitamin-mineral preparation that meets all of your dog's daily requirements for these nutrients. Dog-food companies add a premix to their rations, and you should do the same. Use a daily supplement that meets the minimum daily allowances (MDA). Even though the ingredients recommended with these recipes are already balanced, the supplement is some insurance against "processing" losses. For instance, "processed" rice contains fewer nutrients than the long-grain varieties. Vegetables that are overwashed or overcooked often lose their component of B vitamins. Overcooked meat also loses much of its nutritive value.

Keep all of your rations refrigerated once they are prepared. If you make large batches periodically, you can freeze the food in portions and thaw it as needed. These diets do not contain preservatives, so it is important that you keep them refrigerated. Use the same care for your dog's meals as you would for your own food.

There are no specific feeding guidelines provided with these diets. The actual amount fed will depend on your own pet. Give enough to maintain your dog's normal weight. If your dog loses weight on the amount fed, increase the ration. If he gains weight, reduce the amount.

FOOD PREPARATION

When it comes to food preparation, think healthy. Don't buy a lot of food in advance. Keep it fresh. Prepare vegetables and fruits within the first few days of purchase to maximize their nutritive value. Use frozen foods and canned foods within three months. Vitamin content can decline as much as 75 percent with prolonged storage. When you purchase bulk products, such as dried beans, peas, noodles, rice, and flour, store them in dark containers or in the refrigerator to reduce their exposure to light, heat, and air. Remember—vitamin B_2 (riboflavin) is exceptionally light sensitive. Foods that are not kept refrigerated properly can suffer losses of vitamin A and C and the B vitamins thiamin, pantothenic acid, folic acid, and cobalamin. Air contains oxygen and many nutrients are adversely affected by oxidation. This is especially true of the fat-soluble vitamins, vitamin C, folic acid, biotin, and cobalamin.

The best way to prepare foods is to minimize handling and manipulation of ingredients. The more you "do" to food, the more you stand the chance of losing precious nutrients. For example, slicing and dicing provides more surface area for nutrients to be lost or oxidized. Use the least amount of water possible for cooking. Excess water that gets poured off probably contains most of the B vitamins that were present in the food. Cook foods slowly to at least 140° F to kill bacteria, but don't overcook foods or you will lose most of the nutrients. Cook vegetables until they are tender but still crispy. Cook meats until they are rare or medium using low to moderate heat. Thaw frozen meat, poultry, and fish in the refrigerator before cooking, but do not thaw frozen vegetables first.

Avoid frying whenever possible. All meals need to be cooked, but preferably, you should boil, bake, broil, steam, or microwave them. Avoid cooking with fats, especially the saturated fats of lard or chicken fat. Also avoid coconut oil, which is high in saturated fat. Suitable cooking oils are the monounsaturated canola or olive oils. The polyunsaturated safflower oil and flaxseed oil may be suitable for baking or supplementation but often lose their wholesomeness during cooking.

NOTE: *The following recipes are examples. Contact your veterinarian to make certain the diet is tailored to your dog's needs and his nutritional requirements. Alpine Publications and the author, Lowell Ackerman, assume no responsibility for any of the homemade diets in this chapter.*

GROWTH DIET

Puppies should be on specific growth rations by two months of age. Pups generally remain on these diets until they are twelve to eighteen months of age, depending on the breed. This is the most important time to promote healthy feeding habits. Do not overfeed your puppy, and do not give him dietary supplements unless recommended by your veterinarian. In some ways, it is more difficult to feed a pup nutritiously than an adult because his nutrient needs are so great. His requirements for amino acids, energy, and most vitamins and minerals are greatly increased over maintenance needs.

Do not feed your pup like an adult. He needs specific puppy rations. Also follow the information in Chapter 2.

Puppies should receive a growth ration until 12-18 months of age depending on breed. Photo by Pets by Paulette.

Growth Diet for Pups

Ingredient	Gram Weight	Household Measure
Cottage-cheese curd	85.05	3 oz
Hard-cooked egg	50.0	One
Reg ground beef, med broil	85.05	3 oz
Rice	172.0	1 cup
Carrot	72.0	One large
Corn oil	4.54	1 tsp
Calcium	1.0	1,000 mg
Psyllium husks	4.0	4,000 mg

This diet provides 1.05 lb of food (475 g) with a calcium/phosphorus ratio of 1.28 (mg/mg) and a caloric density of 4.6 kc/gm in the following proportions (on a dry-matter basis):

Crude Protein	40.1%
Fat	21.9%
NFE	34.8%
Fiber	3.2%

Preparation: Select regular ground beef (not lean) for preparation. Cook thoroughly by broiling, baking, microwaving, or barbecuing. Do not add any salt or seasoning. Prepare the rice as usual without adding salt, butter, or other ingredients. Mix the ground beef with the rice and add the cottage-cheese curd and sliced (or mashed) egg. Chop up the carrot or purée in the blender, depending on your dog's preference. Add the carrot pieces and any juices to the mixture. The psyllium husks (available from any health-food store) are added as a source of fiber. Add corn oil to the meal and let in soak in. Be sure to add the calcium and a balanced supplement that fulfills the canine minimum daily requirements for all vitamins and minerals. Calcium supplements at health-food stores are adequate for calcium needs and come in a variety of dosage forms. Feed a sufficient amount of food to maintain normal body weight and to allow for proper weight gain for the particular breed.

MAINTENANCE DIET

A maintenance diet is usually fed to dogs between one and seven years of age, although this is only a general guideline. During this period, most dogs have finished growing and have relatively few special needs. The term "maintenance" is not without controversy. It really describes the dietary situation needed to "maintain" a sedentary dog in a stress-free home environment. If a maintenance diet is formulated appropriately, however, it is suitable for dogs that get regular exercise.

A maintenance diet is relatively easy to formulate, because dogs of this age tolerate wide variations in feeding regimens. They are very forgiving of the nutritional mistakes that you might make when creating your own food without appropriate guidelines. Still, it is recommended that a maintenance diet be "optimal," not just tolerated by your dog. High-calorie, high-protein, and high-salt diets are to be discouraged for most dogs because they have little benefit and a potential risk from long-term use. See Chapter 2 for more information.

Maintenance Diet for Inactive Dogs

Ingredient	Gram Weight	Household Measure
Skinless chicken	86.0	3 oz
Rice	344.0	2 cups
Sunflower Oil	6.81	1-1/2 tsp
Fresh carrots	72.0	1 large carrot
Psyllium husks	7.5	7,500 mg
Calcium	0.5	500 mg

This diet provides 1.1 lb of food (518 g) with a calcium/phosphorus ratio of 1.02 (mg/mg) and a caloric density of 3.95 kc/gm (467.6 kc/1,000 kcal) in the following proportions (on a dry-matter basis):

Crude Protein	20.0%
Fat	8.0%
NFE	62.3%
Fiber	5.7%

Preparation: Select chicken for preparation. Cook thoroughly by broiling, baking, microwaving, or barbecuing. Do not add any salt or seasoning. Prepare the rice and potato as usual without adding salt, butter, or other ingredients. Mix the ground beef with rice. Chop up the carrot or puree it in the blender, depending on your dog's preference. Add the carrot pieces and any juices to the mix. The psyllium husks (available from any health-food store) are added as a source of fiber. Add sunflower oil (rich in linoleic acid) to the meal and let it soak in. Be sure to add the calcium and a balanced supplement that fulfills the canine minimum daily requirements for all vitamins and minerals. Calcium supplements at health-food stores are adequate for calcium needs and come in a variety of dosage forms. Feed a sufficient amount of food to maintain normal body weight. Consider adding supplements such as vitamin E and coenzyme Q after consulting with your veterinarian.

Your dog's weight should be watched very closely to avoid potential health problems. Photo by Corene Atkins.

Maintenance Diet for Active Dogs

Ingredient	Gram Weight	Household Measure
Reg ground beef	113.4	4 oz (1/4 lb)
Rice	344.0	2 cups
Whole-wheat bread	75.0	3 slices
Fresh carrots	72.0	1 large carrot
Safflower oil	6.81	1-1/2 tsp
Psyllium husks	5.0	5,000 mg
Calcium	0.75	750 mg

This diet provides 1.2 lb of food (541 g) with a calcium/phosphorus ratio of 1.21 (mg/mg) and a caloric density of 653.7kc/1,000 kcal.

Crude protein	22.3%
Fat	18.8%
NFE	51.3%
Fiber	3.4%

Preparation: Select lean ground beef for preparation. Cook thoroughly by broiling, baking, microwaving, or barbecuing. Do not add any salt or seasoning. Prepare the rice and potato as usual without adding salt, butter, or other ingredients. Mix the ground beef with the rice. Chop up the carrot or purée it in the blender, depending on your dog's preference. Add the carrot pieces and any juices to the mix. The psyllium husks (available from any health-food store) are added as a source of fiber. Add sunflower oil (rich in linoleic acid) to the meal and let it soak in. Be sure to add the calcium and a balanced supplement that fulfills the canine minimum daily requirements for all vitamins and minerals. Calcium supplements at health-food stores are adequate for meeting calcium needs and come in a variety of dosage forms. Feed a sufficient amount of food to maintain normal body weight. Consider adding supplements such as vitamin E and coenzyme Q after consulting with your veterinarian.

A Papillon clears the jump. Photo by Judith Strom

SENIOR DIET

Dogs are considered elderly when they have reached 75 percent of their expected life span. This differs from breed to breed and dog to dog, but senior diets usually commence at six or seven years of age. These diets are easy to digest and typically contain fewer saturated fats and salt than maintenance rations. The protein source provides ample essential amino acids, but the total protein concentration is reduced to spare liver and kidney function. Most older dogs also need more vitamins and minerals than younger dogs, although phosphorus levels are reduced somewhat. See Chapter 2 for additional information.

Diet for Senior Pets

Ingredient	Gram Weight	Household Measure
Skinless chicken breast	172.0	6 oz
Rice	258.0	1-1/2 cups
Sweet potato	114.0	1 potato
Corn oil	27.24	2 Tblsp
Calcium	1.0	1,000 mg
Vitamin E	100.0 IU	100 IU

This diet provides 1.26 lb of food (572 g) with a calcium/phosphorus ratio of 1.17 (mg/mg) and a caloric density of 4.66 kc/gm (862.7 kc/1,000 kcal) in the following proportions (on a dry-matter basis):

Crude Protein	26.7%
Fat	20.6%
NFE	50.7%
Fiber	0.7%

Preparation: Cook the chicken (with skin) thoroughly by broiling, baking, microwaving or barbecuing. Do not add any salt or seasoning. Prepare the sweet potato as usual without adding salt, butter, or other ingredients. Mix the chicken with the mashed sweet potato. Add corn oil to the meal and let it soak in. Be sure to add the calcium, vitamin E, and a balanced supplement that fulfills the canine geriatric minimum daily requirements for all vitamins and minerals. Calcium supplements at health-food stores are adequate for calcium needs and come in a variety of dosage forms. Feed a sufficient amount of food to maintain normal body weight. Consider adding supplements such as beta-carotene and coenzyme Q after consulting with your veterinarian.

REPRODUCTION/LACTATION DIET

There are few jobs as demanding as pregnancy and lactation. The nutritional status of the bitch is reflected in her pups. By the fourth week of pregnancy, the caloric drain is noticeable, and only a properly formulated diet will meet the nutritional needs of the pregnant bitch.

The diet must be complete and balanced and provide at least 1,600 digestible calories for every pound of food fed. If the meal isn't "energy-dense," the bitch will not be able to eat enough food to meet her needs. During pregnancy and lactation, the bitch may consume two to four times more calories than she did when she wasn't pregnant. This demand subsides when the pups are about three to four weeks of age and beginning to take supplemental feedings. See Chapter 2 for more information.

Reproduction/Lactation Diet

Ingredient	Gram Weight	Household Measure
Chicken breast with skin	172	6 oz
Chicken egg—hard-cooked	50	1 egg
Sweet potato	114	1 potato
Rice	86	1/2 cup
Carrot	72	1 large carrot
Psyllium husks	3	3,000 mg
Calcium	1	1,000 mg

This diet provides 1.1 lb of food (498 g) with a calcium/phosphorus ratio of 1.19 (mg/mg) and a caloric density of 4.67 kc/gm (1,085 kc/1,000 kcal) in the following proportions (on a dry-matter basis):

Crude Protein	31.3%
Fat	23.8%
NFE	38.8%
Fiber	3.2%

Preparation: Cook the chicken breast (with skin) thoroughly by broiling, baking, microwaving, or barbecuing. If you fry the chicken, consider using canola oil. Do not add any salt or seasoning. Prepare the rice and sweet potato as usual without adding salt, butter, or other ingredients. Mix the chicken with the rice and mashed sweet potato. Chop up the carrot or puree it in the blender, depending on your dog's preference. Add the carrot pieces and any juices to the mix. The psyllium husks (available from any health-food store) are added as a source of fiber. Be sure to add the calcium and a balanced supplement that fulfills the canine minimum daily requirements for all vitamins and minerals. Calcium supplements at health-food stores are adequate for calcium needs and come in a variety of dosage forms. Feed a sufficient amount of food to maintain normal body weight.

PERFORMANCE DIET

A performance diet is intended for working dogs that are training hard, working, or competing on a daily basis. This includes sled dogs, racing dogs, and police dogs, as well as others. These dogs have nutritional requirements similar to the pregnant or lactating bitch, and a performance diet should provide at least 1,900 calories of usable energy per pound of food fed. Depending on the circumstances, the diet consists of high-quality protein, complex carbohydrates, and polyunsaturated fats. Most dogs also benefit from nutritional supplements that provide additional amino acids, antioxidants, vitamins, and minerals.

Performance Ration for Working Dogs

Ingredient	Gram Weight	Household Measure
Regular ground beef	454.0	1 lb
Chicken egg—hard cooked	50.0	1 egg
Sweet Potato	114.0	1 potato
Rice	86.0	1/2 cup
Carrot	72.0	1 large carrot
Corn oil	27.24	2 Tblsp
Psyllium husks	10.0	10,000 mg
Calcium	2.5	2,500 mg

This diet provides almost 1.9 lbs of food (858 g) with a calcium/phosphorus ratio of 1.2 (mg/mg) and a caloric density of 5.53 kc/gm (1,141.9 kc/1,000 kcal) in the following proportions (on a dry-matter basis):

Crude Protein	37.5%
Fat	39.7%
NFE	16.4%
Fiber	3.1%

Preparation: Select regular ground beef (not lean) for preparation. Cook thoroughly by broiling, baking, microwaving, or barbecuing. Do not add any salt or seasoning. Prepare the sweet potato as usual without adding salt, butter, or other ingredients. Mix the ground beef with the rice and mashed sweet potato. Chop up the carrot or puree it in the blender, depending on your dog's preference. Add the carrot pieces and any juices to the mix. The egg can be served sliced or mashed. The psyllium husks (available from any health-food store) are added as a source of fiber. Add corn oil to the meal and let it soak in. Be sure to add the calcium and a balanced supplement that fulfills the canine minimum daily requirements for all vitamins and minerals. Calcium supplements at health-food stores are adequate for calcium needs and come in a variety of dosage forms. Feed a sufficient amount of food to maintain normal body weight.

EASY-TO-DIGEST DIET

Dogs with digestive problems obviously benefit from a diet that doesn't overtax their digestive abilities. This diet may be selected for animals with stomach, intestinal, pancreatic, or liver problems or for those recovering from surgery or illness. The ingredients must be easy to digest and absorb and must provide your dog with all of his needed nutrients. Good choices for protein include lean meats, eggs, cottage cheese, and yogurt. The carbohydrates most often used are boiled rice, tapioca, pasta, potatoes, and cooked cereals (such as Cream of Wheat®). More information is given in Chapters 9 and 10.

Easy-to-Digest Diet

Ingredient	Gram Weight	Household Measure
Chicken with skin	113.4	4 oz
Chicken egg—hard-cooked	50.0	1 egg
Rice	344.0	2 cups
Psyllium husks	1.0	1,000 mg
Calcium	1.0	1,000 mg
Vitamin-mineral supplement		Daily Requirement

This diet provides 1.1 lb of food (510 g) with a calcium/phosphorus ratio of 1.36 (mg/mg) and a caloric density of 4.63 kc/gm in the following proportions (on a dry-matter basis):

Crude Protein	28.7%
Fat	17.2%
NFE	53.3%
Fiber	0.8%

Preparation: Cook the chicken thoroughly by broiling, baking, microwaving, or barbecuing. Do not add any seasoning unless you are certain there is no connection with the problem. Prepare the rice (instant preferred rather than whole-grain in this instance) as usual without adding salt, butter, or other ingredients. Cut the cooked chicken into small pieces and mix with the rice. Chop up the egg into pieces or mash it, depending on your dog's preference. Add the egg to the mix. The psyllium husks (available from any health-food store) are added as a source of fiber. Be sure to add the calcium and a balanced supplement that fulfills the canine minimum daily requirements for all vitamins and minerals. Calcium supplements at health-food stores are adequate for calcium needs and come in a variety of dosage forms. Feed a sufficient amount of food to maintain normal body weight. Consider adding plant-based digestive enzymes, if recommended by your veterinarian.

WEIGHT-REDUCTION DIET

A weight-reduction diet is meant to be fed short-term. It usually contains too much fiber for long-term use. If it is fed for too long before being modified, it can cause decreased utilization of other nutrients. After the weight has been lost, it makes more sense to convert to a realistic maintenance diet.

The goal for weight reduction is to provide fewer total calories each day than are needed for maintenance. It takes a reduction of about 3,500 calories to lose one pound of weight. A diet is therefore usually designed to restrict the daily intake by about 250 calories to allow safe weight loss of about one-half pound per week. The high-fiber ingredients do not encourage weight loss. They are there to occupy space and give the dog a full feeling. This is included in the diet so that you don't feel guilty about giving your dog less food than usual. See Chapters 9 and 10 for more information on obesity and nutritional supplements.

Twelve-Week Weight-Reduction Diet

Ingredient	Gram Weight	Household Measure
Skinless chicken breast	84.0	3 oz
Sweet potatoes	224.0	2 potatoes
Carrots	144.0	2 large carrots
Safflower oil	4.54	1 tsp
Psyllium husks	15.0	15,000 mg
Calcium	0.5	500 mg
Vitamin-mineral supplement		Daily requirement

This diet provides 1 lb of food (477 g) with a calcium/phosphorus ratio of 1.21 (mg/mg) and a caloric density of 3.16 kc/gm in the following proportions (on a dry-matter basis):

Crude Protein	24.0%
Fat	6.7%
NFE	56.3%
Fiber	13.0%

Preparation: Cook the chicken thoroughly by broiling, baking, microwaving, or barbecuing. Do not add any seasoning. Prepare the sweet potatoes as usual without adding salt, butter, or other ingredients. Cut the cooked chicken into small pieces and mix with the mashed sweet potato. Chop up the carrots or purée them, depending on your dog's preference. Add the carrot pieces and any juices to the mix. Select safflower oil that is rich in linoleic acid. The psyllium husks (available from any health-food store) are added as a source of fiber. Add the safflower oil to the meal and let it soak in. Be sure to add the calcium and a balanced supplement that fulfills the canine minimum daily requirements for all vitamins and minerals. Calcium supplements at health-food stores are adequate for calcium needs and come in a variety of dosage forms. Feed a sufficient amount of food to maintain normal body weight. Even with the psyllium husks, this diet is low in fiber. Feel free to add popcorn (without butter) and vegetables to the ration as between-meal snacks.

IMPORTANT: This is a temporary diet providing limited calories for a twelve-week weight-reduction program. Do not attempt to feed this diet on a long-term basis. Select the low-energy maintenance diet for long-term feeding of dogs prone to obesity.

Low-Energy Maintenance Diet for Obesity-Prone Dogs

Ingredient	Gram Weight	Household Measure
Skinless chicken breast	86.0	3 oz
Whole-wheat bread	75.0	2 slices
Sweet Potato	114.0	1 potato
Carrot	72.0	1 large carrot
Popcorn	28.0	2 cups
Lettuce	56.0	2 oz
Sunflower oil	4.54	1 tsp
Psyllium husks	10.0	10,000 mg
Calcium	0.75	750 mg
Vitamin-mineral supplement		Daily requirement

This diet provides 1 lb of food (449 g) with a calcium/phosphorus ratio of 1.17 (mg/mg) and a caloric density of 3.42 kc/gm in the following proportions (on a dry-matter basis):

Crude Protein	25.6%
Fat	8.2%
NFE	58.4%
Fiber	7.8

Preparation: Cook the chicken thoroughly by broiling, baking, microwaving, or barbecuing. Do not add any seasoning. Prepare the sweet potato as usual without adding salt, butter, or other ingredients. Cut the cooked chicken into small pieces and mix with the mashed sweet potato. Chop up the carrot or purée it depending on your dog's preference. Add the carrot pieces and any juices to the mix. The psyllium husks (available from any health-food store) are added as a source of fiber. Add sunflower oil to the meal and let it soak in. Be sure to add the calcium and a balanced supplement that fulfills the canine minimum daily requirements for all vitamins and minerals. Calcium supplements at health-food stores are adequate for calcium needs and come in a variety of dosage forms. Feed a sufficient amount of food to maintain normal body weight. Use vegetables and popcorn for between-meal treats. Another option is using high-fiber, low-calorie biscuit treats.

Older dogs have different nutritional requirements. Consult your veterinarian on what type of senior diet is best for your dog. Photo by Judith Strom.

LOW-PROTEIN DIET

A low-protein diet is fed for several reasons, including kidney disease, liver disease, and behavioral problems. There is a common misconception that low protein implies little or no meat in the diet. This, of course, is not usually the case. When a dog needs to have his protein restricted, it is critical that the protein be of the highest quality. This usually means animal-based proteins such as egg, cottage cheese and choice meats. A dog doesn't need protein—he needs essential amino acids. The easiest way to provide those amino acids is in the form of animal protein. It takes a higher quantity of plant protein to provide your dog with those amino acids. Suitable sources of vegetable protein are asparagus, mushrooms, peas, beans, and lentils. Too much vegetable protein is not good for dogs with kidney disease, however, because these proteins contain a lot of phosphorus, which is difficult for the damaged kidneys to handle. The energy needs of the canine kidney patient should be made up of easily digestible carbohydrate such as rice and of fats that provide the essential fatty acids (safflower oil, flaxseed oil).

This diet is suitable for dogs requiring moderate protein restriction. Read Chapters 9 and 10 for specific recommendations regarding diets and supplementation.

Low-Protein Diet

Ingredient	Gram Weight	Household Measure
Creamed cottage cheese	113.4	4 oz
Chicken egg—hard cooked	50.0	1 egg
Rice	344.0	2 cups
Whole-wheat bread	25.0	1 slice
Safflower oil	27.26	2 Tblsp
Psyllium husks	2.5	2,500 mg
Calcium	0.75	750 mg
Vitamin-mineral supplement		Daily requirement

This diet provides 1.3 lb of food (573 g) with a calcium/phosphorus ratio of 1.26 (mg/mg) and a caloric density of 4.94 kc/gm in the following proportions (on a dry-matter basis):

Crude Protein	20.3%
Fat	27.4%
NFE	50.7%
Fiber	1.6%

Preparation: This diet is not suitable for dogs with profound kidney disease that requires ultra-low-protein diets.

HYPOALLERGENIC DIET

A hypoallergenic diet is used for dogs with food allergies, food intolerances, and some cases of colitis. This term is unfortunately often misunderstood. A maintenance hypoallergenic diet only needs to be fed to dogs that have a documented sensitivity to certain foods. The most common causes are protein sources such as beef, milk, corn, soy, poultry, lamb, and pork but can also occur with gluten, whey, and other carbohydrates. A hypoallergenic diet should therefore be limited to the minimum number of ingredients possible, depending on the ultimate cause of the problem. It is imperative that a hypoallergenic diet trial (see Chapter 10) be performed before putting your dog on a long-term hypoallergenic diet for maintenance.

Hypoallergenic Diet

Ingredient	Gram Weight	Household Measure
Lamb meat	113.4	4 oz
Rice	86.0	1/2 cup
Sweet potato	114.0	1 potato
Carrot	72.0	1 large carrot
Safflower oil	4.54	1 tsp
Psyllium husks	5.0	5,000 mg
Calcium	0.75	750 mg
Vitamin-mineral supplement		Daily requirement

This diet provides 1 lb of food (478 g) with a calcium/phosphorus ratio of 1.17 (mg/mg) and a caloric density of 4.15 kc/gm in the following proportions (on a dry-matter basis):

Crude Protein	25.3%
Fat	15.2%
NFE	54.8%
Fiber	4.7%

Preparation: Trim excess fat from lamb meat. Cook thoroughly by broiling, baking, microwaving, or barbecuing. Do not add any seasoning unless you are certain there is no connection with the problem. Prepare the rice and potato as usual without adding salt, butter, or other ingredients. Cut lamb into small pieces and mix with rice and mashed sweet potato. Chop up the carrot or purée it in the blender, depending on your dog's preference. Add the carrot pieces and any juices to the mix. The psyllium husks (available from any health-food store) are added as a source of fiber. Add safflower oil to the meal and let it soak in. Be sure to add the calcium and a balanced supplement that fulfills the canine minimum daily requirements for all vitamins and minerals. Calcium supplements at health-food stores are adequate for calcium needs and come in a variety of dosage forms. Feed a sufficient amount of food to maintain normal body weight.

The suitable protein sources for the hypoallergenic diet are determined during the food trial. They may include lean meats, cottage cheese, and eggs. Rice or potatoes are the preferred sources of carbohydrate. For dogs with colitis, it is also important to limit the amount of fat, which is why cottage cheese is often used in preference to lean meats. For dogs with food allergies, lamb is needed only if the other meat ingredients cause reactions during the food trial. The purpose of the food trial is to determine which foods are acceptable and which cause problems. Lamb is usually not needed for maintenance purposes except in rare instances.

Food allergy in a dog. Photo courtesy of Dr. T. Lewis. From, Ackerman, L.: Guide to Skin and Haircoat Problems in Dogs, *Alpine Publications, 1994.*

LOW-SODIUM DIET

A low-salt diet is useful for any dog with heart disease. When the heart is compromised, circulation is impaired and water and salt are retained. This is counterproductive and causes even more congestion. Commercial dog foods include high levels of salt, which can be harmful to a dog with heart disease. Commercial low-salt diets can be purchased from your veterinarian or prepared at home.

One of the difficulties in feeding a low-salt diet is that most dogs become accustomed to the high salt content and are reluctant to eat meals that haven't been salted heavily. This takes perseverance, and it will likely take several weeks to fully convert a dog to a low-salt food alternative. It is not difficult to formulate a suitable low-salt diet, because many foods are acceptable. Additional supplements may also be helpful. See Chapters 9 and 10 for more information.

Low-Sodium Diet

Ingredient	Gram Weight	Household Measure
Lean ground beef	113.4	1/4 lb (4 oz)
Rice	344.0	2 cups
Carrots	144.0	2 large carrots
Sunflower oil	20.43	1-1/2 Tblsp
Calcium	0.75	750 mg
Vitamin-mineral supplement		Daily requirement

This diet provides 1.4 lb of food (623 g) with a calcium/phosphorus ratio of 1.24 (mg/mg) and a caloric density of 4.92 kc/gm in the following proportions (on a dry-matter basis):

Crude Protein	23.8%
Fat	25.3%
NFE	49.7%
Fiber	1.2%

Preparation: Select lean ground beef for preparation. Cook thoroughly by broiling, baking, microwaving, or barbecuing. Do not add any salt or seasoning. Prepare the rice and potato as usual without adding salt, butter, or other ingredients. Mix the ground beef with the rice and mashed sweet potato. Chop up the carrots or purée them in the blender, depending on your dog's preference. Add the carrot pieces and any juices to the mix. Add sunflower oil (rich in linoleic acid) to the meal and let it soak in. Be sure to add the calcium and a balanced supplement that fulfills the canine minimum daily requirements for all vitamins and minerals. Calcium supplements at health-food stores are adequate for calcium needs and come in a variety of dosage forms. Feed a sufficient amount of food to maintain normal body weight. Consider adding supplements such as vitamin E, L-carnitine, and coenzyme Q after consulting with your veterinarian.

DIABETIC DIET

A diabetic dog needs a diet low in fat and protein but high in complex carbohydrates and fiber. To help regulate insulin levels, the same amounts of the same foods should be fed at the same time of day, each day. Regularity is the key. The diet must be regulated closely to prevent fluctuations in blood-sugar levels, because these dogs are being given insulin.

Several protein sources are suitable for the diabetic dog, but high-quality meats are often combined with vegetables. This provides a minimum of saturated fat as well as a source of fiber.

Supplements are often useful in the diabetic dog, especially chromium (GTF) and L-carnitine. Use a vitamin-mineral supplement that gives your dog his daily requirements, but avoid other water-soluble vitamin products because excessive amounts can inactivate insulin. See Chapters 9 and 10 for additional information.

Diabetic Diet

Ingredient	Gram Weight	Household Measure
Turkey—dark meat	113.4	4 oz
Sweet potatoes	228.0	2 potatoes
Apple—fresh with skin	138.0	1 apple
Corn oil	13.62	1 Tblsp
Psyllium husks	3.0	3,000 mg
Calcium	0.75	750 mg
Vitamin-mineral supplement		Daily requirement

This diet provides 1.1 lb of food (499 g) with a calcium/phosphorus ratio of 1.31 (mg/mg) and a caloric density of 4.03 kc/gm in the following proportions (on a dry-matter basis):

Crude Protein	29.3%
Fat	16.0%
NFE	50.8%
Fiber	3.9%

Preparation: Cook the turkey thoroughly by roasting, broiling, baking, microwaving, or barbecuing. Do not add any seasoning. Prepare the sweet potatoes as usual without adding salt, butter, or other ingredients. Cut the turkey into small pieces and mix with the mashed sweet potatoes. Slice up the apple or purée it in the blender, depending on your dog's preference. Add the apple slices and any juices to the mix. The psyllium husks (available from any health-food store) are added as a source of fiber. Add corn oil to the meal and let it soak in. Be sure to add the calcium and a balanced supplement that fulfills the canine minimum daily requirements for all vitamins and minerals. Calcium supplements at health-food stores are adequate for calcium needs and come in a variety of dosage forms. Feed a sufficient amount of food to maintain normal body weight. Consider adding supplements such as chromium picolinate and L-carnitine if recommended by your veterinarian.

LOW-PURINE DIET FOR DALMATIANS

Many Dalmatians have a metabolic defect that can result in a canine variant of gout. They don't metabolize proteins properly, and uric-acid levels build up in their blood. This can result in skin problems (Dalmatian bronzing syndrome) or in the development of bladder stones consisting of uric-acid by-products. Not all Dalmatians have these problems, but the ones that do benefit greatly from limiting the amount of purines (a family of proteins) in the diet.

Dalmatians with uric-acid problems are best fed a protein-limited vegetarian diet augmented with vegetable oil and small amounts of egg. Depending on the individual, small amounts of lean meat may also be acceptable. Supplemental sources of calcium carbonate (such as eggshells) and potassium chloride (salt substitute) may be needed. Consult with your veterinarian and read the information in Chapter 10 about urinary-tract stones.

Low-Purine Diet for Dalmatians
(from the Dalmatian Research Foundation)

This diet is a combination of vegetable purée and rice. Prepare as follows:

Ingredients	Household Measure
Carrots	3 lb (3 1-lb cans)
Peas	3 lb (3 1-lb cans)
Green beans	3 lb (3 1-lb cans)
Tomatoes	3 lb (3 1-lb cans)
Greens	2 lb (2 1-lb cans)
Broccoli	10 oz (frozen chopped)
Rice	1-1/2 cups
Water	5 cups
Corn oil	1/3 cup
Salt	1 Tblsp

Preparation: 1-1/2 cups of rice in 5 cups water, 1/3 cup corn oil, and 1 tablespoonful of salt in a large sauce pan, mixing thoroughly. Bring to a vigorous boil, stirring only occasionally. Reduce heat to low and cover. Allow to simmer until water has been completely absorbed. Remove cover and set pan aside to cool. The weight of this portion should be approximately 4-1/2 pounds.

The vegetable purée is prepared by first boiling 10 ounces of frozen broccoli in 2 cups of water until tender. Do not drain. The canned vegetables (do not cook or drain!) are combined in a large preserving kettle, mixing thoroughly. Purée this mixture into a second kettle, blending sufficiently to make certain no lumps remain. Thoroughly mix the puréed material. Fill 9 one-quart plastic containers to within 1/2 inch of the top with purée. Cover and freeze until needed. Thaw as needed.

Prepare the meal by mixing 1 quart of vegetable purée with a batch of rice and adding 1 heaping tablespoonful of cottage cheese. Make sure the mixture is thoroughly blended. Dalmatians should be fed modest amounts three times a day. This diet is not suitable for growing puppies or for pregnant/lactating bitches.

STRUVITE UROLITHIASIS DIET

Struvite urinary-tract stones are a common problem in dogs. They form when the pH of the urine is too alkaline and when the magnesium, phosphorus, and protein contents of the diet are too high. Diets have been formulated that not only dissolve struvite uroliths but prevent their recurrence.

Only use a struvite-dissolving diet when the diagnosis has been confirmed by your veterinarian. This is critical, because these diets only reduce struvite crystals and may actually make the situation worse if a different type of urolith is present. It is best to use the prescription diet arecommended by your veterinarian to initially shrink the size of the uroliths. These diets severely restrict magnesium and phosphorus and are not meant to be fed long-term. Urolith-prevention diets are used in dogs at risk of forming struvite urinary-tract crystals and stones. These diets moderately restrict magnesium and phosphorus. The urine is made more acidic by moderately restricting protein and increasing the metabolizable energy level of the diet. Urine pH is then monitored to ensure that an acid urine (6 to 6.5) is maintained for eight hours after your dog eats.

Struvite Urolithiasis Diet

Ingredient	Gram Weight	Household Measure
Chicken breast with skin	141.8	5 oz
Rice	344.0	2 cups
Corn oil	9.08	2 tsp
Psyllium husks	3.0	3,000 mg
Calcium	0.75	750 mg
Vitamin-mineral supplement		Daily requirement

This diet provides 1 lb of food (507 g) with a calcium/phosphorus ratio of 1.16 (mg/mg) and a caloric density of 4.80 kc/gm in the following proportions (on a dry-matter basis):

Crude Protein	26.1%
Fat	23.8%
NFE	48.3%
Fiber	1.8%

Preparation: Cook the chicken thoroughly by broiling, baking, microwaving, or barbecuing. Do not add any seasoning because many are high in phosphorus and magnesium. Prepare the rice as usual without adding salt, butter, or other ingredients. Cut the cooked chicken into small pieces and mix with the rice. The psyllium husks (available from any health-food store) are added as a source of fiber. Add corn oil to the meal and let it soak in. Be sure to add the calcium and a balanced supplement that fulfills the canine minimum daily requirements for all vitamins and minerals. Calcium supplements at health-food stores are adequate for calcium needs and come in a variety of dosage forms. Feed a sufficient amount of food to maintain normal body weight.

IMPORTANT: This diet is not suitable for dissolving urinary-tract stones. Special stone-dissolving diets are available from your veterinarian. They are not suitable for long-term use. This diet moderately restricts protein, phosphorus, and magnesium and helps prevent the development of struvite urinary-tract stones. There is no need to add urinary acidifiers to this diet. Do not use this diet unless approved by your veterinarian. It is only suitable for dogs with struvite urolithiasis. Dogs that have other forms of stones will not benefit from this diet, and the situation could become much worse.

CANCER DIET

No diet has been shown to cure cancer, but certain changes can help your dog if he has cancer. Dogs with cancer utilize carbohydrates, proteins, and fats differently than healthy dogs. They do best when fed high-quality protein coupled with fish oil (containing essential and omega-3 fatty acids) as a source of fat. The fish oil should contain eicosapentaenoic acid (EPA), so make sure that this item in on the label of any fish oil you purchase. It is available from your veterinarian and from select pet-supply outlets and health stores. This diet should also be low in simple sugars but must provide adequate fiber and antioxidant nutrients.

It is highly recommended that you use nutritional supplements if your dog has cancer. You will find more information in Chapters 9 and 10.

Cancer Diet

Ingredient	Gram Weight	Household Measure
Halibut	113.4	1/4 lb (4 oz)
Rice	258.0	1-1/2 cups
Sunflower oil	20.5	1-1/2 Tblsp
Psyllium husks	1.0	1,000 mg
Calcium	1.0	1,000 mg
Vitamin-mineral supplement		Daily requirement

This diet provides 0.9 lb of food (396 g) with a calcium/phosphorus ratio of 1.25 (mg/mg) and a caloric density of 4.8 kc/gm in the following proportions (on a dry-matter basis):

Crude Protein	31.7%
Fat	20.9%
NFE	46.5%
Fiber	0.9%

Preparation: Cook the fish thoroughly by broiling, baking, microwaving, or barbecuing. Add seasoning to enhance flavor if approved by your veterinarian. Prepare the rice as usual without adding salt; butter or gravy can be added sparingly. Cut the fish into small pieces and mix with the rice. The psyllium husks (available from any health-food store) are added as a source of fiber. Be sure to add the calcium and a balanced supplement that fulfills the canine minimum daily requirements for all vitamins and minerals. Calcium supplements at health-food stores are adequate for calcium needs and come in a variety of dosage forms. Feed a sufficient amount of food to maintain normal body weight.

IMPORTANT: This is not a diet to cure cancer. This is a diet that is easily digested and provides the bulk of calories as high-quality proteins and fats. Check with your veterinarian, because some forms of cancer benefit more from high-carbohydrate diets.

VEGETARIAN DIETS

Dogs aren't typically vegetarian by nature, but they can exist on strictly vegetarian cuisine. This diet needs to be formulated very carefully because it takes some effort to combine foods that will meet all nutritional requirements. The term "vegetarian" is vague, because there are many types of vegetarianism. Vegan diets are limited entirely to foods of plant origin. Lactovegetarian diets also include dairy products such as cheese, milk, and yogurt. The lacto-ovo-vegetarian diet adds eggs to the list of acceptable ingredients. All can provide complete nutrition for your dog as long as you plan the diet carefully. This can be complicated if you are feeding growing puppies, working dogs, or pregnant or nursing bitches. The more restrictive the diet, the more difficult it is to formulate balanced rations during demanding times of life.

Vegetarian Diet

Ingredient	Gram Weight	Household Measure
Tofu fried with calcium sulfate	113.4	4 oz
Kidney beans	354.0	2 cups
Whole-grain rice	258.0	1-1/2 cups
Sunflower oil	27.34	2 Tblsp.
Vitamin-mineral supplement Daily requirement		

This diet provides 1.7 lb of food (753 g) with a calcium/phosphorus ratio of 1.36 (mg/mg) and a caloric density of 4.20 kc/gm in the following proportions (on a dry-matter basis):

Crude Protein	20.0%
Fat	20.0%
NFE	56.1%
Fiber	3.9%

Preparation: Fry the tofu in calcium sulfate ($CaSO_4$) and prepare 2 cups of kidney beans as usual. The rice can be an instant variety, but whole grains are preferred if you have the time. Be sure to add the calcium and a balanced supplement that fulfills the canine minimum daily requirements for all vitamins and minerals. Calcium supplements at health-food stores are adequate for calcium needs and come in a variety of dosage forms. Feed a sufficient amount of food to maintain normal body weight.

IMPORTANT: Vegetarian diets for dogs are difficult to balance nutritionally. If you are not a strict vegan, consider supplementing the diet with eggs and cottage cheese, at least occasionally. Make absolutely sure that a vitamin-mineral supplement providing all daily requirements is given on a daily basis.

When formulating a diet without the benefits of meat, milk, or eggs, it is necessary to combine lower-quality protein foods to provide all the essential amino acids. For example, legumes such as beans and peas are low in lysine but high in methionine and cystine. Grains such as wheat and corn are high in lysine but low in methionine and cystine. These legumes and grains can be combined to meet the amino-acid requirements of your dog. Without dairy products, calcium requirements can be met with dark-green, leafy vegetables such as collard greens, kale, and broccoli or with specific mineral supplements. Another option is to add calcium-fortified soy milk to the regimen, perhaps to cooked rice. Cooked broccoli, mushrooms, and fortified cereals can provide the riboflavin needed on a daily basis if you exclude dairy products.

It is wise to add a vitamin-mineral supplement to all vegetarian diets. Vegan diets tend to be low in cobalamin (vitamin B_{12}), iron (in a usable form), and zinc. Obviously, it is much easier to completely balance a vegetarian diet for your dog if you use eggs and dairy products.

PASSOVER DIET

Passover is a Jewish holiday that occurs in the spring, around the same time as Easter. It is the holiday that commemorates the exodus of Jews from Egypt. It is commemorated in part by not using leavened products, such as bread, in the household. There are certain other dietary restrictions as well. The need for a Passover diet is not related to the religious inclinations of your dog, but many foodstuffs are not available in the house during this holiday. Typically, all non-Passover foods are removed from the house prior to the beginning of the holiday.

For the week or so that your dog will be fed a Passover diet, it is not critical that the meal be entirely balanced nutritionally. If he has been fed a nutritious and balanced ration up until then, no nutritional supplements are needed for the week.

Suitable protein sources include meats such as beef, lamb, eggs, or poultry. Appropriate carbohydrate sources include potatoes or matzo meal. Formulate the ration by combining one part protein to two parts carbohydrate and feeding the same amounts as usual.

Introduce the diet immediately before Passover, gradually increasing its proportion in the meal. In this way, your dog is unlikely to have digestive upsets due to a sudden change in his feeding routine.

MORE RECIPES

Daily Diet for a 30-Kilogram Racing Greyhound

Ingredients	Measure
Lean meat	750 g
Cooked rice	450 g
Bone meal	2 tsp
Corn oil	1 tsp
Liver	30-60 g

Add a good one-a-day multiple vitamin/mineral supplement.

[From, Grandjean, D., and Paragon, B.M., "Nutrition of Racing and Working Dogs. Part III. Dehydration, Mineral and Vitamin Adaptations, and Practical Feeding Guidelines." *Compendium on Continuing Education for the Practicing Veterinarian,* 1993; 15(2): 203-211.]

Homemade Maintenance Diet for a 30-Kilogram Nonracing Greyhound

Ingredient	Gram Weight
Red meat	450
Cooked rice	750
Vegetables/fruits	120
Vegetable oil	10
Vitamin/mineral supplement	40

[From, Grandjean, D., and Paragon, B.M., "Nutrition of Racing and Working Dogs. Part III. Dehydration, Mineral and Vitamin Adaptations, and Practical Feeding Guidelines. *Compendium on Continuing Education for the Practicing Veterinarian,* 1993; 15 (2): 203-211.]

Canine Milk Replacer

Skim milk	43.8%
Low-fat curd	40%
Egg yolk	10%
Cooking oil	6%

[From, Kienzle, E.: "Raising of Mother less Puppies and Kittens." *Proceedings of the XVI World Congress of the World Small Animal Veterinary Association,* 1991; 240-242.]

IN SUMMARY

All home-made diets should be supplemented with a vitamin-mineral combination that meets all daily requirements.

Use the freshest foods possible for diets. Prolonged storage decreases nutritive values by as much as 75 percent.

Growth diets are for puppies from two months to 12-18 months of age. Diets must meet needs for increased energy, amino acids, and mostly the correct vitamin and mineral ratios.

High-calorie, high-protein, and high-salt diets should be avoided because of potential health risks from long-term use.

Diets for senior dogs are easily digested, lower in saturated fat and salt, and contain reduced amounts of proteins.

Lower protein diets use a higher quality and lower quantity of protein. Since it takes more plant proteins to provide needed amino acids, animal protein is the best in this case.

Pregnancy and lactation diets must provide at least 1,600 digestible calories per pound of food.

Low sodium diets are indicated for dogs with heart disease.

Intestinal diets are for dogs with digestive disorders or for those recovering from the stress of illness. Diets must have all necessary nutrients and be easily digested.

Supplementation is useful for diabetic dogs, but water-soluble vitamin supplementation can inactivate insulin.

Dogs with cancer utilize carbohydrates, fats, and proteins differently than healthy dogs.

Cancer diets should have high quality protein, adequate fiber, antioxidants, and contain essential omega-3 fatty acids.

Questions to Ponder . . .

Why are table scraps usually not a good choice?

How might you create wholesome table scraps?

Why are dog biscuits not always a reliable choice for part of dental care?

What are the important components of complete dental care?

**Learn the answers to these
and many other nutrition questions
in Chapter 8.**

8

TREATS, TABLE SCRAPS, AND CHEW TOYS

$\mathbb{N}$o discussion of nutrition is complete without mention of treats, table scraps, and chew toys. Treats are often given without knowledge of how many calories they contain. Table scraps are considered an "evil" that most owners give to their dogs even though they believe them to be harmful. Chew toys are given without real appreciation for dental well-being. Let's examine each of these areas individually and see if we can determine the truth about these items.

TREATS

Your dog enjoys treats and giving them is an important way to bond with your dog. It takes so little to make him happy that it is hard to encourage you to go easy when it comes to treats.

It's not that all treats are bad for dogs. In moderation, treats can be an important part of a dog's day. After all, they enjoy getting them and you enjoy giving them. You also may like giving children cookies and candies but realize that there are sensible limits. You may caution your children about "spoiling their dinner" with cookies but may turn around and give your dog a treat without thinking about it.

It really isn't that difficult to "spoil" your dog's dinner with treats, because most treats on the market are relatively high in calories. It may not sound like much, but 100 calories (kcal) per treat or so can really add up over the course of the day. Treats, especially for very small dogs, can provide enough calories that they don't eat enough of their own food to receive adequate amino acids, vitamins, and minerals. If you're paying good money for a quality dog food, it is unfortunate that you could be "unbalancing" the diet with too many treats.

Dogs consider most foods as treats if those items aren't part of their commercial diet. Many dogs could be just as happy receiving carrots or cauliflower without getting the calories, colorings, and preservatives of commercial treats. This requires some experimentation, because dogs have individual tastes. Consider also that most dogs would gladly give up their treats for attention, such as play time or a walk. Exercise is a much superior substitute for the empty calories of treats.

Another option is to make your own treats from wholesome ingredients, going easy on the sugar, fat, and coloring. Although dogs don't digest fresh grains well, the cooked or baked varieties are highly digestible. Whenever possible, use whole grains rather than processed grains to retain the most useful nutrients. This actually has many advantages over commercial treats. The ingredients are going to be fresh and of the highest quality, they are likely to contain much less fat and total calories than their commercial counterparts, and you are more likely to "go easy" with these treats because you are accustomed to limiting baked goods for yourself.

TABLE SCRAPS

Veterinarians recommend against table scraps, because most items considered "scraps" are not very nutritious for your dog. The goal of any feeding plan is to give your dog a balanced diet containing all the vitamins, minerals, fatty acids, and amino acids that he requires in a day. You encourage him to eat his meals that have been balanced specifically to meet this challenge. The last thing you want to do is "unbalance" your carefully constructed meal plan. This is where the concern arises regarding table scraps. What are they really made from? Most of the time, table scraps don't consist of lean meat, vegetables, and grains. Rather, they usually include large amounts of fat and poorly digestible fillers.

There is little problem with feeding your dog table scraps if the ingredients are wholesome and balanced and much like your own meals. Your dog would appreciate a side order of lean meat, rice or potatoes, and cooked vegetables to complement his commercial diet. Adding fat trimmings only gives him saturated fats, cholesterol, and additional calories that he probably doesn't need. Therefore, the whole issue of table scraps revolves around balance and moderation. If the food is prepared in a balanced fashion, the size of the portion is not critical. It can even replace your dog's meal for that day. On the other hand, do not let actual "scraps" comprise more than about 10 percent of your dog's daily caloric intake.

BISCUITS AND CHEW TOYS

There is good reason for encouraging your dog to chew. It is recreational and it helps to keep the teeth clean. It is, however, important to distinguish recreational chewing from tooth cleaning so that you can tell the difference between treats and chew toys. For example, there are many cereal-biscuit companies claiming their products help dogs keep their teeth clean. Should you believe them?

Cereal biscuits are commonly purchased for dental care. This is valid only if your dog actually "chews" the biscuit. Many dogs gulp the biscuits as treats, and they will get calories but little or no tooth cleaning. The cleaning aspect of biscuits comes from their abrasive action on the surface of the teeth. Biscuits don't contain ingredients that promote dental health, so if the biscuit doesn't spend time rubbing up and down against your dog's teeth, don't expect it to clean his teeth.

Hard foods like kibble clean the teeth more than soft foods. If your dog is a "gulper," the kibble will probably not remain in his mouth long enough to get the job done. Many of the commercial biscuits have more than 100 calories each. Use them only as directed by the manufacturer. You also may want to consider the low-calorie varieties. The advantage of biscuits is that most dogs will gladly accept them; some are more particular when it comes to chew toys.

Rawhide chew sticks, strips, and toys are usually helpful because dogs like them and spend more time chewing on them than on biscuits. The longer your dog chews, the more the rawhide comes in contact with his teeth and the cleaner his teeth will become. Rawhide is safe for your dog and is a useful daily tool in keeping his teeth clean. In general, if your dog likes rawhide chew toys, his teeth will get cleaned better and he will consume fewer calories than with biscuits.

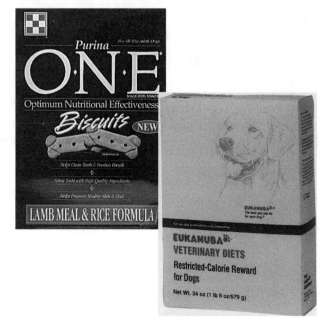

Offer your dog a wide variety of chew toys until you find which type he likes best.

Nylon chew toys are also excellent abrasives for dogs. Some dogs love their chew toys and spend hours a day with them; others seem disinterested. Chew toys come in a variety of sizes and shapes, from bones to balls to flying discs, to provide dogs with chewing exercise and fun. Many of the nylon chew toys have been designed specifically for tooth cleaning. These nylon chew toys are not digested, so they can provide tooth cleaning without calories. The critical issue is to determine if your dog is interested enough in the chew toy to actually spend time chewing it. Throwing it up in the air, chasing it, or batting it around will not get his teeth clean.

Give your dog a variety of chewing options and you will quickly learn which ones he spends the most time chewing. Any safe products that encourage your pet to chew will do their part to help remove plaque and tartar.

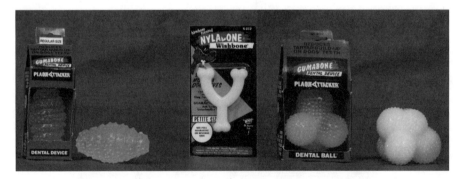

Some dogs prefer nylon bones and toys, which come in a wide variety of shapes and sizes.

Always keep in mind safety. Do not give your dog real bones under any circumstance. Although bones have some desirable cleaning effects, they are potentially very dangerous. They can cause vomiting and diarrhea and can obstruct or puncture the digestive tract. When so many safe chewing supplements are available, it doesn't make sense to risk your dog's health with real bones.

Chewing is great for the teeth, but some teeth benefit more than others from the exercise. Molars and premolars benefit the most because dogs chew with them. The large canine teeth are really designed for ripping and so do not benefit as much from chewing. Remember that chewing helps remove dental tartar. The dog that eats soft food and refuses chew toys needs more dental care by a veterinarian and more home care from you.

Do not rely on any chewing device for complete dental care. All dogs need a dental checkup at least once yearly, and periodic cleanings (prophylaxis) from time to time. Discuss with your veterinarian a total dental health-care program for your dog.

A game of tug-o-war. Photo by Judith Strom.

Rawhide bones are generally safe and, promote healthy teeth. Photo by Tammy Geiger.

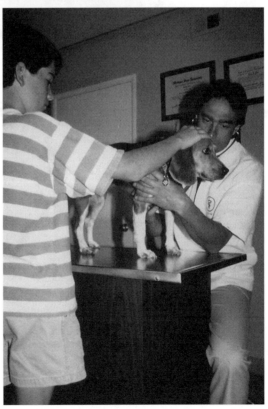

Routine veterinary checkups are very important for promoting good dental care for your dog. Photo © Click the Photo Connection.

IN SUMMARY

Most treats available commercially are high in calories.

Any kind of foods—even healthy vegetables—are treats for dogs if given outside their regular diets.

Nylon chew toys are an excellent part of dental care for dogs. They are noncaloric, they do not splinter like bones, and they provide the abrasive action needed to clean teeth.

Do not give a dog real bones, even cooked bones! Consequences include: diarrhea, vomiting, injury to the digestive tract and suffocation due to bones lodged in the throat.

Questions to Ponder . . .

When should I be giving my dog a nutritional supplement?

What supplement can benefit my dog the most?

What are some good fat supplements for dogs needing high energy diets?

What kind of supplement could help give my dog a glossy coat?

How should calcium supplementation be handled?

What vitamin is known as the *skin vitamin*?

What is a "free radical" and what does it do in the body?

**Learn the answers to these
and many other nutrition questions
in Chapter 9.**

9

NUTRITIONAL SUPPLEMENTATION

Nutritional supplementation is a popular topic, but many misconceptions and myths abound that need to be addressed and corrected.

People supplement commercially prepared diets for some compelling reasons. The very process of commercially preparing pet foods is exacting and potentially destructive to nutrients, especially vitamins. Certainly you would not expect foods that could last for many months on store shelves to have the same nutritional punch as freshly prepared ingredients. Also, the exposure of vitamins and fatty acids to light, oxygen, wide pH changes, heat, and moisture can result in significant loss of potency. Finally, it can be argued that some animals benefit from more "optimal" nutrient sources than the average pet.

Well, then, shouldn't all dogs get nutritional supplements on a daily basis? Most experts in the field of pet nutrition agree that "normal" animals on a good basic nutritional plan reap little benefit from supplementation. Most commercial diets provide more of the "known requirements" for vitamins and minerals than needed by your dog on a daily basis. Why should anyone wish to spend money on supplements if they aren't needed?

One reason is because there are still many unknowns in canine nutrition. What may be considered acceptable now may become significant with additional research. Remember the situation regarding L-carnitine and heart disease in dogs discussed in Chapter 10? This dangerous condition may respond favorably to L-carnitine supplementation. Continual testing may bring to light even more information. Plus there is the argument that some dogs respond to supplements even if there is no dietary deficiency. This is because some nutrients have positive benefits apart from their nutritional claims. For instance, vitamin C does much more than just prevent scurvy. People benefit from fiber intake even though they have no true "fiber deficiency." So there is a big difference between providing nutrients at a level that prevents deficiencies and providing nutrients *with a goal in mind.*

The concept of "nutritional therapeutics" is what often creates a brick wall between conventional medicine and practitioners who seek out more natural alternatives. Of course, no wall is necessary at all. There is more than enough room in health care for both perspectives. A patient who has just recovered from a heart attack would do well to adjust his diet and exercise habits as well as take prescribed medicines. But wouldn't it be advisable to consider diet and exercise *before* a heart attack occurs rather than after?

NUTRIENTS THAT HELP TREAT DISEASE

With the advent of modern medicine, it is difficult to focus on nutrition as a means of treatment. After all, what can nutrition provide that can't be found in pills and capsules? Some basic facts about nutritional therapy are being rediscovered—fiber can help prevent colon cancer, fresh vegetables can help prevent heart disease, and vitamin C helps protect against viral infections.

This really isn't surprising. Nutritional therapy is not new, it is not a "miracle cure," and it is not quackery. Aspirin (acetylsalicylic acid) was originally derived from the bark of willow trees, and digitalis (a heart medicine) comes from the foxglove plant. Even the potent cancer drug vincristine was first isolated from periwinkle. In fact, many of the most popular drugs used today were originally isolated from nature rather than being created "new" in a laboratory.

It is also a healthy trend that poignant questions are being asked regarding health care. Rather than embracing the concept of increasingly stronger drugs, prevention and life-style changes are becoming the focus. It is now time to extend these concepts to your dog. Nutritional therapies should not necessarily replace drug therapy but both might work better together than either one alone. And if nutritional therapies help reduce the dosages of prescriptions needed, they've more than done their job.

This chapter addresses the different roles that nutrition may play in treating disease or, more importantly, in keeping your dog well. So as not to play favorites, the different types of nutrients are discussed in alphabetical order. These include amino acids, enzymes, food factors, fat supplements, herbs, minerals, multinutrient supplements, protein supplements, and vitamins. A few examples are highlighted from each category.

AMINO ACIDS

Amino acids are often called the "building blocks" of protein. Most of the attention is directed at the "essential amino acids," which must be supplied in the diet. This is discussed in detail in Chapter 3. Most of the needed amino acids are produced by the liver, but others must be provided in the diet for your dog to be healthy.

L-carnitine

L-carnitine is a vitamin-like amino acid that is not considered an essential nutrient for dogs, but it is directly involved with energy metabolism. Recent studies imply that carnitine may be limited or inadequate in certain dogs. And dogs, unlike other species, lose in their urine most of the carnitine they ingest. It is not known whether the levels in commercially prepared diets provide all the carnitine needed by dogs on a daily basis.

Recently, families of purebred dogs, in this case Boxers, were diagnosed with a potentially fatal heart ailment. They responded to supplements containing carnitine. How did the researchers know to supplement with carnitine? Did these dogs have low blood levels of carnitine? For most of the dogs studied, blood levels for carnitine were considered normal. The deficiency was predicted from tissue carnitine levels following surgical biopsy of the muscular wall of the heart. Obviously, this test is not likely to be performed in most veterinary clinics.

The study was important because it revealed that a usually fatal condition could be brought under control with a nutritional supplement. Although the *underlying* cause of dilated cardiomyopathy in dogs remains unknown, an inherited defect resulting in carnitine deficiency of the heart muscle may be important, especially in Boxers. Whether this holds true in other breeds has yet to be determined.

Recommendations: Carnitine does not appear to have any side effects, and it can used as a supplement for any dog with dilated cardiomyopathy. This is not an inexpensive supplement. Large breeds are often given 3,000 to 6,000 mg twice daily. Smaller dogs are typically dosed at 100 mg/kg twice daily, but large-scale trials have not been done to determine the optimal dose. Diagnosis of cardiomyopathy is usually made following electrocardiograms and echocardiography (ultrasound examination of the heart). Carnitine has also been used in people to increase athletic ability and as a weight-loss supplement.

Cautions: Side effects from carnitine have not been reported.

Dimethylglycine (DMG)

Dimethylglycine (N,N-dimethylglycine) was originally called vitamin

B_{15} or pangamic acid but is not actually a vitamin at all—it is a tertiary amino acid. It also is not considered essential in the dog and, in fact, has received very little study by the pet-food industry. It is present in minute quantities in sunflower seeds, brewer's yeast, rice bran, wheat bran, whole-grain cereals, oat grits, corn grits, pumpkin seeds, sesame seeds, wheat germ and liver.

DMG is considered to be an "enhancer" and has been used in people to improve the function of the immune and cardiovascular systems. Its main use has been by athletes trying to improve their performance. Presumably it enhances oxygen uptake by tissue and helps remove dangerous free radicals.

Because DMG appears to help oxygen uptake and stimulate the immune response, it also may have a place in the treatment of dogs with immune deficits or heart disease. Competing dogs may also benefit from the nutrient's enhancement of athletic performance.

Recommendations: Dimethylglycine may be helpful in dogs with immune deficits or heart disease. Dogs with cardiomyopathy or in actual heart failure may benefit from supplementation. The other medical application might be for dogs with immune deficits that suffer from recurrent infections. A nonmedical application may be to enhance the athletic performance of animals in competition. The manufacturer's recommended dosage for dogs is 0.8 mg/kg twice daily.

Cautions: Dimethylglycine supplementation appears to be safe.

DL-Phenylalanine (DLPA)

DL-phenylalanine is derived from phenylalanine, a naturally occurring essential nutrient for dogs that claims to be a natural pain-relieving nutrient in people and dogs. The few clinical trials that have been done indicate such a benefit, but few scientific studies have been undertaken.

DL-phenylalanine seems to provide the most relief for arthritis and other chronic pain by prolonging the action of endorphins. Apparently, it inhibits several enzymes (e.g., carboxypeptidase A, enkephalinase) that usually destroy the natural pain-killing endorphins, thus increasing the life span and beneficial effects of the endorphins. Not much benefit occurs in using the supplement for acute pain (such as surgery or trauma). DL-phenylalanine also is vital in regulating hormones and producing protein.

Recommendations: DL-phenylalanine may be an excellent aid for dogs with arthritis, particularly arthritis due to hip dysplasia or osteochondrosis dissecans. DL-phenylalanine can be used in conjunction with other anti-inflammatory drugs such as aspirin (acetylsalicylic acid).

Cautions: Do not confuse DL-phenylalanine with phenylalanine, which is often taken by people seeking weight loss and enhanced vitality.

DL-phenylalanine is the form used for pain relief. Because of its role in hormonal regulation, use DL-phenylalanine cautiously if your pet is pregnant or diabetic or has high blood pressure. Any supplementation should be done under the supervision of your veterinarian.

ENZYMES

Enzymes are forms of protein that make things happen. They are present in all plants and animals. Cooking and processing destroy enzymes in food, but the body makes most of the enzymes it needs from the amino acids at its disposal. Each enzyme has a specific job. Digestive enzymes break down the food that is eaten so that it can be absorbed. Other enzymes help the body remove toxins from the blood, kidneys, liver, skin, and digestive tract. Enzymes also help the body to use oxygen in breathing and then in producing carbon dioxide as a waste product.

Bromelain

Bromelain was originally isolated as a protein-breaking enzyme found in pineapple. It was later shown to have anti-inflammatory properties. Bromelain may work by inhibiting the creation of certain inflammation-causing substances (prostaglandins) as they occur in the body. This is similar to the effect of aspirin (acetylsalicylic acid), yet bromelain does not interfere with blood clotting the way aspirin does.

The main use of bromelain in dogs is to fight the inflammatory reaction that occurs in arthritis, especially that due to hip dysplasia or osteochondrosis dissecans. Bromelain is also used to treat skin infections, allergies, and burns. It may offer benefits following trauma or surgery. Unfortunately, there is a long way to go to completely evaluate this nutrient in dogs. Most of the human research on bromelain has occurred in Europe and Asia. North American research is lagging behind.

Recommendations: Bromelain is an excellent addition to any nutritional formulation intended to treat arthritis in dogs. It may also play a role in alleviating the symptoms of allergies. Bromelain is included in several enzyme supplements.

Cautions: Bromelain can cause stomach upset in some dogs.

Coenzyme Q

Coenzyme Q (CoQ) is an interesting nutrient that doesn't fit neatly into any category. It resembles a vitamin but is not a vitamin. And, it is a coenzyme rather than an enzyme. It is often referred to as ubiquinone because it occurs everywhere that life is found. Chemically, it is a quinone—the same family that includes vitamin K_1.

Coenzyme Q is in every food that has ever "breathed," including all plants, animals, and microbes. The form of CoQ that is needed for dogs and people comes only from vertebrates and is known as coenzyme Q_{10}. Important sources include fresh mackerel, salmon, and sardines. Under normal conditions, dogs and people can make their own coenzyme Q_{10} from other CoQ molecules that they ingest. For instance, most vegetables contain coenzyme Q_9, yeasts contain coenzyme Q_6, and fungi contain coenzyme Q_7. In the liver, these nutrients can be broken down and reassembled to form coenzyme Q_{10}. Foods quickly lose CoQ with processing and storage.

Coenzyme Q is required for energy production by cells and is an important antioxidant. Most research has focused on its role in heart disease and high blood pressure. It appears to be effective in cardiomyopathy and may have a stabilizing role in heart rhythm. Benefits occur from CoQ supplementation in human patients with angina, high blood pressure, allergies, periodontal disease, and even cancer.

Recommendations: Coenzyme Q appears to be a safe nutrient for dogs with heart disease, high blood pressure, immune dysfunction, periodontal disease, or allergies. It might be helpful and safe in helping manage pets with cancer. For your dog to gain the most benefit, supplements should contain coenzyme Q_{10}, the most active form of the nutrient in dogs and people. Some researchers suggest daily does of 30 to 90 mg/day for dogs at risk of heart disease or those experiencing cardiomyopathy or congestive heart failure. Soft gelatin capsules are preferred, because the contents are better absorbed than in hard capsules or tablets.

Cautions: Coenzyme Q appears to be extremely safe.

Digestive enzymes

Digestive-enzyme preparations are available commercially for dogs and include pancreatic and plant-derived enzymes. The three major digestive enzymes—protease, amylase, and lipase—are found in the pancreatic-enzyme preparations. Protease (e.g., trypsin, chymotrypsin) breaks down protein in the diet, amylase digests sugars and starches, and lipase breaks down fats. These enzymes allow food to be digested and later absorbed from the intestines.

Pancreatic enzymes are used in dogs with pancreatic insufficiency, also known as juvenile pancreatic atrophy. This condition seems to run in families, and German Shepherds are the most common breed affected. These dogs start out in life normally, but by one to two years of age they develop chronic diarrhea and lose weight because they cannot digest their meals. This condition can often be controlled effectively by supplementing with the pancreatic enzymes.

More recently, plant-based digestive enzymes have been used in geriatric dogs and in dogs with skin disease, coprophagia and arthritis. Supposedly animals with borderline enzyme levels may not be able to take full advantage of what they're eating and therefore may manifest vitamin and mineral imbalances. Some circumstantial evidence indicates that marginal pancreatic-enzyme deficiencies might allow sufficient protein remnants to sensitize the lining of the intestines, increasing susceptibility to food allergies or intolerances. Clearly, many owners feel their pets have benefited from enzyme supplementation even though the reasons are seldom apparent.

Recommendations: The principal reason to use pancreatic-enzyme therapy is when your dog has been diagnosed through blood and fecal tests with pancreatic insufficiency. Because pancreatic insufficiency can also result in malabsorption of cobalamin (vitamin B_{12}), supplementation with this vitamin is also recommended. Treatment should be under the supervision of your veterinarian.

The use of plant-based digestive enzymes for the treatment of arthritis, coprophagia or skin diseases can be attempted for four to six weeks to see if any benefit occurs. If it does, any long-term treatment should be under the direction of your veterinarian.

Cautions: Most enzyme supplements are applied to the food before it is eaten, not given directly to the dog. Apply the enzymes to the food for several minutes before feeding so that they can digest the proteins, carbohydrates, and fat in the meal before it is consumed.

Superoxide Dismutase

Superoxide dismutase and its companion enzyme catalase are produced naturally by the body and help revitalize cells and remove dangerous free radicals. They are found in Brussels sprouts, cabbage, barley grass, and other food items that dogs rarely consume.

Superoxide dismutase and catalase reach their highest levels in young dogs and are gradually depleted as the animals age. Additional supplies can be consumed in the sources listed above but they are rarely part of a pet's diet. Another alternative is to give your dog supplemental superoxide dismutase and catalase as needed.

Supplements have been prepared exclusively for dogs, yet only limited research has been done. The main problem with taking any enzyme in pill form is that it needs to be enteric-coated so that it is not destroyed by stomach acids. Otherwise, any potential benefits will terminate within a few minutes.

Recommendations: Studies support the contention that superoxide-dismutase levels decrease with age, meaning that this compound may help keep your older dog young in spirit. The ability of this enzyme to remove dangerous free radicals may make it helpful in the management of dogs with cancer.

Cautions: The supplements appear to be safe. The only concern is whether your dog can fully absorb the superoxide dismutase and catalase present in supplements.

FAT SUPPLEMENTS

Fats are a great source of fuel and supply more than twice as much energy (calories) as either proteins or carbohydrates. They provide essential fatty acids and act as carriers for fat-soluble vitamins like vitamins A, D, and E. Fats also make foods tastier.

Essential Fatty Acids

Essential fatty acids (EFAs) are those that must be provided in the diet to avoid deficiencies. The most important ones are linoleic acid, alpha-linolenic acid, and arachidonic acid. These EFAs, sometimes referred to as polyunsaturated fatty acids (PUFAs), are needed for healthy skin and fur and to promote normal kidney function and reproduction.

Linoleic acid is the major unsaturated fatty acid in most vegetable oils and makes up 15 to 25 percent of poultry and pork fat. It is also a major ingredient in commercial fatty-acid supplements. The body, however, does not need much fatty acid. In fact, only 2 percent of the calories needed by a dog are required as essential fatty acids. Too much fat in the diet may mean that your dog doesn't eat enough of the foods he really needs to meet his other nutritional requirements.

There are definite needs for fatty acids. Poor-quality pet foods, especially dry foods, may be deficient in fatty acids. The best way to avoid fatty-acid deficiency is to give a good-quality food with adequate fat content. Canned foods are less likely to cause deficiencies than dry foods. If necessary, purchase a fatty-acid supplement or formulate one by adding small amounts of vegetable oils (e.g., flaxseed, soybean, safflower, sunflower or corn oil) to your dog's diet. The best source of essential fatty acids is fortified flaxseed oil, which is low in saturated fats and calories and contains no cholesterol. Soybean oil also contains lecithin. It doesn't take much of these oils to supplement the diet—one teaspoon to one tablespoon daily is sufficient for most dogs. Too much can cause upset stomach and diarrhea and can impair the metabolism of vitamin E. Use caution in giving supplemental fats if your dog has a medical condition such as pancreatitis, gall-bladder disease, or malabsorption syndrome.

Recommendations: High-quality essential fatty acids may help provide a glossy coat. In dogs with normal enzyme function, these fatty acids can be converted into the important omega-3 and omega-6 fatty acids.

Cautions: Too much fatty-acid supplementation may cause diarrhea and other potential digestive upsets. Large amounts may impair the metabolism of vitamin E. Because dogs eat to meet their energy requirement and fats provide much energy (calories), too much supplemental fat will mean that other necessary nutrients will be short-changed in the diet. Give all fat supplements cautiously if your dog has pancreatic disease, gallbladder disease, or malabsorption syndrome. Do not purchase fatty acid supplements in clear containers. Exposure to light renders the essential fatty acids useless. Purchase all fatty acids in opaque containers only.

Omega-3 and Omega-6 Fatty Acids

Essential fatty acids can have another important function. They can be converted in the body into compounds that help relieve inflammation. To accomplish this wonderful feat, however, they must first be converted by enzymes into their active form. This means that linoleic acid eventually gets converted into gamma-linolenic acid (GLA), and alpha-linolenic acid gets converted into eicosapentaenoic acid (EPA), both of which have some anti-inflammatory properties.

Omega is the name for the system of describing fatty acids based on their chemical structure. The omega-3 (n-3) series is derived from alpha-linolenic acid, while the omega-6 (n-6) series is derived from cis-linoleic acid.

If your dog has adequate levels of the pertinent enzymes, substances like EPA and GLA are produced to help relieve inflammation naturally. Unfortunately, there is no practical way of knowing whether your dog has the enzymes necessary to fight inflammation. You can, however, supply him with the correct forms of the fatty acids. This is done most often for dogs that have allergies or arthritis, although even "normal" dogs may benefit from supplementation. It is estimated that perhaps 20 percent of allergic dogs benefit significantly from supplementation with omega-3 and omega-6 fatty acids. But don't be fooled by imitations. Most commercial fatty-acid supplements do not contain the *functional* forms of the essential fatty acids.

Eicosapentaenoic acid (EPA) originates in plankton and algae, which is then eaten by fish. Many fish, such as cod, concentrate these fatty acids in their livers. The problem is that cod-liver oil, although it contains 9 to 20 percent EPA, also contains enough fat-soluble vitamins to be toxic in doses that would truly provide adequate levels of EPA. Therefore, omega-3 supplements are usually made from fish that concentrate the fatty acids in their muscles rather than in their livers. Krill, herring, mackerel, and salmon are all suitable sources. Omega-3 fatty acids may decrease serum cholesterol and the risk of hypertension, atherosclerosis, stroke, and heart disease in people. Some benefit may also be derived for gout, rheumatoid arthritis, psoriasis, and asthma.

The omega-6 fatty acids, especially gamma-linolenic acid, are derived from seed oils, and some are much better than others. Evening primrose oil, borage oil, and black-currant seed oil are the usual sources. Like EPA, GLA is a natural substance that helps fight inflammation. They work in a complimentary fashion but on different aspects of the immune system and therefore are usually supplemented together.

Recommendations: Supplements containing eicosapentaenoic acid and gamma-linolenic acid are safe and potentially beneficial in managing dogs with allergies and arthritis. It is also possible that eicosapentaenoic acid could be useful for dogs with high blood pressure (hypertension), heart-worm disease, or other heart ailments. These supplements provide the essential fatty acids necessary for a shiny coat. Don't be fooled by imitations—look for gamma-linolenic acid and eicosapentaenoic acid on the label.

Cautions: Follow the recommended doses carefully. Too much fat supplementation can result in diarrhea and other digestive upsets. Do not purchase fatty acid supplements in clear containers. Exposure to light renders the essential fatty acids useless. Purchase all fatty acids in opaque containers only. The use of polyunsaturated fatty acids in the diet increases the need for vitamin E. The fish oils that contain the omega-3 fatty acids create more need for vitamin E than the plant-derived omega-6 fatty acids.

Lecithin

Lecithin is a phosphatide, a form of fat. It contains choline, a nutrient that helps the body safely utilize fat and cholesterol. It also "emulsifies" fats by breaking them into smaller droplets. Lecithin may also provide some of the essential fatty acids. The best natural source of lecithin is soybean oil, which also contains useful levels of linoleic acid and alpha-linolenic acid.

Lecithin is frequently used in people because of its effect on cholesterol, especially patients with arteriosclerosis. Because of its concentration of choline, it is also helpful in the treatment of liver disease, especially when the liver contains large amounts of fat.

Recommendations: Lecithin, or its derivative choline, is very useful for dogs that are overweight, because it helps the body safely utilize fat. For this reason, it is also useful in dogs with liver disease. Lecithin is an excellent addition to the diet of any elderly pet, since it helps protect against cardiovascular disease.

Cautions: Lecithin appears to be exceptionally safe.

FOOD FACTORS

Aloe Vera

Aloe vera is derived from members of the aloe plant, and there are more than two hundred species worldwide. It has been advocated as a natural remedy for at least one thousand years. Its most popular application is for treating cuts, burns, and other skin problems but it can also be taken internally. This treatment is often used for patients with digestive problems, arthritis, and allergies.

The scientific study of aloe vera has confirmed that it increases the rate of healing of burns and cuts, but fewer studies have been done to show the merit of internal use. Aloe vera contains a hodgepodge of alkaloids, saponins, glycoproteins, and terpenoids, making it difficult to determine which fraction contains the most active ingredients.

Recently, a complex carbohydrate derived from aloe called acemannan has been found to be a potent stimulator of the immune system. Research has shown that acemannan stimulates the release of interleukin-1 and tumor-necrosis factor, two products of the immune system that help defend against infections and cancers. It has been used experimentally in the treatment of infectious diseases, immunologic diseases, periodontal disease and some cancers. In coming years, the official results of these studies should help document the benefits of this natural treatment.

Recommendations: Aloe vera makes an excellent topical remedy for cuts, burns, and inflamed skin. It may also be useful in dogs with arthritis, digestive problems, and allergies, but confirmatory clinical trials are lacking. In a very limited clinical trial of ten allergic dogs, none benefited from aloe vera given internally. Acemannan appears to be an extremely safe derivative of aloe that may have benefits for dogs with immunologic diseases, chronic infections, periodontal disease, and some cancers. It is the first licensed treatment for the cancer fibrosarcoma in dogs.

Cautions: Aloe vera is very safe when applied topically. Internal use is generally safe but may cause digestive upset in some dogs. Acemannan has been given intravenously in some cases, with allergic-type reactions (anaphylaxis) being reported. These can probably be minimized by pretreatment with antihistamines, but intravenous use is not an approved route to administer the product.

Bioflavonoids

Bioflavonoids are similar to vitamins and are even sometimes referred to as vitamin P. They are not vitamins, however, but rather are polyphenolic plant compounds. Most of the bioflavonoids are derived from the white material just beneath the peel of citrus fruits. These citrus flavonoids include the chemicals hesperidin, hesperitin, catechin, eriodictyol, kaempferol, and rutin. The bioflavonoid quercitin is found in blue-green algae.

Bioflavonoids reduce inflammation and pain. They are used extensively in treating athletic injuries in people, where use of prescription drugs could result in disqualification. Eriodictyol, quercitin, and catechin are excellent antioxidants, protecting cells from oxidative damage.

Quercitin, rutin, catechin, and hesperidin also inhibit hyaluronidase, an enzyme that causes damage in joints and skin. The bioflavonoids also stabilize the blood capillaries, making them less permeable (hence the name vitamin P), and this, in turn, stabilizes the mast cells and basophils that release histamine and cause allergic reactions. In this way, they create a similar effect to antihistamines. Bioflavonoids act most effectively when given together with vitamin C. Quercitin and catechin seem to be the most effective bioflavonoids in treating allergies and asthma in people, and the same appears to be true in dogs.

Recommendations: Bioflavonoids are safe and effective nutrients in managing dogs with allergies, injuries, and bone or joint pain. To have maximum effectiveness, bioflavonoids should be administered with vitamin C.

Cautions: Bioflavonoids appear to be very safe and, because they are water-soluble, excesses are excreted in the urine.

Brewer's Yeast

Brewer's yeast is a nutritional supplement as well as a safeguard against fleas. As a nutritional supplement, it contains high levels of the amino acids lysine, tryptophan, and threonine, but it is deficient in the important sulfur-containing amino acids methionine and cystine. It is rich in B vitamins except for cyanocobalamin (vitamin B_{12}). It is not well fortified in vitamins A, C, or E. Approximately half of its weight is in the form of protein, making it a better protein supplement than a total nutritional supplement. Brewer's yeast is also high in phosphorus, which means that you shouldn't administer large amounts to growing pups or elderly dogs because of its potential adverse effects on calcium levels and kidney function, respectively.

The claim that brewer's yeast is an effective treatment for fleas has been advocated aggressively by pet owners but has never stood up to scientific scrutiny. The reason why it should repel fleas is also a mystery. Perhaps because it has chromium and B vitamins, it enhances the immune system and, thereby, the body's own response to fleas.

Recommendations: Brewer's yeast is rich in many vitamins and amino acids but is not a complete supplement for either category. It is a high-protein supplement and a good natural source of chromium. Many pet owners and breeders feel that it is effective in treating and preventing flea infestation, but laboratory studies have not confirmed this claim.

Cautions: Brewer's yeast is considered a safe supplement but because it contains large amounts of phosphorus, use it cautiously in young pups and elderly dogs. Brewer's yeast is noticeably lacking in vitamins A, B_{12}, C, and E and in the important amino acids methionine and cystine. Use brewer's yeast cautiously if your dog has recurrent yeast infections because sensitivity (allergy) may become a problem.

Kelp

Kelp is a type of seaweed (*Ascophyllum nodosum*) and can be eaten raw or prepared in granules or powders. It is a rich source of vitamins, minerals and trace elements and is particularly rich in iodine. It also contains appreciable amounts of the amino acids aspartic acid, methionine, arginine, and leucine.

Many people claim that kelp supplementation is beneficial for dogs. It is believed that the trace minerals in kelp help construct enzymes in the body, which then optimize digestion. It is also thought that the minerals in kelp are naturally chelated, making them easier to digest, absorb, and use.

Kelp is used in treating a variety of skin problems and, because of its iodine content, for managing patients with marginal thyroid function. Few scientific studies have explored these claims.

Recommendations: Kelp may be a good general supplement to provide vitamins, minerals, and trace elements, but it is not nutritionally complete on its own. It is considered to be safe.

Cautions: Administer kelp cautiously to dogs that are already receiving more than adequate levels of iodine. In some dogs, kelp may cause diarrhea or constipation, and it commonly changes the stool to a green color.

HERBS

Herbal remedies have been around for centuries and are the basis for many of our most common medications. Aspirin (acetylsalicylic acid) was derived from the bark of willow trees but, with modern technology, it can now be formulated in a laboratory setting in a purer form. The same can be said for digitalis which was isolated from the foxglove plant and is now produced synthetically. The most current example is the drug taxol (Bristol-Myers Squibb) which is used in the treatment of ovarian cancer. It is derived from the bark of the Pacific yew tree. Four of these trees must be cut down to provide enough bark to treat one patient. Research is underway to explore the use of European yew trees as well as extracting from yew needles a substance that can be turned into taxol.

There are both advantages and disadvantages to converting herbal remedies to conventional medicines. The major advantage is that conventional medicines are easier to study, because they can be standardized based on their active ingredients. For instance, digitalis is quite toxic and therefore there is much value in knowing exactly how much of the active ingredient is being consumed. This is impossible with the herbal preparation since the actual concentration of active ingredient may vary considerably between plants or even between leaves on the same plant.

On the other hand, some herbal remedies cannot be distilled into one active ingredient. For example, garlic has been credited with many healing attributes and yet no one ingredient in garlic has been identified that may account for all of the benefits. Perhaps its the allicin, the germanium, the allyl disulfides, the volatile oils or a combination of these. Conventional medicine will no doubt purify the beneficial ingredients when they'reidentified, but until then, garlic will persist as a herbal remedy.

Thus, herbal medicine, like nutrition does have its base in true science even though it might not be considered as such by everyone in the medical profession. The fact is that you can administer rose hips, or its active ingredients (vitamin C and bioflavonoids) to get an effect. The main difference is how standardized a dosage is necessary.

Echinacea

The roots and leaves of the *Echinacea angustifolia* plant contain betaine, echinacen, fatty acids, and polysaccharides. Echinacea is credited with stimulating the immune system and protecting the body against viruses and bacteria. It is thought that the immune-stimulating qualities are present in the polysaccharide (sugar) portion of the extract. Because alcohol tinctures destroy the polysaccharide portion, freeze-dried preparations are preferred when the immune-stimulating properties are desired.

Research indicates that the immune-stimulating effect is caused by potentiation of the reticuloendothelial and T-lymphocyte defense mechanisms. The antibiotic properties of Echinacea are found in the echinacoside fraction and are most effective against streptococci and staphylococci bacteria. Echinacea has been scientifically shown to increase levels of interferon (an immunologic fighter of viruses and cancers) in the body as well as properdin, a protein that destroys bacteria and neutralizes viruses. A compound, echinacen B, has also been found to inhibit inflammation in the body, especially that caused by hyaluronidase. This might make Echinacea supplementation helpful when treating skin or joint problems.

Recommendations: Echinacea may be beneficial in dogs with poorly functioning immune systems and for those with allergies (and perhaps arthritis). Dogs prone to recurrent infections are prime candidates.

Cautions: This herb appears to be safe. Ideally, echinacea should be preserved by freeze-drying rather than by alcohol tinctures. Although Echinacea is extremely safe, use it only periodically, giving the immune system a chance to respond on its own.

Garlic

Garlic is probably the most prescribed herbal remedy and acts as a natural antibiotic, immune stimulant, regulator of digestion, and detoxifier. Contained within the garlic bulb are numerous chemicals including unsaturated aldehydes, volatile oils, vitamins, and minerals.

Garlic has been found to be beneficial in many clinical trials, but the underlying reason has always been elusive. Much research has focused on allicin and the allyl disulfides, but they only account for part of the picture. Research on people suggests that garlic might lower cholesterol and triglyceride levels and block the ability of cancer-causing chemicals (carcinogens) to turn normal cells into cancerous ones. Other studies have shown that garlic stimulates various immunologic factors and protects cells against damage from free radicals.

Recommendations: Garlic is an excellent supplement to give dogs with immune problems, digestive upsets, or recurrent infections. Newer versions even lack the odor that has plagued garlic use for centuries. In clinical trials performed at medical institutions in China, garlic was found to be as effective in treating some fungal infections as conventional prescription drugs.

Cautions: Garlic appears to be a very safe herbal remedy.

Goldenseal

Goldenseal is derived from the roots and rhizomes of the eyebalm plant, *Hydrastis canadensis*. Like garlic, it purportedly helps to fight infection, stimulates the immune system, and detoxifies the body. It is also used for digestive problems and as a natural anti-inflammatory agent. Extracts of goldenseal contain hydrastine, berberine, volatile and essential oils, and several vitamins and minerals. It was first introduced to westerners by the Cherokee Indians, who used it to treat arrow wounds and ulcers. Hydrastine, the alkaloid derivative of goldenseal, was later used in the treatment of gonorrhea.

Recommendations: Goldenseal might prove useful for dogs with immune deficits, digestive upsets, or recurrent infections.

Cautions: Goldenseal appears to be very safe, but because of its effectiveness against bacteria, long-term use may impact on the normal bacterial flora of the intestines.

Turmeric

Turmeric is derived from the plant *Curcuma longa*, not to be confused with *Cucumis sativa*, the cucumber plant. It is a primary ingredient in many varieties of curry powders and sauces. Its main use is as an anti-inflammatory agent, and the active ingredient isolated recently is known as curcumin. Recent studies suggest that curcumin may be as effective as cortisone or phenylbutazone in its anti-inflammatory capabilities, with many fewer potential side effects. Laboratory studies indicate that curcumin lowers levels of inflammatory substances (prostaglandin E_2 and 5-HETE), and perhaps this is why it is effective. Much research has been done regarding the protective effect of turmeric on liver function and on its ability to stimulate bile secretion. The scientific basis for these conjectures has been proposed but not definitively proven.

Recommendations: Turmeric is an excellent herbal remedy for dogs with inflammation and pain, especially those with arthritis. Turmeric may also be beneficial in dogs with liver disease or digestive disorders, especially pancreatic insufficiency, but no studies have been done to support this hypothesis.

Cautions: Turmeric appears to be very safe. Studies indicate that turmeric does not cause stomach bleeding, which is a problem with the current steroidal and nonsteroidal anti-inflammatory agents.

MINERAL SUPPLEMENTS

Calcium and Phosphorus

Calcium and phosphorus are so interrelated nutritionally that they need to be discussed together. This principle is unfortunately often neglected when calcium supplements alone are given. These minerals provide the rigid framework for bones and teeth, and it is critical that calcium and phosphorus exist in the correct ratio to get the job done right. For dogs, the correct ratio is about 1.3 parts calcium to every 1 part phosphorus.

The most common reason for calcium deficiency could be prevented entirely—by *not* supplementing your dog's diet at all unless recommended by your veterinarian. Calcium should not be added to the diets of most dogs, especially those that are growing rapidly or are pregnant. These, however, are usually the ones given excess amounts of calcium. The fact is that calcium levels in the body are carefully regulated by hormones (such as calcitonin and parathormone) and vitamin D. Supplementation disturbs this normal regulation, causing many problems. For instance, it has been well documented that calcium supplements given to rapidly growing pups can interfere with cartilage and bone formation. Calcium supplementation can also interfere with the proper absorption of zinc from the intestines.

Another way that you could get into problems with calcium is by making your own diet for your dog without proper direction. Homemade diets tend to be high in meat content, and meat usually is low in calcium. It also throws off the important calcium:phosphorus ratio. Rather than a ratio of 1.3 parts calcium to 1 part phosphorus, a hamburger-based diet may provide a completely inappropriate blend of 1 part calcium to 15 parts phosphorus.

In short, there is no reason to supplement the diet with calcium unless instructed to do so by your veterinarian. This is very rarely required, even in breeding bitches. The lesson to be learned—not all supplements are good for your pet!

Recommendations: Do not supplement your dog with calcium unless instructed to do so by your veterinarian.

Cautions: Calcium supplementation has been shown to cause bone and joint disorders and to impair the absorption of zinc from the intestine. Use only under the direction of your veterinarian.

Zinc

Zinc is an important mineral that is critical in making proteins, enhancing the function of enzymes, and promoting normal immune function. Some ingredients in dog foods (e.g., fiber) as well as supplements containing calcium, iron, tin, and copper, can decrease zinc absorption. This is another reason why general supplements that include a multitude of nutrients may actually do more harm than good. Anything that interferes with the absorption of zinc, affects its function in the body, or enhances its loss will reduce the body stores of zinc.

In recent years, zinc has probably received more attention than any other mineral. It was documented that some skin diseases in dogs, which did not respond to other forms of therapy, cleared entirely with appropriate zinc supplementation. The condition is called zinc-responsive dermatosis rather than zinc deficiency, because most of these dogs had "normal" levels of zinc in their blood. The more studies that were done, the more it appeared that there may be several reasons for these observations.

Most of the affected dogs were sled-dog breeds—Siberian Huskies, Malamutes, and Samoyeds. It was believed that they might have a genetic defect that results in a decreased ability to absorb zinc from the intestine. Another group of dogs had problems related directly to diet. For instance, dogs given calcium supplements by their owners had problems that would clear up when supplementation was stopped. Other dogs were fed high-cereal diets that apparently caused a zinc imbalance. This is because phytates (fibers) which are present in cereals interfere with the absorption of zinc. This seemed to be most acute in rapidly growing breeds such as Doberman pinschers and great Danes. Yet another closely related problem was seen in dogs fed generic diets. Many of these dogs developed skin problems about two to four weeks after being on these generic diets as the sole dietary source. They appeared healthy and happy but were covered with scabs and sores. Putting them on a "brand-name" diet remedied the problem.

There are many lessons to be learned from these experiences with zinc. First, it is important for all dogs to receive a properly balanced, nutritious diet. Second, supplementing with calcium or feeding a high-cereal (high-fiber) diet can impair the ability of the body to absorb zinc, even if it is present in adequate amounts in the diet. Third, zinc alone may be a useful supplement when a dog has chronic skin problems or some immune deficit. Finally, it may be helpful even when there is no deficiency. That's because zinc levels can be lowered by diarrhea, kidney disease, liver disease, or diabetes that might not be linked to any nutritional problem, and because of zinc's beneficial effects on the immune system.

Zinc is sometimes used in treating other conditions. Recently, it was determined that zinc acetate supplementation could be helpful in managing dogs with liver disease caused by copper toxicity. This condition, which is most common in Bedlington Terriers and West Highland White Terriers, has some similarities to Wilson's disease in people. Although the pattern of inheritance is not precisely known in all breeds, affected dogs store copper in their livers and eventually poison themselves. Zinc acetate can block the absorption of copper from the intestines. Previously, only drugs such as penicillamine and trientine were used in treatment, but they have toxicities of their own. Zinc acetate has been used successfully, and without side effects.

Recommendations: Zinc is a useful supplement for dogs suspected of having immune problems, as well as for a variety of crusting skin diseases. Zinc has also been incorporated into a dental mouth rinse, combined with ascorbic acid (vitamin C) and cysteine, and found to be an excellent aid in preventing tartar buildup and promoting healthy gum tissue. Zinc acetate can be successfully used to manage dogs with liver disease associated with copper accumulation and toxicity. Enzyme supplements may increase blood levels of zinc by increasing absorption of zinc from the diet.

Cautions: Too much zinc in the diet can result in either diarrhea or constipation and can affect the levels of other vitamins and minerals in the body. If you are unsure about dosing, consult your veterinarian.

Cases of zinc-responsive dermatitis. Above is hyperkeratotic footpads. From, Ackerman, L.: Guide to Skin and Haircoat Problems in Dogs, *Alpine Publications, 1994. To the left is a mild case with scaling on the bridge of the nose. From: Ackerman, L.,* Practical Canine Dermatology, *American Veterinary Publications, 1989.*

Germanium

Organic germanium (bis-beta-carboxyethyl germanium sesquioxide) is not typically discussed in books on dog nutrition, but it has many important functions. It is present in a number of plants, including garlic, aloe, comfrey, ginseng, waternut, shelf fungus (Shiitake mushroom), and Chlorella (algae). Germanium is present in whole grains but not in refined flours. It is probably nonexistent in many commercial pet foods.

Germanium may enhance the immune response and act as an antioxidant, helping to preserve foods (and bodies) naturally. It also acts as a detoxifier by chelating mercury, cadmium, and other metals. It helps ensure that cells in the body have adequate amounts of oxygen so that they can resist the effects of toxins in the system. As a bonus, it may have pain-relieving properties.

Germanium is a supplement worth considering in dogs with ongoing infections. It is likely that these dogs have impaired immune systems that might benefit from supplementation. At present, germanium is available from health-food stores, but relatively little work has been directed at dogs.

Recommendations: Germanium holds promise as a natural immune stimulant and can be used in dogs with immune deficits or other debilitating diseases.

Cautions: Germanium appears to be exceptionally safe.

Chromium

Chromium is important in energy production. Because it is involved in the metabolism of glucose (sugar), it is sometimes referred to as glucose tolerance factor (GTF). Chromium is found in brewer's yeast, brown rice, and whole grains. The American diet is generally low in chromium. This may impair regulation of blood-sugar levels and may, in part, account for the preponderance of hypoglycemia and diabetes in North America. On the other hand, beer is high in chromium and the long-term toxic effects on the heart are sometimes referred to as beer-drinkers' cardiomyopathy. In proper amounts, chromium helps maintain normal blood-sugar concentrations, promotes normal coronary artery function, and provides energy.

Recommendations: Chromium might be useful in dogs with diabetes mellitus.

Cautions: Chromium is considered very safe unless administered in excessive doses.

MULTINUTRIENT SUPPLEMENTS

Nutritional supplements for dogs abound, yet few actually meet the requirements of a dog with specific problems. In normal, healthy dogs fed a good, balanced ration, supplementation of vitamins and minerals is likely unwarranted. Dogs have a certain maintenance requirement for vitamins and minerals. During growth and times of stress, this requirement is essentially doubled. Despite the vast number of supplements on the market, it is still rare to see one that meets the requirements for the important vitamins, minerals, and fatty acids. Most supplements generally augment the diet with a multitude of vitamins and minerals but not necessarily for stress levels or for specific disorders. It is always advisable to supplement your dog with individual ingredients rather than with a potpourri of nutrients unless they have been formulated for a specific purpose.

Recommended Daily Allowance (RDA) Supplements

Many commercial supplements provide a combination of vitamins and minerals that meet the daily nutritional requirements of dogs. If your dog is receiving a well-balanced diet that includes some exposure to fresh vegetables and grains, he probably does not need a daily vitamin-mineral supplement. Where these supplements do have their place is when you are giving your dog a homemade diet that has not been evaluated thoroughly for nutritional balance and completeness.

Vitamin-mineral supplements are not likely to be useful in managing any health-care problems even though they may contain helpful nutrients. This is because there is a big difference between the amount that will prevent deficiencies and the doses often used to treat problems. For example, the dosage of vitamin C used in medicine may be 500 to 1,000 mg daily or more, even though there is no recommended daily allowance. The recommended daily allowance for vitamin E for a twenty-pound dog is about ten IU, yet during treatment, 200 IU two to three times daily may be used to get the desired effect. This same dog may have a nutritional requirement for vitamin A of 1,000 IU, but probably ten times this amount would be given for a specific medical problem. It is therefore very unlikely that the dosages in a daily vitamin/mineral supplement will help an animal with a specific medical problem.

Recommendations: Nutritional supplements that provide the recommended daily allowances of nutrients are useful additions to diets that are prepared at home that have not been evaluated thoroughly for nutritional balance and completeness.

Cautions: These supplements are unlikely to cause problems, but it is also unlikely that they will aid in managing any specific health problems.

SPECIFIC COMBINATION PRODUCTS

Specific combinations of nutrients are the practical way to approach many health care problems. If they have been formulated intelligently, they should contain nutrients in the correct balance to best manage the problem for which they are intended.

Elderly pets, for example, would benefit from supplements that take into account the changing dietary needs of aging dogs. Moderate increases in vitamin A, thiamin, pyridoxine, cyanocobalamin, and vitamin E are all indicated. Zinc is often added for its role in bolstering the immune system. Phosphorus and sodium should be reduced in older dogs because of the stress that these nutrients place on the kidneys and heart, respectively. Too much protein, phosphorus, and sodium have all been shown to enhance the progression of kidney disease in older dogs. A properly formulated supplement, intended for elderly dogs, should take all of these factors into account.

The same is true for supplements intended for other health-care problems. We know, for example, that dogs (and people) with heart disease should be on a low-salt diet. These same dogs may also benefit from antioxidants and other nutrients that help ensure that tissues receive adequate amounts of oxygen even when circulation is impaired. Recent research has suggested that the amino acid L-carnitine may be an important element in dilated cardiomyopathy, one of the leading causes of heart disease in dogs.

Dogs with kidney disease also benefit from intelligent nutritional supplementation. They should receive only high-quality protein and in moderate amounts. Too much protein taxes the kidneys and is counterproductive. Phosphorus and sodium supplementation can be hazardous as well. Vitamin A, although it is an antioxidant, is not a good choice for dogs with kidney disease because it may increase the release of a hormone (parathormone) that will cause adverse changes in the kidneys. These dogs should receive liberal amounts of the water-soluble vitamins, especially vitamin C, folic acid (folate), and pyridoxine. Calcium, phosphorus, and vitamin D should not be administered because they can result in further deterioration of kidney function. In these kinds of diseases, it is important to know the hazards and the benefits of nutritional supplementation.

Skin diseases are probably the most common condition for which nutritional supplementation is sought. Although many skin problems benefit from specific supplements, few are the result of actual nutritional deficiencies. A well-formulated supplement will provide high-quality amino acids, vitamins, and minerals needed for optimal skin care. These levels are not achieved with supplements that meet the recommended daily requirements. Most research has focused on the use of omega-3 and omega-6 fatty acids in treating allergic dogs, but the use of zinc, vitamin E, the sulfur-containing amino acids, and the bioflavonoids is also of great interest.

Recommendations: A well-formulated combination product that takes into account the nutritional needs of your dog with a specific condition is the best option for supplemental use.

Cautions: Follow any recommendations by the manufacturer and your veterinarian regarding specific products.

PROTEIN SUPPLEMENTS

Proteins are needed as a source of amino acids, the building blocks of body proteins. Without a steady supply of protein, the body cannot manufacture its own particular blend of needed proteins. The skin and hair alone take 25 to 30 percent of the total daily protein intake just for maintenance. Animals have a lot of fur, and that fur is made up of protein.

Shouldn't you therefore feed your dog a high-protein diet? Not really. Total protein *quantity* is not nearly as important as protein *quality*. The fact is, if you shaved your dog and fed him his own fur, he would receive lots of protein but would derive little benefit. So, in nutrition, the important thing is bioavailability—how much of the nutrients you are giving are actually being digested and absorbed. Take a look at the ingredient list on the dog food and be more concerned with protein quality than with the actual percentage of protein in the diet. If the source of protein cannot be digested, absorbed, and utilized, the actual percentage listed on the package is irrelevant.

Protein deficiency is rare in animals and is seen only in individuals fed a poor-quality diet or in animals that are ill and unable to eat properly. Changing to a better-quality diet is more realistic than trying to supplement a poorly-formulated homemade or commercial diet.

Recommendations: Protein supplements are of limited use unless your pet is exceptionally debilitated and unable to eat a healthy diet on his own. If his diet is only marginal in quality, it makes more sense to convert to a better diet than to use a protein supplement.

Cautions: Generally safe but rarely needed.

VITAMIN SUPPLEMENTS

Vitamin A

Vitamin A has always been considered an important "skin vitamin," but it also regulates immune function and promotes health of the eyes and reproductive system. In many ways, vitamin A resembles a hormone more than a vitamin. Dogs can use either vitamin A or its precursor, beta-carotene, in their diets.

Vitamin A has many uses as a dietary supplement, but it does carry some risks. It is a fat-soluble vitamin and, if given in large amounts, can accumulate in the liver and cause toxicities. Large doses of vitamin A should be given only under the direction of your veterinarian.

There are good reasons to treat some dogs with vitamin A. A specific skin disease, vitamin A-responsive dermatosis, can occur in dogs. This skin condition simply responds to larger doses of vitamin A than are present in the diet. It especially affects the Cocker Spaniel, but other breeds have also been implicated. It causes dandruff, hair loss, and marked crusting, especially on the back. The diagnosis is confirmed when a dog responds completely to supplementation with megadoses of vitamin A.

Vitamin A has long been described as a nutrient that helps "normalize" the skin. In recent years, derivatives of this vitamin (retinoids) have been formulated with even more specific activities. Isotretinoin (Accutane®), a vitamin-A derivative, has been used in treating serious acne in people, and its sister compound etretinate (Tegison®) has been used in treating psoriasis.

Because of the potential problems with vitamin A, attention has focused on beta-carotene, which can be converted in the body to vitamin A. The risk of overdose is diminished, because the unconverted beta-carotene is just excreted. This makes beta-carotene (found in deep-green, leafy vegetables, carrots, cantaloupes and sweet potatoes) an excellent antioxidant, but it may not permit high enough levels of vitamin A in the body to treat diseases of the skin, eyes, or reproductive tract.

Many supplements designed for skin and immune problems include appreciable amounts of vitamin A. These are often helpful, but be careful not to add additional vitamin A or problems could result. Megadose vitamin A therapy should only be done under the supervision of your veterinarian. Periodic blood tests will be necessary to document that no side effects result from the therapy.

Recommendations: Megadose vitamin A is important in treating a variety of skin, reproductive and eye diseases, but should be used only under the direction of your veterinarian. Periodic blood tests are necessary to ensure that it is being used safely. Beta-carotene is an excellent nutrient to help promote the antioxidant actions of vitamin A in the body.

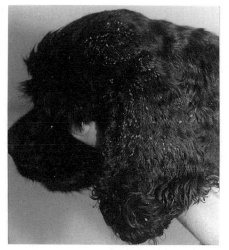

Vitamin A responsive dermatosis in a Cocker Spaniel. Note the scale which clings to the hair. From, Ackerman, L.: Practical Canine Dermatology, *American Veterinary Publications, 1989.*

Cautions: Vitamin A is a fat-soluble vitamin that can cause toxicity. It should be administered cautiously to dogs with liver disease and to pregnant bitches. Use only as recommended by your veterinarian. Blood-test monitoring is an important aspect of treatment. Beta-carotene may not result in sufficiently high levels of vitamin A in the body to treat certain disorders of the skin, eyes, and reproductive tract.

B Vitamins

The B vitamins are familiar to almost everybody. They include thiamin (B_1), riboflavin (B_2) and niacin (B_3). Other important B vitamins that are less familiar are pantothenic acid (B_5), pyridoxine (B_6), and cyanocobalamin (B_{12}). Related compounds are biotin, choline, folic acid, and inositol. The B vitamins are often discussed as a group but many have distinct benefits individually.

Niacin, and its companion form niacinamide, are needed for proper circulation and healthy skin. Niacinamide has been used in treating lupus (systemic and cutaneous lupus erythematosus), sebaceous adenitis, and dermatomyositis in dogs and in other immune-mediated diseases in people.

Pantothenic acid is known as an "antistress" vitamin and helps to convert fats, carbohydrates, and proteins into energy. It also aids in the formation of antibodies and adrenal hormones.

Pyridoxine activates many enzymes and helps the immune system. It also assists in maintaining sodium and potassium balance and in making new red blood cells. In fact, pyridoxine is probably the busiest of the B vitamins, although it often takes a backseat to thiamin, riboflavin, and niacin in name recognition.

Cyanocobalamin is an essential nutrient for all cells and helps build red blood cells. It is not present in any significant levels in vegetables or grains but only in animal products such as milk, eggs, organ meats, and seafood. Therefore, dogs maintained on a vegetarian diet are at risk of developing vitamin-B_{12} deficiency. Probably the most common reason for reduced vitamin B_{12} in dogs is from parasites (worms) or bacterial overgrowth in the intestines that inhibit the absorption of B_{12}. Malabsorption can also result from pancreatic insufficiency.

Folic acid provides energy and is a key ingredient in the formation of red blood cells. Folic acid is often used together with cyanocobalamin in treating anemia.

Biotin is important for healthy skin and fur, and deficiencies are rare. Feeding raw eggs to dogs has been blamed as a contributing factor to biotin deficiency but this is unlikely if you seldom do it. The reason is because avidin, which is present in raw eggs, can bind biotin in the intestines and make it unavailable. Cooking the eggs removes the danger. There is probably more danger of biotin deficiency from chronic administration of sulfa drugs and antibiotics than from feeding raw eggs.

Choline is most important because of its role in lecithin formation and hormone production. It also helps remove fat from the liver and enhances nerve transmission. Accumulations of fat in the liver can overwhelm choline requirements and result in deficiencies. Keep your pet fit and trim!

Inositol, like choline, is important in lecithin formation and helps remove fat from the liver. It is vital for hair growth and may be included in dietary supplements intended to promote healthy skin and haircoat.

Recommendations: It is rare to see B-vitamin deficiencies in dogs fed commercial pet foods, but supplementation can be helpful in managing many health problems. Dogs with hair loss or nail disorders often benefit from supplemental inositol. Niacinamide has been used to treat several skin disorders in dogs and other immune-mediated disorders in humans. It is often combined with tetracycline for its anti-inflammatory effect. Inositol and choline are indicated for dogs that are overweight or have liver problems. Pantothenic acid may help dogs with allergies and is also helpful in dogs with hormonal disorders. Pyridoxine is useful in animals that need a boost to their immune system and to help increase energy levels in dogs recovering from disease. Cyanocobalamin, folic acid, and pyridoxine are helpful nutrients in managing dogs with anemia. New research on humans has focused on the role of folic acid (folate) in preventing neurological defects of newborns such as spina bifida and anencephaly. A link has also been made between folic acid and the prevention of cervical cancer. Little research has been done on the potential value of folic acid to dogs, other than in the management of anemia. Biotin is used to manage a variety of skin diseases, especially those that produce excessive scaling.

Cautions: The B vitamins are water-soluble and pass into the urine if they are given in excess. Some, such as niacin, can cause rashes if given in truly excessive amounts.

Vitamin C

Vitamin C (ascorbic acid) is a water-soluble vitamin and is probably familiar to almost everyone. It is a potent antioxidant that is required for tissue growth and repair, normal immune function, and adrenal gland function. Recent research has produced some evidence that vitamin C may promote the production of interferon, a substance important in ridding the body of viruses and cancers.

Unlike humans, dogs do not have an absolute requirement for vitamin C and are not at risk for developing scurvy. Does this mean that there are no benefits from vitamin-C supplementation? Most of the recommendations for giving dogs supplemental vitamin C are anecdotal. Breeders often claim that it is helpful in dogs with bone and joint problems, such as hip dysplasia and hypertrophic osteodystrophy. For the most part, these have not been studied scientifically, and valid conclusions are not available. On the other hand, there is a fair amount of research to support the contention that ascorbic acid will not prevent orthopedic diseases. A study with growing Labrador Retrievers found that ascorbic acid supplementation of 500 milligrams per day had no effect on the development of skeletal disorders. Some researchers have even claimed that ascorbic acid supplementation may actually increase the risk of developing orthopedic problems in dogs. Similar claims about using vitamin C to protect dogs from kennel cough or viruses are also difficult to defend but not necessarily without merit.

There are many documented benefits in using vitamin C. Dogs with alkaline urine that tend to form struvite crystals may be able to effectively acidify their urine by taking vitamin C. This may also decrease urinary tract infections, which occur most commonly in alkaline urine. For some dogs, though, this practice may not be safe. It is not desirable for the urine to acidify in breeds that are prone to forming oxalate crystals (e.g., Schnauzers), uric-acid crystals (e.g., Dalmatians), or cystine crystals (e.g., Dachshunds).

Although scientific studies in dogs have not proven the value of vitamin-C supplementation, there are many reasons to supplement. Dogs that have recurrent infections, those with immune-system problems, and those recovering from injuries or surgery may all derive some benefit from vitamin-C supplementation.

Recommendations: Vitamin C is an important supplement even though dogs can make their own internally. Vitamin C is an antioxidant that helps prevent fats in the body and in the diet from going rancid. For this reason alone it is added to many supplements for many different problems. It also may be given for its acidifying effects. This may be helpful in dogs with urinary-tract infections and bladder stones, or when combined with drugs that work better in an acidic environment. Drugs such as ketoconazole may be given with vitamin C to help increase the absorption of the medication. Finally, many breeders and pet owners are convinced that vitamin C helps dogs with arthritis and respiratory infections. Although large clinical trials have not been done to support this contention, vitamin C is a very safe nutrient to administer and is worth trying, whether it works or not.

Cautions: Vitamin C is very safe. Excess intake is excreted in the urine. Vitamin C should be administered cautiously and under veterinary direction in dogs with a tendency to form oxalate, cystine, or uric-acid crystals in their urine.

Vitamin E

Vitamin E is a fat-soluble vitamin that acts as a natural antioxidant and is a mild anti-inflammatory agent. Good natural sources include wheat germ, soybeans, vegetable oils, enriched flour, whole wheat, whole-grain cereals, and eggs. Vitamin E, of all the vitamins, appears to have the most significant effect on immune function. Supplementation at levels several times above actual requirements helps stimulate immune reactivity.

Dogs with experimentally induced vitamin E deficiency show scaling (dandruff), increased susceptibility to infection, redness of the skin, and visual defects (resembling progressive retinal atrophy). This has only been seen experimentally, and vitamin-E deficiency would have to be considered extremely rare in dogs fed good-quality diets.

Antioxidants must be added to commercial dog foods, especially dry foods, to keep the fats from going rancid. Vitamin E can accomplish this naturally if it is added in sufficient quantity and if it is not expected to keep the food fresh for more than a month or so. Vitamin E is unfortunately more expensive than chemical antioxidants and doesn't provide enough preservation for the many months that a dry food might be expected to sit on store shelves.

Excessive supplementation with fatty acids, especially commercial preparations designed to promote a glossy coat, can actually render vitamin E less available in the body. This is another reason why indiscriminate supplementation is not advised.

The stability of vitamin E varies considerably among the different forms. This is one vitamin, however, that has been used to treat many different diseases in dogs, including discoid and systemic lupus erythematosus, demodicosis, acanthosis nigricans, dermatomyositis, and epidermolysis bullosa simplex. Vitamin E is rarely successful alone in managing these conditions but offers a relatively nontoxic aid to therapy.

Recommendations: Vitamin E is often given for its powerful antioxidant effects. In veterinary medicine alone, it has been used to treat discoid and systemic lupus erythematosus, demodicosis, acanthosis nigricans, dermatomyositis, and epidermolysis bullosa simplex. It does not necessarily control these conditions alone but is frequently combined with other medications to get the job done. The body requires adequate levels of zinc to maintain proper levels of vitamin E in the blood.

Cautions: Vitamin E is very safe, but large doses should be used cautiously in dogs with overactive thyroids (i.e., hyperthyroidism), high blood pressure, or diabetes.

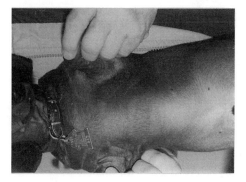

Acanthosis nigricans in a Dachshund. Note the darkening of the skin in the armpits. Vitamin E in the correct dosage helps this condition. From, Ackerman, L.: Guide to Skin and Haircoat Problems in Dogs, *Alpine Publications, 1994.*

POTENTIAL USES FOR NUTRITIONAL SUPPLEMENTATION

CONDITION	NUTRIENT	CATEGORY
ALLERGIES	Vitamin C	Vitamin
	Bioflavonoids	Food Factor
	L-methionine	Amino Acid
	Pantothenic Acid	Vitamin
	Turmeric	Herb
ANTI-INFLAMMATORY AGENTS	Vitamin C	Vitamin
	Bioflavonoids	Food Factor
	Bromelain	Enzyme
	Coenzyme Q	Enzyme
	Vitamin E	Vitamin
	Zinc	Mineral
	Turmeric	Herb
HEART DISEASE	L-carnitine	Amino Acid
	Lecithin	Fat
	Pyridoxine	Vitamin
	Coenzyme Q	Enzyme
	Dimethylglycine	Amino Acid
	Chromium	Mineral
	Echinacea	Herb
IMMUNE STIMULANT	Vitamin C	Vitamin
	Germanium	Mineral
	Pantothenic Acid	Vitamin
	Dimethylglycine	Amino Acid
	Zinc	Mineral
	Vitamin E	Vitamin
	Garlic	Herb
	Goldenseal	Herb
INTESTINAL DISEASE (CHRONIC)	Vitamin C	Vitamin
	Inositol	Vitamin
	Folic Acid	Vitamin
	Enzymes	Enzyme
	Goldenseal	Herb
	Garlic	Herb
KIDNEY DISEASE (CHRONIC)	Vitamin C	Vitamin
	Folic Acid	Vitamin
	Pyridoxine	Vitamin
	Zinc	Mineral
	Bioflavonoids	Food Factor
	Lecithin	Fat
SKIN DISEASE (CHRONIC)	Inositol	Vitamin
	Niacinamide	Vitamin
	Pyridoxine	Vitamin
	Zinc	Mineral
	L-methionine	Amino Acid
	Vitamin C	Vitamin
	Biotin	Vitamin
	Brewer's Yeast	Food Factor
	Echinacea	Herb
	Goldenseal	Herb

FREE RADICAL

The term "free radical" is frequently used in discussions of nutrition and it is a term worth understanding. It is not a simple concept but it accounts for a great deal of damage to the body and is one of the main reasons for degenerative diseases.

Oxygen constitutes about 21 percent of the air we breathe and without it we would die. But, there are circumstances in which oxygen can pose a danger as well. Within the body tissues, oxygen must get along with all of the other elements present.

All molecules consist of protons and neutrons with small electrons circling them like planets around the sun. The protons are positively charged, the neutrons are neutrally charged and the electrons carry a negative charge. When the number of electrons equals the number of protons, the system is neutral and all is as it should be. However, some molecules can steal electrons from other molecules and some will donate their electrons to other molecules. When oxygen loses an electron, we refer to it as "oxidation"; when it gains an electron, it is called "reduction." When oxygen exists with an unpaired electron in its outer orbital, it is referred to as "superoxide," a dangerous element indeed.

Within the body, this "pass the electron" game can become dangerous when it causes a chain reaction of "oxygen-derived free radicals." These oxygen-derived free radicals are very reactive and cause much damage within the body. Oxygen-derived free radicals can cause breaks in DNA, enhance inflammatory reactions within tissues and cause damage to cell membranes. They are therefore implicated in disorders such as rheumatoid arthritis, other autoimmune diseases, acute pancreatitis, and some cancers.

A good balanced diet will promote good health, good skin and haircoat. Photo by Tammy Geiger.

Oxygen-derived free radicals occur for a variety of reasons, including tissue damage, excessive exposure to the ultraviolet rays of the sun or x-rays, exposure to tobacco smoke, car exhaust and other environmental pollutants, and from the effects of saturated fats in the body. To deal with the natural risk of free radicals, the body produces a number of "scavengers" including superoxide dismutase, catalase, peroxidase and ceruloplasmin. Superoxide dismutase, which is a protein containing copper and zinc, and catalase, which contains selenium, are discussed further in this chapter. Unfortunately, anything that stresses the system can lead to free radicals that overpower the available scavengers. Then, the responsibility for protecting the body falls into the hands of the antioxidants.

ANTIOXIDANTS

Antioxidants are a groups of vitamins, minerals and enzymes that help protect the body from the formation of free radicals. Some of the more important ones are vitamins A, C, and E, gamma-linolenic acid, L-cysteine, L-glutathione, selenium and superoxide dismutase.

Vitamin A or its precursor beta-carotene have been shown to destroy cancer-producing substances (carcinogens). In research done in people, it was shown that eating foods high in beta-carotene lessened the risk for developing several different types of cancer. The same benefit is suspected in the dog.

Vitamin C is a powerful antioxidant that has been shown in laboratory experiments to decrease the risk of benign tumor cells converting to malignant ones. It is a water-soluble vitamin and works in the bloodstream more than in the fat stores.

Vitamin E helps prevent fat from going rancid and also protects the cell membrane which is the covering for every cell in the body. In the language of science, this is described as "blocking lipid peroxidation." Recent research has also shown that vitamin E promotes a healthy immune system and increased resistance to disease.

Therefore, antioxidants play an important role in keeping the body healthy and avoiding the dangers posed by oxygen-derived free radicals.

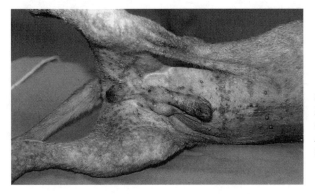

Generic dog food disease. From, Ackerman, L.: Practical Canine Dermatology, American Veterinary Publications, *1989.*

IN SUMMARY

Nutritional therapies used with drug therapies in some diseases may benefit the animal more than when compared to animals treated with the drug therapy alone.

The important fatty acids or polyunsaturated fatty acids, such as linoleic acid, alpha-linolenic acid, and arachidonic acid. Linoleic acid is abundant in most vegetable oils, and also found in poultry and pork fat (containing approximately 15-25 percent linoleic acid).

Garlic is the most prescribed herbal remedy and acts as a natural antibiotic, immune stimulant, regulator of digestion and detoxifier.

It is very important that calcium and phosphorus exist in the correct ratio (canine requirements: 1.3/1 = calcium/phosphorus ratio) in any animal ration.

Some skin diseases that did not respond to any other therapy were completely healed with zinc supplementation.

Vitamin C is a potent antioxidant that is required for tissue growth and repair, normal immune function, and adrenal gland function. Vitamin C may also promote the production of interferon, which rids the body of viruses and cancers.

ADDITIONAL READING:

Ackerman, L., "Effects of an Enzyme Supplement (Prozyme™) on Selected Nutrient Levels in Dogs." *Journal of Veterinary Allergy and Clinical Immunology,* 1993; 2(1):25-29.

Ackerman, L., "Enzyme Therapy in Veterinary Practice." *Advances in Nutrition,* 1993; 1(3):9-11.

Ackerman, L, "Fatty Acid Supplements—Practical Applications." *Advances in Nutrition,* 1993; 1(2):9-11.

Aguilera, J., "Omega-3 Unsaturated Fatty Acids—Therapeutic Uses." *Annales de Medecine Interne,* 1994; 145(1):44-49.

Beisel, W.R., et al., "Single-Nutrient Effects on Immunologic Functions." *Journal of the American Veterinary Medical Association.* 1981; 245(1): 53-58.

Brewer, G.J., "Use of Zinc Acetate to Treat Copper Toxicosis in Dogs." *Journal of the American Veterinary Medical Association.* 1992; 201(4): 564-568.

Brown, R.G., "Vitamin and Mineral Supplements."*Canadian Veterinary Journal,* 1987; 28(11): 697-698.

Buffington, C.A., "Therapeutic Use of Vitamins in Companion Dogs." In *Current Veterinary Therapy X,* edited by Kirk & Bonagura. W.B. Saunders Co., Philadelphia, 1989, 40-47.

Crane, F.L., Sun, I.L., and Sun, E.E., "The Essential Functions of Coenzyme Q." *The Clinical Investigator, 1993; 71:* S55-S59.

Fritsche, K.L., Cassity, N.A., and Huang, S.C., "Dietary (n-3) Fatty Acid and Vitamin E Interactions in Rats: Effects on Vitamin E Status, Immune Cell Prostaglandin E Production and Primary Antibody Response." *Journal of Nutrition,* 1992; 122: 1009-1018.

Gedek, B.R., "Probiotic Agents for Regualtion of Intestinal Flora." *Tierarztliche Umschau,* 1993; 48(2): 97-104.

Gonzalez, M.J., et al., "Lipid Peroxidation Products are Elevated in Fish oil Diets Even in the Presence of Added Antioxidants." *Journal of Nutrition,* 1992; 122: 2190-2195.

Gratz, H., "Results of Treatment with Enzymes of Animal Origin in Small Animal Practice." *Praktische Tierarzt,* 1993; 74(8): 704-707.

Harris, E.D., "Regulation of Antioxidant Enzymes." *Journal of Nutrition,* 1992; 122: 625-626.

Hitt, M.E., "Oxygen-Derived Free Radicals: Pathophysiology and Implications." *Compendium on Continuing Education for the Practicing Veterinarian,* 1988; 10(8): 939-946.

Keene, B.W., "L-carnitine Supplementation in Therapy of Canine Dilated Cardiomyopathy." *Veterinary Clinics of North America, Small Animal Practice,* 1991; 21(5): 1005-1009.

Kolb, E; Kramer, T; Kuba, M, et al., "Concentration of ascorbic acid in blood plasma of lambs and dogs before and after oral application of ascorbic acid and ascorbylphosphate—Compounds and excretion in the urine of dogs 8 hours after." *Monatshefte fur Veterinarmedizin,* 1993; 48(8): 395.

Maki, P.A. and Newberne, P.M., "Dietary Lipids and Immune Function." *Journal of Nutrition*, 1992; 122: 610-614.

Mandelker, L., "Immunomodulation: The New Frontier." *Veterinarian Forum*, 1992; July: 68-69.

Mandelker, L., "L-carnitine—therapeutic or theoretical?" *Veterinary Forum*, 1994; August: 54-55.

Michell, A.R., Sodium in health and disease—What can we learn from animals?

Pociot, F., Reimers, J.I., Andersen, H.U., "Nicotinamide—biological actions and therapeutic potential in diabetes prevention." *Diabetologia*, 1993; 36: 574-576.

Rumore, M.M., "Vitamin A as an immunomodulating agent." *Clinical Pharmacy*, 1993; 12: 506-514.

Sheffy, B.E., "Nutrition, Infection, and Immunity." *Compendium on Continuing Education for the Practicing Veterinarian*, 1985; 7(12): 990-996.

Steiner, M., "Vitamin E: More than an antioxidant." *Clinical Cardiology*, 1993; 16 (Suppl. I): I16-I18.

Taussig, S., "The Mechanism of the Physiological Action of Bromelain." *Medical Hypotheses*, 1980; 6: 99-104.

Different breeds and even different dogs have varying nutritional requirements. Bouvier des Flandres herding ducks. Photo by Judith Strom.

QUESTIONS TO PONDER . . .

Could my dog's behavior be linked to his/her diet?

What can I do to decrease the risk of my dog bloating?

Are there diets that can ease pain in a dog that has cancer?

What type of diet should a dog consume when recovering from colitis?

What is the correct way to determine if my dog has a food allergy?

What is the number one nutritional disorder in North American dogs that is completely preventable?

What are some good wholesome treats that are not packed full of calories?

What is pancreatitis and how can it be prevented?

**Learn the answers to these
and many other nutrition questions
in Chapter 10.**

10

DIETS FOR MEDICAL CONDITIONS

Every year in North America, consumers spend nearly $10 billion on pet foods. All companies do research showing that their product is best. Their commercials attest to the fact that dogs like their food best or that they consulted with veterinarians when formulating their diets. Could they all be telling the truth? Will those diets prevent the ills to which domestic dogs are prone?

This chapter deals with special diets and nutrients used for specific medical problems. The material is comprehensive but fairly generic, and specific company names are not included. Commercial therapeutic diets have been formulated for many of the conditions discussed and may be available from veterinarians and specialty pet outlets. Discuss the situation with your veterinarian before putting your dog on a therapeutic diet.

BEHAVIORAL PROBLEMS

There has long been a perceived relationship between diet and behavior, but few scientific studies have been conducted to provide meaningful conclusions. Recently, the term "animal psychodietetics" has been advanced to describe the relationship between nutrition and behavioral changes in scientific terms. It is not outlandish to assume that some dogs might have behavioral problems related to their diet. After all, many dogs eat high-calorie, high-protein commercial diets liberally laced with additives, flavorings, preservatives and other processing enhancements.

Most concerns of veterinary behavioral specialists focus on the role of protein, including the quantity fed, the quality of the protein, and the extent of processing. There appears to be some breed susceptibility. Golden Retrievers are often suspected of being especially sensitive to dietary factors.

The hypothesis that high-protein diets contribute to behavioral problems can be tested easily by feeding a high-quality but low-protein-quantity diet for as little as seven to ten days. The protein sources include boiled chicken, lamb, fish, or rabbit combined with boiled white rice or mashed potatoes. Mix one part meat to four parts carbohydrate and feed in the same amount as your dog's regular diet. Provide only fresh water during the trial. Give no supplements, treats, or snacks. This diet is not nutritionally balanced, but that should make little difference for the seven to ten days in which the trial is being conducted. If there is improvement, your veterinarian can recommend a balanced low-protein diet. However, don't expect protein to affect most behaviors. A recent study on the role of protein in canine aggression determined that a low-protein diet was only beneficial when managing dogs with territorial aggression that resulting from fear. There was no effect seen in dogs with dominance aggression or hyperactivity.

Another concern, often posed by dog trainers, is that training problems are more common in dogs fed dry food than those fed a canned ration. They conclude that the problem has to do with the low-moisture content of the dry kibble, but it is more likely that the problem is related to preservatives. Canned food is heat sterilized before packaging, and preservatives are not needed. In dry foods, which are expected to last for months on store shelves without being refrigerated, many chemicals, especially antioxidants and flavor enhancers, must be added to keep the food edible. Only recently has any scientific research been directed in this area.

The "extranutritional activities" of food are also being investigated. For example, casomorphine is derived from the digestion of casein, and exorphine from the digestion of gluten. These substances, together with hormones, hormone-like substances, and pheromones, are naturally present in many dog foods. All have been scientifically shown to alter normal dog behavior. Casomorphine and the exorphines, which are provided by milk proteins and cereals respectively, can trigger behaviors in dogs not unlike giving them morphine or other opioids.

Flat-Coated Retriever, with a retrieved duck. Photo by Judith Strom.

Research is also being compiled on nutrition as it relates to neurotransmitters, chemical substances in the blood that can affect brain activity. For example, high-meat diets can result in lowered levels of the neurotransmitter serotonin in the brain, which can make some animals more aggressive. Serotonin is made from the amino acid tryptophan, and, although meat is relatively high in tryptophan, competition between the amino acids tyrosine, leucine, and tryptophan result in tryptophan being short changed and not reaching appreciable levels in the brain. This, in turn, results in lowered levels of serotonin in the brain. On the other hand, a high-carbohydrate diet reduces this competition among amino acids, tryptophan reaches the brain in higher amounts, and serotonin is produced. This has a calming effect on the dog making him less aggressive. It might be beneficial to supplement the diet of this dog with vitamin B_6 (pyridoxine), because it aids in the production of serotonin. When the diet is low in vitamin B_6, the nerve cells cannot produce adequate amounts of serotonin.

RECOMMENDATIONS

The effects of diet on behavior are only now being investigated seriously, and several areas deserve further scrutiny. Many parts of your dog's diet may be implicated in behavioral problems. In general, high-protein diets, especially those based heavily on meat, are most likely to result in abnormal behavior. Dry dog foods, with their extensive use of preservatives and additives, pose their own concerns.

Until more information is available, it is advisable to consider a nutritional basis if your dog has abnormal behavioral patterns, is aggressive, or fails to train properly. You can test this hypothesis by feeding a low-protein mixture of boiled chicken and rice for as little as seven to ten days. This also limits problems that might occur with high-cereal diets (e.g., exorphines), milk proteins (e.g., casomorphine), and preservatives.

BLOAT

Gastric dilatation-volvulus (GDV), more commonly referred to as bloat, is a life-threatening disorder in the dog. Large and giant-breed dogs are especially affected. Breeds at increased risk include the Basset Hound, Borzoi, Bouvier de Flandres, Boxer, Collie, Doberman Pinscher, German Shepherd, German Shorthaired Pointer, Gordon Setter, Great Dane, Irish Setter, Irish Wolfhound, Labrador Retriever, and Saint Bernard. GDV is a two-step problem. The stomach fills with gas, and the bloated stomach twists on itself. This then kinks blood vessels and organs and causes death if not dealt with immediately. More than 60,000 dogs are affected yearly in North America alone. Whether or not they survive is directly related to how soon they receive veterinary attention. If rapid, aggressive, and specific treatment is not instituted within three hours, the patient usually dies.

There are many causes of GDV. Some are genetic, some are physiological, some are environmental, and others are diet-related. The most accepted theory is that a number of mechanisms can be responsible for decreased motility (movement) of the stomach and a delay in the emptying of the stomach contents into the intestine. For example, the pH of the stomach contents is normally low because the stomach produces acid used in digestion. Few bacteria survive in the stomach because of this acid content. On the other hand, when a very large meal is eaten, the stomach absorbs much of the acid and the pH then rises making it more hospitable for bacteria. If the food does not make its way to the intestines quickly, the bacteria start to ferment the food in the stomach. This produces gas and the stomach distends (dilates). If not treated, the dilated stomach can twist, compressing the blood vessels and organs associated with the stomach. With the blood supply effectively cut off by the twisting (torsion), the tissue quickly dies from oxygen deprivation and shock results. Without appropriate attention, death occurs.

Theories have tried to explain the prevalence of GDV by focusing on commercial dog foods and breeding practices. This is largely because GDV is unknown in wild dog populations. Perhaps the highly fermentable, cereal-based, commercial dry dog foods make dogs more prone to bloating. This has not been documented, however, in several controlled studies performed to date. Perhaps some lines of dogs have a genetic abnormality in the contractions of their stomachs (gastric dysrhythmia), making them more prone to bloating. This hypothesis has merit and is being investigated in several veterinary teaching hospitals. Other studies have suggested that stress makes bloat-prone dogs more likely to bloat. Stressful events to a dog might include visitors coming to the house, a bitch in heat, or other occurrences that might not be perceived as stress by the owner.

What does diet have to do with bloat, and why is bloat being included in a book about nutrition, if no diet-related causes are suspected? Nutrition is important because dietary management is needed after a bout of GDV and perhaps might prevent further episodes in dogs that are prone to the problem.

The goal of dietary management is to create a scenario in which gas is unlikely to accumulate in the stomach at all. It is therefore recommended that you feed your dog an easily digested meal with moderate amounts of protein, fat, and carbohydrate and that you give him smaller meals several times a day. Also, do not give him water for thirty minutes before or after eating, because this may cause the stomach contents to swell, and more time will be needed for the contents to empty into the small intestines. It is recommended that you not exercise your dog within an hour of eating if he is prone to GDV, because all of his energies should be devoted to digesting the meal. Exercising might delay the emptying of the stomach contents, making bloat more likely to occur. It must be emphasized that these recommendations are still not scientifically validated. Nevertheless, they remain a reasonable guide to prevention, albeit not sufficient to completely prevent GDV. For dogs that have experienced GDV, there are some nutritional supplements that might be helpful in recovery. Antioxidants such as vitamin E, coenzyme Q, germanium, and dimethylglycine may help limit damage to other tissues and organs. Give supplements only under the direction of your veterinarian, because GDV is life-threatening.

RECOMMENDATIONS

GDV is a life-threatening condition in the dog, the ultimate cause of which is still being investigated. Diet does not appear to be directly involved, but nutritional management may be helpful in preventing occurrences.

For dogs prone to GDV, meals should be easily digestible and fed several times a day. Neither water nor exercise should be provided around mealtime. Supplements may be helpful in resisting some of the degenerative changes associated with GDV, but must be administered cautiously and under the supervision of a veterinarian.

BONE AND JOINT DISORDERS

Disorders of the bones and joints, especially arthritis, hip dysplasia, and osteochondrosis, are not caused directly by diet but can be related to overfeeding and inappropriate supplementation.

Canine hip dysplasia is a developmental abnormality of the hip (coxofemoral) joint that is partly inherited and partly due to environment. According to recent scientific studies, one of the major environmental influences affecting dogs prone to hip dysplasia is food consumption. Dogs that are fed more calories than needed, or given food throughout the day, have a higher incidence of hip dysplasia than those fed restricted diets. Studies show that limiting food consumption could significantly reduce the incidence of hip dysplasia in susceptible animals.

Recently, a relationship was established between the electrolyte content of the diet and the incidence of hip dysplasia. In one study, five different breeds were fed diets with different electrolyte concentrations that represented various dietary anion gaps (DAGs). The basic equation was formulated by adding the concentrations of the positively charged electrolytes (sodium and potassium) and subtracting chloride, a negatively charged electrolyte. Feeding diets with a low anion gap to large-breed dogs resulted in less femoral head subluxation, on average, at six months of age. This beneficial effect was maintained in the group of dogs fed lower DAGs from six months to two years of age. Thus, although elimination of hip dysplasia by genetic selection is preferred, the incidence and severity may be lessened in susceptible breeds by dietary modification. The goal is to provide a nutritionally balanced diet with a dietary electrolyte (DEB) balance below 20 milliequivalents per 100 grams of food, preferably below 10 meq/100g.

Osteochondrosis (also called osteochondritis), a disorder of joint cartilage, has also been linked with overnutrition. Recent studies conclude that the primary problem is weak bone that cannot provide adequate bony support for joint cartilage. This tendency to form weak bone is exaggerated by overfeeding, which increases the rate of skeletal growth. In addition, the increased weight (both muscle and fat) caused by overfeeding further overloads the joint surfaces that were inadequate to begin with. Once again, a sensible diet is beneficial in limiting osteochondrosis in susceptible animals.

Overfeeding your dog is one way in which you can inadvertently contribute to problems of the bones and joints. Another is by providing supplements that can have harmful effects. It has been well-documented that calcium supplementation in rapidly growing dogs can interfere with cartilage and bone maturation and bone remodeling during the growing process. It has been similarly well-documented that calcium excesses interfere with the absorption of zinc and magnesium in the intestines. Nature has developed a way for the body to respond to an increased demand for calcium during times of active growth, pregnancy, and lactation. More harm than good is done by trying to give nature a helping hand.

If your dog is a breed at risk for hip dysplasia or osteochondrosis, make dietary management a top priority. Meals should contain moderate levels of protein, carbohydrate, and fats, while high-protein and high-fat diets are to be strictly avoided. Feed your dog enough to maintain his normal weight, but split the daily ration into two or more meals. Keep your pet lean, especially for the first two years of his life, and you could spare youself and your dog a lot of future heartache.

Water quality may also play a role in degenerative joint diseases. A recent study showed that the risk of osteochondritis is increased if dogs drink well water rather than city water. This may be a function of "hardness," with well water containing more calcium. Other factors may also be significant. It may be best to give your dog distilled water if you live in an area where the water supply is naturally "hard."

If your dog suffers from bone and joint problems, nutritional management can also prove helpful. Keep your dog lean so that he does not further compromise his joint function by carrying extra weight. Several different supplements might be helpful. These include the antioxidants, especially vitamins C and E, superoxide dismutase, dimethylglycine, and germanium. The effect of vitamin C can be potentiated by combining bioflavonoids, as described in the previous chapter. Digestive enzymes, including bromelain and papain, have been advocated for arthritis, but scientific studies in dogs have been slow to materialize. The same can be said for the use of an amino acid, D,L-phenylalanine and the omega-6 fatty acid, gamma-linolenic acid.

A sensible approach to exercise is also important. Recent studies have shown that playing with other dogs and exercising excessively during growth phases can increase the risk of osteochondritis. Exercise should be regular and controlled, especially during the first two years of life.

Many drugs used to treat arthritis and pain in people have been used in dogs, but caution must be exercised. Many of the nonsteroidal anti-inflammatory drugs, such as naproxen (e.g., Naprosyn®), ibuprofen (e.g., Motrin®), and piroxicam (Feldene®) have caused serious medical problems, especially stomach and intestinal ulcers in dogs. They can also cause high and unsafe blood levels of potassium, especially in dogs with kidney disease. Better choices include etodolac (Etogesic®) and carprofen (Rimadyl®).

Feeding your puppy a correct and balanced diet, while keeping him in an appropriate body condition, will decrease the possibilities of bone and joint disorders later in life. Photo by Cindy Nolan.

RECOMMENDATIONS

A few simple rules can go a long way in preventing many bone and joint disorders in dogs. If your dog is prone to these conditions, avoid high-protein and high-fat diets. Feed a low-DAG diet. To calculate the DAG, you need to know the amounts of sodium, potassium, and chloride in the diet, expressed in milliequivalents per 100 g of diet. Then, the DAG is calculated as sodium (meq/100 g) + potassium (meq/100 g) – chloride (meq/100 g). Dogs kept lean, especially during the first two years of life, have a much reduced incidence of hip dysplasia and osteochondrosis (osteochondritis).

Dietary supplementation is a mixed blessing when it comes to bone and joint problems. Indiscriminate use of calcium is one of the easiest ways to upset the body's delicate balance of bone production. No dog should receive calcium supplements unless explicitly instructed by a veterinarian for medical reasons. On the other hand, antioxidants, bioflavonoids, digestive enzymes, gamma-linolenic acid, and D,L-phenylalanine may all have their place in lessening some of the discomfort associated with arthritis and other bone and joint ills.

CANCER

No diets or supplements have been shown to *cure* cancer. Yet, there are many nutrients that may help *prevent* some cancers and others that may help improve the quality (and perhaps length) of life.

The study of cancer (oncology) is difficult to appreciate, because even the word "cancer" creates a sense of fear. There is not one type of cancer. Cancers evolve from different cells of the body. Breast cancer (mammary carcinoma) is as different from bone cancer (osteosarcoma) as a cat is from a dog. In the development of cancer, specific body cells are converted to abnormal forms that grow faster than their normal counterparts. Some of these growths are harmless (benign), while others are much more worrisome (malignant).

There are two distinct phases to cancer development in people and dogs. The first stage is known as "initiation," in which a normal cell transforms into a cancerous one. This happens daily and is usually not a cause for alarm because the body has evolved to recognize these cellular mutants and remove them before they can do harm. The second stage, which has the most bearing on the outcome of a cancer, is "promotion." This stage determines the ultimate outcome of the cancer and the phase at which nutrition makes its most important contribution. Different ingredients in a diet can initiate, promote or inhibit the development of cancers.

Circumstantial evidence indicates that dogs kept on a high-calorie diet are more prone to developing cancer. In research studies, reducing the caloric intake reduces the incidence of some tumors, including breast cancers and possibly skin tumors and leukemia. Dietary saturated fats may act indirectly as tumor promoters, whereas other nutrients such as vitamin A seem to inhibit tumor promotion. Research in laboratory animals and people has demonstrated a correlation between dietary fats and cancers of the breast and colon. These studies are unfortunately not available for dogs, which tend to ingest large quantities of saturated fats in their diet.

Clearly there are many additives in pet foods, and their role in initiating, promoting, or inhibiting cancers is incompletely understood. Some investigators attribute cancer-causing properties to preservatives such as ethoxyquin, while other studies suggest that the antioxidant properties may actually inhibit some cancers. Dietary nitrosamines are derived from plant nitrates and have been isolated from commercial rations. These nitrosamines are not intentionally added to the diet. Nitrites are frequently found in processed meats and can then be converted to nitrosamines once in the body. If vitamins C and E are adequate in the diet, nitrosamine formation, which is believed to be cancer promoting, can be blocked in the stomach.

One of the best ways to lessen the incidence of cancer in dogs (and in people) is to feed a diet low in saturated fats and dietary additives and adequate in fiber and antioxidant nutrients (vitamins A, C, and E, beta-carotene, and selenium). This does not guarantee that your dog will not develop cancer, but it is the most effective prevention available.

Dietary guidelines are also helpful for dogs that have developed cancer. Cancers grow faster than normal tissues, and they preferentially sap the nutrient content of diets so that other cells don't receive optimal nutrition. Also, drugs that are used in the treatment of cancer may have detrimental effects on the nutritional status of dogs.

Dogs with cancer experience alterations in the way they manage dietary carbohydrates, proteins, and fats. They are prone to "cancer cachexia," which is a loss of weight even though adequate calories are being consumed. In fact, there is a net energy gain by the tumor and a net energy loss by the dog. Cancers love sugar (glucose), which means that insulin levels often climb. Lactic acid (lactate) forms in tissues, and the body must exert energy to turn this lactate back into glucose, draining the body of energy to supply the tumor with its preferred nutrients. This suggests that dogs with cancer would do better on diets low in simple carbohydrates (sugars).

Dogs with cancer also misuse the proteins in their diets. The cancers use the amino acids for their own needs, while the rest of the body experiences amino-acid deficiency. This is why cancer patients often lose muscle mass and have difficulties with wound healing. Amino acids are also needed for antibody formation, which is why cancer patients are more susceptible to infections. It is important to note that most animals that have been successfully treated for their cancers may still have abnormal amino-acid levels. Correcting these deficiencies with appropriate supplements (e.g., arginine) can go a long way in improving immune function.

Even though carbohydrates and proteins are heavily impacted by the cancer process, most weight loss in cancer patients is due to alterations in fat metabolism. There is a greater breakdown of fats and an increase of fatty acids in the blood, even though cancers don't prefer fat as a source for their nutrition. This is important in practical terms, because tumors don't like to use fats for their own fuel, yet the other body tissues have no problem at all. Feeding a diet high in fish oils that contain polyunsaturated fatty acids and the omega-3 fatty acids (eicosapentaenoic acid and docosahexaenoic acid) may be very effective in promoting weight gain in dogs with cancer.

Nutritional supplements will not cure cancer, but they are often invaluable in increasing the quality of life in cancer patients. The antioxidants, such as vitamins A, C, and E, beta-carotene, and selenium, are indispensable because they help control the free radicals that promote the degenerative process. Vitamin B_6 and zinc are often used to bolster the immune process and folic acid is the key to normal cell growth. Cancers eat away at the protein supply in the body, making amino-acid supplementation critical. The amino acid arginine might slow the growth of cancers and improve survival time. Similarly, glutamine, although not an essential amino acid, is rapidly lost from muscle tissues in patients with cancer. When muscle wasting occurs, about 25 percent of the amino acid loss is glutamine.

Certain nutritional supplements are recommended for dogs with cancer, even though confirming evidence is lacking. For example, coenzyme Q appears to improve animals clinically and may increase the effectiveness of anticancer drugs. Also, immune stimulants such as dimethylglycine and germanium may be helpful. It may be argued, however, that if a patient has cancer, these products are very unlikely to be harmful even if there is no benefit. What is there to lose?

There *are* many potential nutritional side effects from typical anticancer drugs. For example, cisplatin (Platinol®), often used for bone cancers, can lead to magnesium depletion. Trimetrexate (Trimetrexate®) can interfere with folic acid. Doxorubicin can cause heart problems, which in rats can be reversed with supplemental vitamin E. This protection is not as profound in dogs or people.

RECOMMENDATIONS

Cancer prevention is much more important than cancer treatment. Diets that contain adequate fiber, vitamin A, vitamin C, vitamin E, beta-carotene, and selenium and that are low in saturated fats are the best safeguards available. Most of these nutrients are antioxidants, and this is the perceived reason for their role in cancer prevention. Other nutrients, such as pyridoxine (vitamin B_6), folic acid, and zinc, are important in cancer prevention and useful in managing cancer patients. Preliminary evidence suggests that folic acid helps prevent the conversion of normal cells to cancerous ones. Vitamin B_6 and zinc are recommended because they bolster the immune system.

Whereas low-fat diets are suggested for cancer prevention, certain fats are very important when dogs have already developed cancer. These dogs should be on diets that are low in simple sugars and that provide certain fats, especially the omega-3 fatty acids found in specific fish oils. Amino acids may be needed in treatment, because deficiencies are common in cancer patients. Supplementation should be performed under the direction of a veterinarian, because some amino acids are required more than others. For example, arginine and glutamine are required more than lysine. This should be planned on an individual basis. Immune stimulants such as dimethylglycine and germanium and antioxidants such as coenzyme Q might also be valuable in managing dogs with cancer.

DIABETES MELLITUS

Diabetes mellitus is relatively common in dogs. Diabetic dogs have high blood-sugar levels, and the sugar (glucose) overflows into the urine. Most treatment options have involved the injection of insulin. Oral hypoglycemic agents, commonly used in people, have not been completely evaluated in dogs.

Dietary therapy has an important role in the successful management of diabetes mellitus. Obesity must be corrected, because excess weight complicates the successful regulation of blood-sugar levels. Diets low in fats and proteins but high in complex carbohydrates and fiber promote weight reduction. It is also important that feeding schedules are regular. Diabetic dogs should be fed the same amounts of the same food at the same time each day to prevent fluctuating blood-glucose levels. *Regularity is the key.* Diets should contain small amounts of high-quality protein, and vegetable sources are preferred to lessen the intake of saturated fats.

A moderately high fiber content helps improve the regulation of blood-sugar levels in dogs of normal weight. In people, soluble fiber sources such as pectin and gums are superior to insoluble fiber (e.g., cellulose) for diabetic control, but this distinction has not been definitively proven for dogs. It appears that both sources of fiber benefit diabetic dogs.

Fructose (oligofructose) is not classified as fiber but shares many similarities. Because of its structural conformation, fructose in not digested by enzymes; it is broken down by bacteria in the colon, specifically *Bifidobacteria* and *Bacteroides.* This produces short-chain fatty acids (just like fiber) that affect glucose and fat metabolism. Thus, fructose seems to be a much more beneficial form of sugar to use in diabetic patients. It also supports the use of fruit as a treat for diabetic dogs.

Nicotinamide, a derivative of niacin (vitamin B_3) is being carefully evaluated in people for its preventive effect on the development of diabetes if given early enough to susceptible individuals. Once diabetes occurs, supplementation is unlikely to be of any real benefit. Perhaps one day research will show the same preventative effects for dogs.

There are some guidelines for the use of supplemental nutrients in diabetic dogs. Chromium (GTF) may be beneficial in stabilizing blood-sugar levels and increasing energy. Studies in people have shown that diabetics tend to have lower levels of chromium in their bloodstream than healthy individuals. Supplementation with chromium can potentiate the effects of insulin and can overcome the insulin resistance seen in some diabetics. The preferred form of this mineral supplement is as chromium picolinate. The amino acid L-carnitine is also recommended, because it mobilizes fat. Large doses of the water-soluble vitamins (the B vitamins and vitamin C) are to be discouraged, because they may inactivate insulin and encourage urination.

RECOMMENDATIONS

The ideal diet for diabetic dogs contains more than 50 percent complex carbohydrates and fiber levels of approximately 15 percent. Fruits, oats, barley, legumes, and whole grains are the ideal sources of fiber. These moderately high-fiber diets must be administered only under veterinary supervision, because they do pose some risk of interfering with the absorption of other essential nutrients in the diet. Chromium and L-carnitine may be useful dietary supplements, but excessive amounts of the B vitamins and vitamin C are to be avoided. Diabetic dogs should be maintained at their normal weight and fed according to a very rigid schedule. Be careful with treats—consider slices of fresh fruit (high in fructose) rather than biscuits.

DIGESTIVE-TRACT DISEASE

The digestive tract stretches as a long tube between the mouth and the rectum. When food is ingested, it passes down the esophagus into the stomach, where digestive acids help break down the food particles. The meal then passes into the intestines, where it is acted upon by digestive enzymes from the pancreas and bile from the gallbladder. Most of the nutrients in the food are absorbed in the small intestine (small bowel). The large intestine (colon or large bowel) is the final part of the system. Here, water is absorbed and the remaining material is packaged as stool for excretion. This section discusses problems in the small intestine and colon. Problems of the pancreas and liver are covered in separate sections.

ENTERITIS

The small intestine provides a maximal surface area from which nutrients can be absorbed. It is therefore looped and coiled, and the inner surface has many little fingers or "villi" that extend outward to make intimate contact with the food. The small bowel is composed of the duodenum, the jejunum, and the ileum.

When food enters the small intestine from the stomach, it is acted upon by enzymes from the pancreas and bile from the gallbladder. Nutrients are broken into smaller portions that can then be absorbed by the small bowel. Some nutrients are absorbed better than others. For instance, fat is extremely well absorbed, but most types of fiber resist digestion and therefore are only poorly absorbed.

Any disease that affects the small intestine also affects the ability of the small intestine to absorb nutrients. Disorders of the pancreas or gallbladder that inhibit the digestion of nutrients also impair the ability of the body to absorb those nutrients. The small bowel is the gateway to nutrients entering the bloodstream, which means that any disease affecting this region can also affect nutrient levels. Several bizarre immune-mediated diseases also affect the small intestine, and these can be difficult to diagnose without intensive studies. They include lymphocytic-plasmacytic enteritis, immunoproliferative enteropathy of basenjis, eosinophilic gastroenteritis, and granulomatous enteritis. Wheat-sensitive enteropathy of Irish Setters, food allergies, and a variety of cancers can affect this region, too.

Small intestinal bacterial overgrowth (SIBO) is emerging as a potentially important cause of chronic diarrhea in the dog, particularly German Shepherd Dogs. The initiating cause is still being debated, but the proliferation of bacteria in the small intestine affects the absorption of nutrients from this region of the bowel. Affected dogs may have difficulty digesting starch, fats may be broken down to hydroxy fatty acids, and bile salts may be deconjugated. All can result in diarrhea. The diagnosis is not straightforward and may require blood levels of folate and cobalamin, culture of intestinal fluids and, occasionally, biopsy. Researchers are currently evaluating a hydrogen breath test, similar to the one used in people. Treatment includes antibiotics and feeding a diet low in carbohydrates and fats. Good-quality protein sources and rice usually make up the basis of a therapeutic diet. Fructooligosaccharides (FOS) are natural compounds found in various plants and make an excellent alternative to starch, when used in diets for dogs with SIBO.

One of the most common causes for small-intestinal disease (enteritis) is infection with parvovirus or coronavirus. These viruses selectively attack the absorptive surface of the small intestine, resulting in profuse diarrhea as food is ingested but not absorbed. Even after intensive treatment, affected dogs may have impaired absorption and may not recover well. Whatever the actual cause, however, small-bowel disease often results in profuse diarrhea and loss of important nutrients and electrolytes. These dogs can quickly become malnourished and lose body condition.

Because of the severe nature of small intestinal disease, diagnostic testing must be thorough and comprehensive. This will likely require blood tests and tests of stool for parasites, microbes, and chemical analysis. Radiography and endoscopy may also be necessary to pinpoint a diagnosis. The approach to all cases of enteritis is greatly facilitated by a correct diagnosis. Then, specific treatment can be introduced, greatly improving the chances for success. All dogs with small-intestinal disease have some features in common, including impaired absorption of nutrients, and therefore they all are likely to benefit from intelligent nutritional management. Most dogs with this disorder have diarrhea, which means that some dietary modification is required. It is probably best for dogs with enteritis to initially receive fluid therapy, because they quickly become dehydrated. This also provides calories (usually as glucose or dextrose), which are drastically needed, and corrects any electrolyte imbalances. Food intake is restricted for twenty-four hours or so, giving the intestine a much needed rest. When oral feeding is resumed, the diet should be bland and low in fat and fed in small amounts three to four times daily. This way the intestine will not be overtaxed as it tries to absorb nutrients. Appropriate foods include lean meat, eggs, cottage cheese, or yogurt combined with boiled rice, tapioca, pasta, Cream of Wheat®, or potatoes. Prescription diets from veterinarians provide highly digestible ingredients in canned or kibble form. As the problem resolves, your dog can be gradually weaned back onto his original diet.

Nutritional supplements can be very helpful when a dog has diarrhea. Pectin, often combined with kaolin, is recommended for the first few days, because it helps improve the consistency of the stool; in cases of small-bowel diarrhea, it is wise to supplement with B vitamins, because these can be quickly lost from the body. Vitamins A and E can be depleted, too, if the diarrhea persists for weeks, but because they are stored in the body, deficiency is unlikely in the short term. Kelp is a good source of microminerals, which can also be depleted rapidly in dogs with diarrhea. Digestive enzymes are also sometimes added to the food to help break it down into the simplest nutrients possible, facilitating absorption. Similarly, *Acidophilus/Lactobacillus* can be given on an empty stomach to assist with the uptake and manufacture of nutrients.

Chronic enteritis *requires* nutritional management. These dogs may need amino-acid supplements, specific fat supplements, and multivitamin and mineral supplements. The fat used for supplementation is often derived from coconut oil and sold as Medium Chain Triglyceride (MCT) oil, which is more easily absorbed than regular fats. Unfortunately, people often tolerate MCT oils better than dogs. If large amounts are given, dogs may vomit or have a reduced appetite. Suitable protein sources include lean chicken, fish, wild game, cottage cheese, or eggs. Yogurt is sometimes recommended but has a fairly high content of lactose, which might be difficult for some dogs to digest. The most easily digestible carbohydrate is rice. Supplements worth considering in long-standing cases include the fat-soluble vitamins A, D, E, and K, folic acid, vitamin B_{12} and calcium.

COLITIS

Colitis is inflammation in the large intestine (also known as the colon or large bowel). The main function of the colon is to act as a storage chamber, allowing the body to complete absorption of fluids and electrolytes that started in the small intestine. The main stimulus for material to move through the colon and then be excreted is bulk. The more material that is present in the colon, the more the walls of the large bowel are stretched (distended), and this stimulates the colon to contract and move the contents toward the rectum.

The large bowel is also home to many microbes, most of which perform valuable functions. The large bacterial population in the colon, often billions of microbes per gram of stool, helps prevent disease-causing (pathogenic) bacteria from gaining a stronghold. Some of the important microbes include *Bacteroides, Bifidobacterium, E. coli,* streptococci, and lactobacilli. These microbial populations can be adversely affected by changes in diet or by the use of antibiotics that change the population dynamics in the colon.

Colitis can be caused by different diseases including parasites, microbial infections, inflammatory diseases, cancers, and others. Some of the more common disorders are whipworm *(Trichuris vulpis)* infection, *Giardia* infection, food allergy/intolerance, and inflammatory disease. Proper diagnosis is imperative, and testing might include stool evaluations, blood tests, radiography, endoscopy, and biopsy procedures. "Scoping" of the colon (colonoscopy) with biopsy is the most likely test to provide a definitive diagnosis. Only with proper diagnosis can management be optimized.

Regardless of the underlying cause, nutritional management is helpful in all cases of colitis. Initially, the colon is rested by withholding food for a day or so. This fasting helps reduce the workload of the colon and allows the healing process to begin.

Homemade diets are introduced slowly, and single sources of protein and carbohydrate are used to minimize potential allergic reactions in the colon. Cottage cheese is the preferred source of protein, and rice is the preferred carbohydrate source. The fat content must be kept low to maximize the opportunity for the fat to get absorbed and to prevent excess fat from being altered by bacteria in the colon to actually promote diarrhea. This diet is often fed for three to four weeks when it has been confirmed that no parasites are implicated. Proving that there are no parasites can be tricky, and a single fecal examination is not sufficient. Dogs that respond well to this hypoallergenic diet can often be converted to a commercial or alternate diet in time.

The use of high-fiber diets in cases of colitis is controversial. Although fiber tends to bulk up the colon and get it moving, it can also bind bile acids and helpful bacteria, and therefore make the problem worse. Some forms of fiber cause production of short-chain fatty acids, like butyrate, which might be beneficial in treating colonic inflammatory bowel disease. At present, moderate to low levels of fiber are recommended, and psyllium (Metamucil®) is a useful and convenient additive.

Animals with colitis have diarrhea but typically not as profuse as dogs with small-bowel disease. Dogs with colitis are therefore less likely to become severely malnourished as those with enteritis. Dogs with colitis are likely to benefit from supplements of vitamins B and C to help in the healing phase. Vitamins A and E may also be needed in long-standing cases. The use of digestive enzymes and *Acidophilus* are likely to be helpful, although supportive studies are not yet available.

RECOMMENDATIONS

Enteritis is a disease of the small intestines which may originate from several different sources. Dogs with enteritis have difficulty absorbing nutrients from the digestive tract. To manage the problem successfully, foods must be low in regular fats and easy to absorb. As the problem resolves, most dogs can be gradually weaned onto their original diets. A variety of supplements may be helpful depending on the extent of malabsorption and how long the problem has continued.

Colitis is an inflammatory disease of the large intestine and also results from a variety of underlying diseases. Initial dietary management consists of a one- to two-day fast and gradual re-introduction of single sources of protein and carbohydrate. This diet must often be fed for three to four weeks until regular bowel function resumes. Occasionally, high-fiber diets or "bulking agents" are necessary.

Drugs used to treat digestive-tract disorders can cause nutritional upsets. For example, long-term use of antacids such as aluminum hydroxide can lower blood levels of phosphorus. Cimetidine (Tagamet®) can cause cobalamin (vitamin B_{12}) depletion and increase the risk of bleeding if there is a simultaneous vitamin-K deficiency. Sulfasalzine, a drug commonly used for colitis, can induce folic-acid deficiency with long-term use, especially in dogs with malabsorption. Even safe products like psyllium gum (Metamucil®) can impact on nutrition; with long-term use, riboflavin absorption is reduced.

ENTERAL/PARENTERAL NUTRITION

Enteral nutrition means providing food by nasogastric tube directly into the stomach for dogs that are critically ill, malnourished, or unable to eat yet are capable of digesting and absorbing food. Parenteral nutrition means providing nutrients intravenously to animals that, for medical reasons, cannot eat, digest, and absorb food by the usual mechanisms. It is reserved for dogs with severe disorders of the stomach or intestines that temporarily require receiving their essential nutrients directly into the bloodstream.

ENTERAL NUTRITION

Enteral nutrition is often referred to as "tube" feeding and can be an important way to maintain nutritional status in dogs that can't eat because of illness, surgery, or trauma. Dogs can develop severe malnutrition within a few days, with decreased resistance to infection and increased susceptibility to shock. These patients can recover faster and with less complications and can go home from the hospital sooner if they receive

*Making diet adjustments very gradually,
and only giving "good table scraps,"
no fat or rich foods, will decrease the
chances of your pet experiencing colitis
or pancreatitis.
Photo by Tammy Geiger.*

their nutrition enterally, before they become malnourished. Most animals experience no side effects with enteral feeding. The most common problem is diarrhea, likely associated with feeding a strictly liquid diet or gruel. Obstruction of the feeding tube is also possible but less likely if only used to instill liquified diets. Adding foods and medications to the tube increases the likelihood of blockage.

PARENTERAL NUTRITION

Parenteral nutrition is sometimes referred to as hyperalimentation in people, but this is inaccurate. There is also a major difference between parenteral nutrition and intravenous therapy. Whereas intravenous therapy may provide fluids, electrolytes, and even a source of calories (e.g., dextrose, glucose), parenteral nutrition attempts to provide all of the essential amino acids, essential fatty acids, caloric needs, electrolytes, trace minerals, and B-complex vitamins that a dog requires on a daily basis. Fat-soluble vitamins are not usually added to the solutions because they are stored in the body and are unlikely to be depleted during the temporary duration of parenteral nutrition.

Parenteral nutrition is potentially life-saving but is a difficult and expensive system to maintain. The placement and maintenance of a catheter for intravenous feeding make infection a concern. Also, estimating the total nutrient needs for a dog and providing them in a form that can be used without digestion requires difficult and calculating decisions. Most of the caloric needs are provided by glucose (dextrose) and fats (safflower and soybean oils). The total number of calories to administer must be calculated by estimating levels of activity, stress, metabolic requirements, and energy expenditures.

Once the dog has recovered and is able to eat, he is slowly weaned off parenteral nutrition and periodically offered food. He is not removed entirely from parenteral feedings until his blood-sugar levels are stabilized and he is eating on his own.

RECOMMENDATIONS

Enteral nutrition is a far simpler procedure than parenteral nutrition and involves placing a nasogastric tube through which liquid diets can be fed. This provides short-term nutritional support to critically ill dogs or those recovering from surgery so that they do not become malnourished.

Parenteral nutrition is an intensive form of life-support nutrition for dogs that cannot eat on their own. It is used predominantly in dogs that are unable to eat for at least five days. There are many side effects to parenteral nutrition, including problems with catheters, infections, and maintenance of normal glucose and electrolyte levels.

FOOD ALLERGY/INTOLERANCE

It is not unusual for dogs to react adversely when fed certain foods. Sometimes they vomit, sometimes they get diarrhea, and sometimes they develop itchy patches or hives. Not all of these problems are allergic in nature. Many diet-related problems may be caused by intolerance as well.

Adverse food reactions, whether caused by allergy or intolerance, are not uncommon in dogs. It is estimated that diet-related problems may account for 10 percent of hypersensitivity reactions in dogs. Occasionally, diet-related problems can affect the respiratory and nervous systems. The most common manifestations are itchiness with redness and scaling, recurrent ear infections, and pyotraumatic dermatitis (hot spots). Additional possibilities include urticaria (hives), vomiting, diarrhea, anal itch (pruritus ani), flatulence, sneezing, asthmalike conditions, behavioral changes, and even seizures. Allergy-related conditions include wheat-sensitive enteropathy, eosinophilic gastroenterocolitis, and lymphocytic-plasmacytic enterocolitis.

When it comes to allergy and intolerance to foods, individual ingredients are always to blame. A common mistake is to try changing the brand of dog food to see if there is any connection, but it is unlikely that your dog is allergic to any particular brand name of diet. He is more likely allergic to specific ingredients in that diet, such as beef, chicken, soy, milk, corn, wheat, etc. You may not associate your dog's symptoms with a food because the problem may not be worsened at mealtime or the diet may be one that you have fed for months or years without diffi-culty. The correct way to diagnose food allergy/intolerance has been greatly misinterpreted by commercial dog-food companies in the past several years. Experts in the field agree that a hypoallergenic diet trial must be homemade and consist of ingredients to which the dog has never been exposed. The rationale is simple—you can't be allergic to something you've never eaten before, and neither can your dog. If your dog has never eaten lamb, then it is a suitable protein source for the trial. This doesn't mean that just because a dog food contains lamb, it is acceptable. This single protein source (i.e., lamb) can be combined with a carbohy-drate source such as rice or potatoes and the entire diet fed for four to twelve weeks. If your dog improves substantially, further investigation is warranted. If there is no improvement, diet is not a significant part of the problem and the diet can be discontinued. Newer hypoallergenic diets have been formulated that ultilitze small protein fragments rather than whole proteins. This represents an exciting prospect in the diagnosis and management of food allergies.

The use of lamb in food trials is simply a matter of convenience. Lamb is rarely a part of the diet for most dogs in North America. Where lamb is commonly fed to dogs (e.g., Great Britain, Australia), it can cause as many allergic reactions as any other protein source. Hence the misinterpretation of the facts by many dog-food companies. They are now producing lamb-based diets and selling them to the public as superior foods for skin prob-lems. This is hogwash. Lamb is not fed because it is good for the skin; it is used in food trials only because most dogs haven't eaten it before. To com-pound the problem, many lamb-based diets contain other ingredients, (corn, wheat, soy) that may contribute to food allergy/intolerance. To reit-erate, there is nothing magical about lamb! It is used in a food trial only if a dog has never eaten it before.

To conduct a hypoallergenic diet trial properly (if your dog has never eaten lamb), mix lamb with rice or potatoes and feed him this home-cooked meal for at least four, and preferably twelve weeks. The lamb can be boiled, broiled, baked, or microwaved (but not fried), and the rice should be boiled prior to serving. Mix one part lamb to two parts rice or potatoes. Feed the mixed ingredients in the same total volume as your dog's normal diet. Once cooked, the meal can be packaged in individual portions, frozen, and then thawed as needed, greatly decreasing the need for cooking daily. Dur-ing the trial, hypoallergenic foods and fresh, preferably distilled, water must be fed exclusive of all else. *Absolutely nothing else*—including treats, snacks, vitamins, chew toys, and even flavored heartworm-preventative tablets—must be fed. Access must also be denied to food and feces of other dogs and cats in the household. Although this is clearly not a fun job, and few enjoy the headaches involved in a controlled food trial, it is the pre-ferred way to reliably identify adverse reactions to foods.

For dogs that have been on varied homemade diets, nonmeat diets can be prepared with vegetables (carrots, celery, broccoli, kale, dock, peas, pinto beans, green beans), fruits (grapes, dates, pears, plums, peaches), fillers (potatoes, sweet potatoes, coconut, sesame or sunflower seeds), and flavor enhancers (raisins, honey, maple syrup). These diets are difficult to balance nutritionally, yet the four to twelve weeks necessary for a food trial should not prove detrimental unless your pet is pregnant, lactating, growing or performing strenuous activities. Not *all* seemingly innocent foods *are* innocent. Products like tofu contain soy, vegetable oil and margarines often contain corn, and cheese, cottage cheese, and ice cream often contain milk or milk by-products.

These diets should not be fed indefinitely, because they are not balanced nutritionally for long-term feeding. They are only meant to be fed for the four to twelve weeks necessary to determine if food is implicated in the medical problem. If your dog's condition improves while he is on the diet, you will need to follow up with challenge feeding to determine which ingredient is causing the symptom. For example, if your dog reacts to beef in the diet, a beef-free dog food will be recommended. If the problem is soy, a soy-free diet will be recommended. There is little need to feed a lamb-based diet long-term unless it is your personal preference. And during the testing period, commercial lamb-based diets are definitely not the best way to diagnose the problem.

Another inaccurate but well-marketed testing procedure is the new series of blood tests (RAST, ELISA) that claim to be able to predict food-related problems with a small sample of blood. Unfortunately, these tests can be very misleading, because the results are reliable perhaps only 10 percent of the time. It is hard to justify spending money on a test that will be wrong nine times out of ten. If these tests predict that your dog is allergic to beef or to soy, there is very little assurance that the diagnosis is correct. This is not surprising, because not all diet-related problems are allergic (these tests don't identify intolerance), and those that are allergic are not necessarily caused by the antibodies measured in the blood tests. Blood tests should **never** replace a hypoallergenic food trial as a screening test in dogs.

RECOMMENDATIONS

Testing for food allergies is worthwhile, but misinformation is so abundant that few people perform a hypoallergenic diet trial correctly. Selecting a commercial diet that includes lamb or paying for a "convenient" blood test is no substitute for a proper diet trial. The test diet should include a single protein source to which your dog has never been exposed. The protein is combined with a carbohydrate source such as rice or potatoes and fed for four to twelve weeks. An alternative is to use the new commercial low molecular weight diets available from veterinarians. If improvement occurs in that time, further investigation is warranted. If there is no improvement, and if the diet trial was done correctly, you can be satisfied that your dog does not have a food allergy and he can be returned to his original diet.

HEART DISEASE

Nutrition plays an important role in managing dogs with heart disease. Some supplementation might also prove beneficial. The heart is a muscle that is responsible for circulating blood to all areas of the body, all day, every day, throughout your dog's life. When the function of the heart is compromised by disease, the blood cannot be pumped as efficiently as needed to the different organs of the body. This sets up a series of events in which the heart tries to compensate—to do the best job it can—under difficult circumstances.

For a dog with heart disease, in order for the heart to be as full of blood as possible when it pumps, the body tries to conserve fluid by signaling the kidneys to retain water and sodium. Of course, this is no real solution, because the heart still pumps inefficiently. Eventually, this conservation of fluid becomes counterproductive, causing swelling (edema) in the lungs or liver. This is called congestive heart failure.

Although some heart diseases can be cured (e.g., heartworm disease), most heart problems are chronic and progressive. Many dogs with heart failure, however, can be managed successfully with medications and proper diet. Therapy is aimed at making the heart pump more efficiently and removing obstacles to this goal. Medications such as digitalis increase the efficiency of the pumping actions, while other medications may be dispensed to help excrete fluids (e.g., diuretics) and lower the blood pressure. Diet is used to help reduce swelling (edema), and antioxidant supplements may provide vital nutrients needed to maintain a healthy heart.

Dogs with heart disease are given a low-sodium diet, just as people are. Salt can increase fluid retention, making the heart work harder to get its job done. Decreasing the salt content of the diet reduces the workload of the heart, which is already working to capacity. Unfortunately, most commercial dog foods are heavily salted, providing approximately thirty times the amount of sodium that dogs really need. This makes the diets tastier, but they also can be deadly for a dog with heart disease.

Step one for any dog with heart failure is to commence a low-sodium diet. This is not always easy, because dogs that have been fed commercial diets become accustomed—almost addicted—to the salt content and may shun low-salt meals. It may take several weeks to convert your dog from a regular commercial diet to one low in sodium. These diets are available commercially, often from veterinarians, or can be made at home. Provide fresh water, preferably distilled, at all times. Use of water softeners is to be discouraged because they add sodium to the water, in exchange for calcium.

Step two is to introduce medications that help the heart beat more efficiently and decrease the amount of fluids collecting in the body. Other drugs may be necessary to lower the blood pressure so that the blood can circulate around the body under less tension. All of these medications need to be administered under the careful supervision of your veterinarian. All of these products are potentially harmful, and patients must be monitored and the doses altered as needed.

Step three is to make sure that your dog maintains his appropriate weight. Animals that are considerably overweight are more likely to have further impaired heart and lung function. With diseases such as cardiomyopathy or mitral regurgitation, obese dogs are more likely to accelerate actual heart failure. On the other hand, dogs with long-standing heart failure are often underweight, with so-called "cardiac cachexia." This may result from the disease itself or from drugs (e.g., digitalis, captopril) that depress the appetite or promote loss of minerals (e.g., diuretics). Also, dogs given a low-salt diet will eat less initially because they have been accustomed over the years to eating highly salted foods.

Step four is to supplement the diet with nutrients that will help the heart to function optimally. Some supplements have specific actions, whereas most serve in a supportive role. One nutrient with specific actions is L-carnitine, a vitaminlike amino acid. Several years ago it was reported that a family of Boxers with dilated cardiomyopathy, a fatal heart ailment, improved with supplementation of L-carnitine alone. It was found that the heart muscles in these dogs were deficient in this important amino acid, even though blood levels were usually normal. It was believed that these dogs might have an inherited defect in carnitine metabolism that resulted in decreased levels of carnitine in their heart muscle and eventual heart disease.

To further complicate matters, dogs have more difficulty than most species in conserving L-carnitine. Much of it is excreted in the urine daily, and it is poorly reabsorbed by the canine kidney. Carnitine is therefore an important supplement for any dog with dilated cardiomyopathy, especially Boxers, but possibly Cocker Spaniels, Doberman Pinschers and Great Danes as well. Carnitine is found naturally in meat and dairy products, but a typical diet provides only a fraction of the amount needed to treat this condition. Carnitine can also be synthesized in the liver from the amino acids methionine and lysine if sufficient ascorbic acid, niacin, pyridoxine, and iron are present. Taurine supplementation may also be important in dogs with cardiomyopathy, especially Cocker Spaniels. Overall nutrition, as you can see, is an important consideration as well.

Antioxidants, especially beta-carotene (or vitamin A), vitamin E, and vitamin C, are also important for dogs with heart disease. These substances require micronutrients to be effective, including zinc, copper, manganese, iron, and selenium. Antioxidants help remove the free radicals that contribute to many degenerative diseases, including heart disease.

Additional nutrients that provide adequate oxygenation of heart muscle include coenzyme Q, germanium, dimethylglycine, and superoxide dismutase. Recent studies strongly support the value of Coenzyme Q_{10} supplementation in dogs with heart disease.

Supplements may also serve to counteract some of the adverse effects of the heart medications your dog is taking. For example, diuretics (e.g., Lasix (furosemide) cause a loss of potassium from the body into the urine and work to lower blood levels of magnesium and sodium. Your veterinarian may recommend that you give your dog oral supplements of potassium chloride or food sources rich in potassium (e.g., bananas). Also, drugs that promote directed blood flow may cause less blood to flow to the intestines and liver, leading to impaired absorption or metabolism of nutrients. This may result in a significant loss of protein and B vitamins. Drugs such as digoxin (digitalis) decrease the appetite, which in turn lessens nutrient intake. Calcium channel blockers such as diltiazem (Cardizem) can be inactivated by calcium supplements or high-calcium diets.

RECOMMENDATIONS

Although there are many different types of heart disease, some generalizations can be made regarding nutritional management. A low-salt diet is recommended, and this can either be purchased commercially or made at home. Some dogs with dilated cardiomyopathy may benefit from specific supplements such as L-carnitine, but antioxidants (especially coenzyme Q_{10}) may be helpful in providing additional oxygen uptake by the heart muscle. Other supplements may be needed, especially when multiple drugs are used in therapy.

KIDNEY DISEASE

The kidneys act as important filters, removing unwanted material from the blood for excretion in the urine and returning crucial factors back to the blood. For instance, protein and glucose (sugar) are important nutrients that pass through the kidneys but inevitably are returned to the blood. Waste products, on the other hand, pass through the kidneys into the urine, where they are then excreted from the body.

Many different diseases can affect the kidneys and interfere with their important filtering functions. When approximately two-thirds of the kidney function has been compromised, renal (kidney) insufficiency results but can still be compensated for by dogs drinking and urinating more than normal. When three-quarters of the kidney function has been compromised, kidney failure results, toxins accumulate in the bloodstream, and nutrients are not conserved. Destroyed kidney tissue cannot be regenerated or replaced. Pets in kidney failure can never be cured, but dietary management is critical. It is therefore important that a diagnosis be reached as soon as possible.

Diagnostic tests include blood tests, urinalysis, radiography, and, occasionally, biopsy. The kidney is not only a filter, but also plays a central role in regulating calcium and phosphorus levels. It produces a critical enzyme that converts vitamin D (important in calcium/phosphorus regulation) to its active form. Also, a major regulating hormone, parathyroid hormone or PTH, normally tells the kidney when to conserve calcium and excrete phosphorus. Progressive kidney diseases can therefore result in renal secondary hyperparathyroidism, in which calcium is gradually lost from the body and phosphorus is retained. Calcium is removed from bone to keep blood levels normal, which in turn weakens the bones and makes them more brittle.

Kidney disease must be recognized early if management is to be successful, and dietary therapy is one of the chief tools used in management. All dogs with documented kidney disease should be fed a diet low in total protein, but the protein source must be of high quality to ensure that amino-acid requirements are met. This low-protein diet is essential to minimize the work of the already stressed kidney in filtering protein by-products. It also reduces the total amount of toxins circulating in the blood. Low-protein diets also tend to be beneficial low-phosphorus diets, because meat proteins are often high in phosphorus.

It is critical that careful attention be paid to the protein given to dogs with kidney disease. On the one hand, high-protein diets stress the kidney further and advance the progression of the disease. On the other hand, dogs with kidney disease frequently lose protein in their urine and are at risk of developing protein deficiency. The answer is to provide *high-quality protein* but in *small amounts*. These diets often furnish approximately two grams of protein daily per kilogram of body weight (roughly one gram per pound). Eggs are considered the protein of choice for dogs with chronic kidney disease, although cottage cheese, yogurt, and small amounts of meat protein are acceptable. High-quality sources of vegetable protein include asparagus, mushrooms, peas, beans, and lentils. The balance of the meal must be made up of easily digestible carbohydrate and fat sources, such as rice, and a form of essential fatty acids (e.g., flaxseed oil, evening primrose oil, safflower oil). High-fiber diets are to be discouraged because they contain phosphorus-containing phytates.

Disturbances of calcium and phosphorus regulation commence early in the course of kidney disease and progress as kidney function deteriorates. With kidney disease, phosphorus is retained rather than excreted. Blood levels of calcium decrease, absorption from the intestines is impaired, and calcium is removed from bones to meet the deficit in the blood. This is obviously a dangerous change, and a low-protein (and therefore low-phosphorus) diet is critical. When dietary protein restriction is not enough, supplements of calcium-containing, phosphate-binding agents may be prescribed. These interfere with phosphorus absorption from the intestines and provide an important source of calcium. Phosphate restriction is a worthwhile goal, because it prevents the progression of kidney damage and increases the life span of affected dogs.

High-salt diets were often recommended in the past for dogs with kidney disease to help flush out the kidneys and remove protein by-product waste. Recent research has shown that high-sodium diets cause increased blood pressure (hypertension), which can complicate the already mild hypertension commonly seen in dogs with kidney disease. For this reason, diets intended for dogs with kidney disease should contain normal levels of salt. Neither low-sodium nor high-sodium diets are recommended for dogs with impaired kidney function.

Nutritional supplements are essential for the dog with impaired kidney function. Deficiencies in the water-soluble vitamins are common, especially vitamin C, folic acid, and pyridoxine. Vitamin-D supplementation may be required but should only be introduced on the recommendation of a veterinarian. Indiscriminate supplementation can actually result in additional kidney damage. Vitamin A should not be given to dogs with kidney disease because of the possibility of toxicity. If vitamin-A supplementation is required, only the emulsion form should be used.

It may seem to make sense to add calcium to the diet of dogs with kidney disease, but this is not always a smart move. If blood levels of phosphorus are elevated, calcium supplementation can actually promote kidney injury and mineralization of other tissues. Hypercalcemia—too much calcium in the blood—is an all-too-common complication of calcium supplementation. Calcium should only be administered to dogs with normal blood phosphorus levels, and only on the instructions of a veterinarian.

Amino-acid supplements and immune stimulants are also worth considering for dogs with kidney disease. The amino acids L-arginine and L-methionine are particularly indicated, because they may become deficient when protein levels are severely restricted. Vitamins E and C are important antioxidants and immune stimulants, and zinc promotes healing of the damaged kidney.

RECOMMENDATIONS

Dogs with kidney disease benefit from a diet low in total protein and phosphorus but with a high-quality source of protein. A source of essential fatty acids is also necessary. Nutritional supplements that might be helpful include vitamin C, folic acid, pyridoxine, zinc, L-arginine, and L-methionine.

LIVER DISEASE

The liver is the body's purifying system, and it filters toxins that are absorbed from the intestines and circulate in the bloodstream. It is also an important manufacturing plant for most of the body's store of proteins, enzymes, and clotting factors.

Most cases of liver disease in dogs reflect chronic damage, but this may not be apparent immediately because of the incredible regenerative capacity of the liver. Although many problems are lumped together under the generic term "liver disease," there is not one cause or one treatment for all liver ailments. Problems with the gallbladder and bile ducts are often lumped together with liver disease because they are so intimately associated with one another.

Canine Selected Protein Diet With Lamb & Rice

PRODUCT DESCRIPTION
WALTHAM™ VETERINARIUM™ Canine Selected Protein Diet With Lamb & Rice is a complete and balanced canned meat food for adult dogs and features lamb and brewers rice as main ingredients. The product is available in 375 g (13.2 oz) cans.

INDICATIONS/RATIONALE
WALTHAM™ VETERINARIUM™ Canine Selected Protein Diet With Lamb & Rice is carefully formulated to aid in the diagnosis and management of dietary intolerance or hypersensitivity (allergy) in dogs. The product is also suited for use in a protocol designed to identify a food-borne allergen. Protein is supplied by lamb and brewers rice, which also provides usable carbohydrates. Cellulose powder provides dietary fiber. Selected Protein Canine Diet is highly palatable.

WALTHAM™ VETERINARIUM™ CANINE SELECTED PROTEIN DIET WITH LAMB & RICE

Approximate Calories ME¹	360 kcal/can (96 kcal/100 g)
Palatability² vs Hill's® Prescription Diet® Canine d/d®³	Parity
Digestibility	
Dry Matter, %	83
Protein, %	80
Fat, %	93
Energy, %	87

¹ME = calculated metabolizable energy.
²Independent testing.
³Hill's®, Prescription Diet®, and d/d® are registered trademarks of Hill's, Division of Colgate-Palmolive Company.

GUARANTEED ANALYSIS

Crude Protein, % Min.	5.5
Crude Fat, % Min.	1.5
Crude Fiber, % Max.	1.0
Moisture, % Max.	78.0
Ash, % Max.	3.5

This is an example of a low protein diet that is available from your veterinarian.

When there is chronic damage to the liver, the body has decreased concentrations of substances produced by the liver, including cholesterol, the important blood protein albumin, glucose, urea, and the clotting factors. These can pose serious dangers.

The first goal is to identify the cause of the problem and correct it, if possible. Then, supportive care and dietary manipulation are important so that the liver can have the best chance to repair itself. Attempts are made to reduce the workload of the liver by providing needed nutrients that require the least amount of processing and detoxification.

Dogs with liver disease should be on a diet high in easy-to-digest carbohydrates, moderate in protein, and low in fat. Ideally, the carbohydrate source should not be too high in fiber, because bacterial digestion of fiber in the intestine requires filtering by the liver. Boiled white rice is a excellent carbohydrate source, because its nutrients are easily absorbed from the intestines and are usable without processing by the liver.

A suitable protein source is critical when feeding dogs with liver disease. If too much meat is fed, the meat protein is converted to ammonia in the body and can be toxic. The ideal protein source is of vegetable origin (e.g., rice, corn grits, soy flour) or is a high-quality animal protein such as cottage cheese or eggs.

The diet needs to be low in sodium, because fluid tends to accumulate (edema, ascites) in dogs with liver disease. If possible, homemade diets are preferred, because additives and chemicals in commercial diets may be converted to substances that are toxic to the liver. Lactulose, a form of sugar that is not metabolized by animals but that *is* metabolized by bacteria in the intestines, is often given long-term to dogs with liver disease. Lactulose helps remove ammonia from the body. Ammonia, a by-product of protein metabolism, is toxic and can result in abnormal behavior in dogs with liver disease.

Nutritional supplements can be beneficial for a dog with liver disease. The B vitamins, especially choline and inositol, are essential for normal liver function. The amino acid L-cysteine is also useful, because it helps detoxify poisons in the system. Supplements such as dimethylglycine, superoxide dismutase, coenzyme Q_{10}, and germanium improve the level of cellular oxygenation. Lecithin helps protect the cells of the liver and helps remove fatty deposits from liver tissue. You may also want to consider adding digestive enzymes of plant or animal origin to your dog's diet to help him digest the ingredients in the food, making them easier to absorb and less likely to require processing by the liver. Supplementation with vitamin K may also be necessary for blood clotting in dogs with severely impaired liver function.

There are some concerns when supplementing dogs with liver disease. Vitamin A, which is stored in the liver, must be given cautiously, because toxicity can result. Also avoid beta-carotene because it is converted by the liver to vitamin A. If you must give vitamin A, use the emulsion form because it bypasses the liver and is safer than beta-carotene or regular vitamin A. Fatty-acid supplements should be administered cautiously to pets with liver disease. Only the highly unsaturated forms, such as evening primrose oil, should be used. Amino acids are essential for life, but certain amino acids can be toxic when administered to dogs with liver disease. Methionine given orally can be converted by bacteria in the intestines to mercaptans, which are toxic in this situation. The aromatic amino acids phenylalanine, tyrosine, and tryptophan should also not be administered to dogs with liver disease, because they upset the already tenuous balance the body is trying to maintain with the branched-chain amino acids leucine, isoleucine, and valine.

RECOMMENDATIONS

Animals with liver disease benefit from a diet that provides high-quality protein with easily digestible carbohydrate. Homemade diets are preferred so that additives and preservatives can be avoided. Excellent ingredients include eggs, cottage cheese, rice, soy flour, and corn grits. Lactulose may be added to the diet to help prevent ammonia formation, a potentially devastating effect of liver disease.

Consider supplementation carefully. The most important supplements are the B vitamins (especially choline and inositol) and the nutrients that help promote normal oxygen use by cells.

OBESITY

It's a sad fact that the number-one nutritional disorder in North American dogs is obesity. The condition is sometimes referred to as "overnutrition," but the results are the same—more than 25 percent of dogs in North America are overweight.

Everyone knows the dangers of obesity in people but the same rationale is not applied to pets. Clearly, obese pets don't live as long as dogs of normal weight. They suffer more from heart problems, they fatigue easily, and they are at increased risk of developing diabetes mellitus. Obese dogs also have a decreased resistance to infection and are more prone to anesthetic complications during surgery. A link with many other clinical problems has been suggested but has not yet been clearly demonstrated. Today, more than ever, dogs are being "killed with kindness" as their owners allow them to become obese.

Part of the problem is due to marketing by pet-food and pet-food-supplement manufacturers, but the rest of the blame belongs to consumers. They have bought into the "more is better" philosophy and often provide their dogs high-calorie meals, followed by high-calorie snacks and perhaps even high-calorie dietary supplements. There is much more risk to your dog's health from obesity than there is a likelihood of his suffering a nutritional deficiency.

Dogs are obese when they weigh 20 percent more than their ideal body weight. Obesity becomes more common as pets get older. Females are more prone to obesity than males, and neutered pets are more likely to become obese than intact pets. Unfortunately, obese people are much more likely to have obese pets, attesting to the significance of environmental factors promoting obesity.

Genetic factors likely have some role in the development of obesity in the dog. Labrador Retrievers, Cocker Spaniels, Collies, Dachshunds, Beagles, Basset Hounds, Shetland Sheepdogs, and some terriers are more prone to obesity than other breeds. Some breeds, most notably the German Shepherd Dog and Boxer, actually have a lower incidence of obesity than other breeds.

Clearly the most significant causes of obesity are excessive calories and inadequate physical activity. Obesity is rarely seen in wild dogs and wolves and only infrequently in working dogs. The household pet that is rarely exercised, confined to the home, and fed a high-quality diet is the most prone to obesity.

The pet-food industry has come a long way in making diets that are tasty and calorie-dense so that obesity is readily achieved. It is easy to be swayed by advertising and believe that your dog deserves the best, which often means a high-protein diet. What could be healthier than a diet loaded with protein? Well, the fact is that excess protein is either converted to fat or excreted in the urine. And diets high in meat protein are also high in meat fat, often saturated fats. These diets are therefore loaded with calories!

This problem is often compounded by inappropriate feeding practices. The food is often left available to the dog all day, and snacks are given regularly. Compound the problem by adding a fatty-acid supplement to help make the coat shiny, and you can begin to see why most pet dogs receive more calories in a day than they could possibly know what to do with.

Obesity can be dealt with intelligently and effectively if you pay attention to the facts. All weight-reduction programs should be performed under the supervision of a veterinarian to reduce the risk of complications from the obesity or the weight loss.

Weight loss is best achieved with a three-facet approach. First, a lifestyle change must occur between you and your pet. You must be committed to helping your dog lose weight and realize that he will be healthier and happier if the effort is made. The difficult time is when you first implement the plans, because you feel guilty by depriving your dog of food rewards. So you must be committed to providing a reasonable amount of calories to your dog, exercising him more, and cutting back on fattening supplements and treats. Your dog may not thank you immediately, but you will be paid back with many more healthy and active years of companionship.

The second part of the program is to increase the amount of physical exercise your dog is getting. Severely obese dogs will not be able to exercise normally and will quickly become fatigued. The goal is to slowly accommodate him to regular exercise, not to stress him to exhaustion. A daily walk of one to three miles is exhilarating and healthy for most dogs. If your lifestyle does not permit this, consider teaching your dog to retrieve, then use this game for fifteen to twenty minutes, twice a day. When your dog asks for a treat, reward him with an outing instead. Most dogs prefer the companionship to the treat anytime.

The third part of the program is to decrease the number of calories your dog receives on a daily basis. In fact, to burn off the fat that is already present, you must use a feeding regimen that provides about 60 percent of his normal daily caloric requirements. This allows your dog to lose the required weight over a safe twelve-week period. This is done for most commercial "Lite" diets by providing fiber for bulk so that a regular portion only provides a fraction of the calories. Do not feed high-fiber diets long-term to your dog, however, because this can eventually lead to other nutrient deficiencies. The other way you need to reduce your dog's caloric intake is to give him access to his food for only thirty minutes twice daily. Do not feed him between meals.

If you are serious about a weight-loss program for your dog, and you want to be totally involved in the process, it is important to *count calories* (actually, Kcal). A typical ten-kilogram dog (twenty-two pounds) requires about 750 calories (kcal) each day for maintenance. If you want your overweight pet to lose weight safely, you need to design a diet that provides about 500 to 625 Kcal per day. If you create a calorie deficit of about 250 calories per day, your dog should lose about half a pound per week safely. It takes a total calorie reduction of about 3,500 calories for every pound of weight loss (7,700 Kcal per kilogram of weight loss).

There are some important guidelines to follow in selecting a weight-loss diet. When your dog loses weight, he may lose muscle as well as fat. It is therefore important to select a dog food that has adequate protein (at least 22 percent, although amino-acid content is more critical) so that lean muscle mass can be regenerated. Diets that contain fiber levels higher than 10 percent are common in "Lite" formulations, but this might interfere with the absorption of essential nutrients. Some commercial products unfortunately claim appropriateness for dieting dogs that really are inadequate in protein and fiber. You can only choose wisely if you are an informed consumer.

Once your dog has safely lost the weight, it is important not to resort to the old behaviors that resulted in obesity in the first place. It is usually recommended that the calorie content of the diet be left at 90 percent of requirements rather than 100 percent because snacks are bound to creep back into the diet at some point. If you are aware of how many calories you are providing your dog, you won't be as surprised if the weight problem returns. Of course, a program of moderate exercise is highly recommended, because it allows *both* you and your dog to burn off many of the calories you ingest on a daily basis.

Watching your dog's weight will promote a good, healthy, long life. Photo by Tammy Geiger.

It is also important that you consider the impact of dietary supplements and treats. For the most part, dogs do not require fatty-acid supplements, which are often very high in calories. If a coat-care supplement is truly needed, select vegetable oils that provide the essential fatty acids. These include flaxseed oil, safflower oil, and evening primrose oil. These highly polyunsaturated fatty acids provide the most value for coat care and carry the least health risks. For treats, consider popcorn, carrots, broccoli, cauliflower, celery, cucumbers, or other vegetables, or the new low-calorie snacks. When using any snack, check the ingredient label for calorie information. If it is not provided, the snack might not be suitable. For chewing enjoyment, give your dog a nylon or rawhide chew toy rather than a biscuit treat.

Despite the warnings on the use of supplements, some nutrients may help your overweight dog. Supplements such as vitamin E, lecithin, choline, and inositol are often helpful in managing the fat by-products that are produced as the fats are being boken down in the body. These include the amino acids L-ornithine, L-lysine, and L-carnitine which might help "burn up" the fat stores in the body. L-phenylalanine and L-arginine are also helpful as long as your dog is not diabetic. Vitamin C and the B vitamins are often recommended, because calorie restriction may also limit the amount of these important water-soluble vitamins.

RECOMMENDATIONS

Obesity is the number-one nutritional problem affecting dogs, and it is entirely preventable. Your dog counts on you for his health-care needs. Unfortunately, weight loss in pets is no easy matter. Proper nutrition requires a basic philosophical change so that you understand the difference between optimal nutrition and overnutrition.

PANCREATIC DISEASES

The pancreas is a long, thin gland that serves two main functions. It produces hormones—insulin and glucagon included—which regulate the level of sugar (glucose) in the bloodstream, and it releases digestive enzymes into the intestine. It is this second function that is explored here. Pancreatic juices contain not only digestive enzymes, but also substances that play a role in the absorption of vitamin B_{12}, zinc, and perhaps other nutrients.

PANCREATIC INSUFFICIENCY

The pancreas produces a number of enzymes that break down proteins, carbohydrates, and fats so that they can be absorbed more easily. Without these enzymes, maldigestion occurs (as opposed to malabsorption), and nutrients pass through the intestines and out in the stool without being properly utilized. This is referred to as exocrine pancreatic insufficiency (EPI). The exact cause is unknown, but an inherited form of the disorder is seen in the German Shepherd. Many hypotheses try to explain why the pancreatic tissue is no longer able to produce enzymes, with a nutritional imbalance being proposed but not confirmed.

Dogs with pancreatic insufficiency, regardless of the cause, do not digest their food properly and eventually become malnourished. Their appetite is increased, but they continue to lose weight and often have semiformed stools if not frank diarrhea. The diagnosis is made by fecal evaluations and specific blood tests.

Most cases of EPI fortunately do not affect the insulin-producing cells of the pancreas and hence can be managed medically by dietary modification. The pancreatic enzymes can be provided by commercially available dried pancreatic extracts or by adding chopped raw ox or pig pancreas to the meals immediately before feeding. These enzymes work well but still digest fats incompletely. Highly digestible diets are therefore recommended for dogs with EPI. Medium-chain triglyceride oil is often added to the diet, because it can be absorbed without further breakdown.

Intelligent supplementation is definitely warranted because dogs with EPI are prone to malnutrition. It is especially important to provide supplemental vitamin E and vitamin B_{12}. Because fat absorption may never return entirely to normal, supplementation with vitamins A, D, and K might also be necessary but should be attempted only under veterinary supervision.

PANCREATITIS

Pancreatitis is an inflammatory disease of the pancreas. The exact cause is still a matter of debate, but the clinical signs (symptoms) appear to be due to the release of digestive enzymes that actually digest the pancreatic tissue itself. The progressive damage done to the organ is enhanced by oxygen-derived free radicals that further damage the pancreatic cells (through lipid peroxidation). These free radicals usually are kept under control by scavengers such as superoxide dismutase and catalase, but when the response is insufficient, pancreatitis results. Other proteins in the body (e.g., alpha-macroglobulins) protect the other tissues from the potentially life-threatening situation of roaming and destructive protein-digesting enzymes released from the pancreas.

Diet is a major contributor to the onset of pancreatitis in dogs. Obese dogs are much more commonly affected, and high-fat meals are thought to promote pancreatitis in dogs that are prone. Some breeds with a tendency toward high blood-fat levels, such as hyperlipoproteinemia in Schnauzers, are also more susceptible. There are, of course, many other causes for pancreatitis, including drug reactions, infections, trauma, high blood levels of calcium, and hereditary factors.

Pancreatitis usually causes vomiting and abdominal pain, and veterinary attention is mandatory. The diagnosis can often be confirmed with radiographs and blood tests.

Treatment for pancreatitis involves both medical and nutritional approaches. Initially, most dogs are put on intravenous therapy, which provides electrolytes and gives the pancreas a much needed rest. In very severe cases, blood or plasma transfusions may be necessary to provide alpha-macroglobulins that will protect the body from the ravaging digestive enzymes. At present, these compounds are not commercially available and so transfusions must suffice.

Within one to two days of controlling vomiting, small amounts of water are introduced, and then small amounts of food are gradually provided. The food should be almost entirely carbohydrate (e.g., rice, pasta, potatoes) because protein and fat stimulate pancreatic function. As the dog improves, a low-fat, low-protein diet is commenced and, if nutritionally balanced, can be used for a maintenance diet.

Some dietary supplements may be helpful in pancreatitis, especially because the damage done by free radicals can be severe. Antioxidants, especially vitamin C, dimethlyglycine, superoxide dismutase, and germanium may be helpful. Care should be taken in supplementing with any fat-soluble products (e.g., vitamins A and E, essential fatty acids), because fats can worsen the problem.

RECOMMENDATIONS

Pancreatic insufficiency results when the pancreatic enzymes needed to digest foods are no longer produced in sufficient quantities. Treatment consists of providing a good-quality diet that is low in fat and adding digestive enzymes to the meal before feeding.

Pancreatitis is an inflammatory disease of the pancreas in which the digestive enzymes produced by the pancreas are released and damage the pancreatic tissue itself. Veterinary therapy is essential, because most dogs with pancreatitis benefit from intravenous-fluid therapy. When food is reintroduced, diets should be low in fat and protein. Antioxidant supplementation is warranted, but caution is the rule when considering fat-containing products.

SKIN PROBLEMS

There is a virtual explosion of dog foods on the market that claim to be good for dogs with skin problems. They supposedly provide a shiny coat, rid the skin of dandruff, and stop dogs from scratching. Most of these foods contain lamb, which the ads say is good for skin problems. The only problem is that these advertising claims are bunk. Lamb is no better for skin than any other protein source. It's not richer in the essential amino acids, and it certainly doesn't provide the essential fatty acids required for a healthy coat. Lamb-based diets have some merit in managing dogs with proven food allergies (see section on food allergy/intolerance), but lamb itself is not a skin-helping protein source.

The best approach for chronic skin problems is to seek veterinary attention. If the problem persists, request a referral to a dermatologist, a specialist in pet skin problems. The truth is that only a very small percentage of skin problems, perhaps 10 percent, can be controlled by dietary change alone.

The best diet for a dog with skin problems should contain ample amounts of the essential amino acids, especially the sulfur-containing varieties. If 2 percent of the calories in the diet are provided by linoleic acid, the essential fatty acid requirement for healthy skin will be met. The diet should also contain easily digestible, high-quality protein in moderate amounts, low levels of saturated fats, and the least amount of preservatives possible.

Supplements for skin conditions are in no short supply either, but most are completely unnecessary. A source of essential fatty acids may be helpful, but most retail products are mixtures of vegetable oils that are high in saturated and monounsaturated fats. The preferred sources of polyunsaturated fats include safflower oil, sunflower oil, sesame-seed oil,

Left: Mild symptoms of inhalant allergies. Note the dark patches around the eyes.
Right: More severe changes associated with long-standing and poorly controlled allergies.
From, Ackerman, L.: Guide to Skin and Haircoat Problems in Dogs, *Alpine Publications, 1994.*

flaxseed oil, and soy oil. The omega-3 fatty acids are provided in cold-water fresh fish oils, and gamma-linolenic acid (an omega-6 fatty acid) is plentiful in evening primrose oil, borage oil, and black-currant seed oil.

Fatty acid supplementation works best for inflammatory skin conditions such as allergic inhalant dermatitis (atopy), keratinization disorders (seborrhea), and some immune-mediated skin conditions. The allergic diseases respond best to supplements that include a high dose of marine oils containing eicosapentaenoic acid (EPA). Whereas trials using combinations of EPA and gamma-linolenic acid (GLA) typically report success rates of about 20 percent, fixed ratio diets (such as Eukanuba Veterinary Diets™Response Formula FP™) seem to enjoy a success rate of about 40 percent. A trial using high-dose fish oil was able to earn a success rate of over 50 percent. EPA/GLA supplementation appears to cause few if any adverse effects. The biggest problem seems to be owner compliance, since dosing with gelatin capsules and liquids aren't welcomed by most dogs. Fatty acids in chewable tablet form (e.g., VetriDerm™) have done much to improve the palatability of these supplements. Feeding a commercial diet in which there are controlled ratios of EPA to GLA is another option.

Keratinization disorders of many types seem to partially respond to fatty acid supplementation. Preliminary studies suggest that dogs with keratinization disorders (frequently referred to as seborrhea) have higher concentrations of oleic acid and lower concentrations of linoleic acid in their skin. At least one study has shown that supplementing the diet with sunflower oil, a rich source of cis-linoleic acid was beneficial in treating dogs with keratinization disorders. The results of using supplements in people with psoriasis have been more equivocal. Dietary supplementation with very-long-chain n-3 fatty acids was no better than corn-oil supplementation in treating psoriasis. Thus, keratinization disorders are best supplemented with vegetable oils (such as sunflower, safflower or corn oils) rather than the more expensive sources of EPA and GLA.

RECOMMENDATIONS

Skin problems in dogs, probably more than any other medical condition, prompt people to change their dog's diet and seek nutritional advice. New fad diets promise dermatologic health but can deliver in only a small percentage of cases. Similarly, dietary supplements for skin problems line the shelves of pet-supply outlets, but only relatively few contain appro-

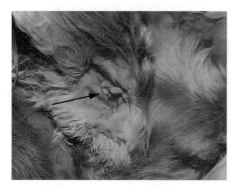

Ceruminous otitis in a dog with a keratinization disorder. Photo courtesy of Dr. T. Lewis.

priate ingredients in correct amounts. Much time and expense can be saved by visiting your veterinarian and, if necessary, requesting a referral to a veterinary dermatologist.

URINARY-TRACT STONES (UROLITHIASIS)

Minerals accumulate in the urine of some dogs, resulting in "stone" formation. For the most part, these stones collect in the bladder, but occasionally they form in the kidney itself. Interestingly enough, different types of stones appear to preferentially affect different breeds of dogs.

The most common mineral found in uroliths (urinary-tract stones) is magnesium ammonium phosphate (MAP), frequently referred to as "struvite." These account for about 60 percent of urinary-tract stones, and they tend to form in alkaline urine. Calcium-oxalate stones are probably next most common and have been reported most often in Dalmatians, Lhasa Apsos, Miniature Schnauzers, Poodles, Shih Tzus, and Yorkshire Terriers. Uric-acid or ammonium-urate stones are relatively rare in dogs, but Dalmatians are uniquely at risk because they may have an inherited defect in uric-acid metabolism. Cystine stones are even less common, but certain breeds, especially Dachshunds and English Bulldogs, are at increased risk. Cystinuria, the loss of cystine into the urine, is an inherited metabolic defect. Other less common sources of urolithiasis in dogs are silica, calcium phosphate (apatite), xanthine, and calcium carbonate.

What does diet have to do with urinary-tract stones? Lots! Most stones form when the pH of the urine changes. Some stones are more prevalent in acid pH, and some when the urine is more alkaline. Although many uroliths can be surgically removed, nutritional management is an excellent way to dissolve the stones and thereby control the problem. For example, struvite crystals can often be dissolved by feeding a diet low in urea, phosphorus, and magnesium. These diets have reduced protein and increased salt and should be given only under the direction of a veterinarian.

Dogs with oxalate stones benefit from a diet with normal calcium levels that does *not* include calcium supplements or calcium-rich foods (e.g., milk, yogurt, cheese). High-salt diets are also discouraged, because this may lead to additional calcium being excreted into the urine. Soybeans are especially high in oxalates and therefore are best avoided in dogs prone to developing calcium-oxalate uroliths.

Attempts to dissolve oxalate uroliths through dietary change have been disappointing. Because magnesium may be antagonistic to the effects of calcium, magnesium supplements may have a role in managing dogs with oxalate urolithiasis. Also, vitamin B_6 (pyridoxine) may be beneficial, because it lowers the amount of oxalic acid in the urine and therefore might reduce the risk of kidney-stone formation.

Dogs with cystine uroliths have a metabolic disorder that results in this amino acid being shed into the urine. These dogs are usually not amino-acid deficient, but cystine uroliths form because this amino acid is not very soluble in urine, especially not at the usual pH range of 5.5 to 7.0. Most of the stones can be dissolved and excreted by providing potassium citrate (sodium bicarbonate would be a second choice) and raising the pH to about 7.5. A low-protein diet, especially low in methionine (which converts to cystine), coupled with a potassium-citrate supplement, may help prevent a future recurrence of cystine uroliths in dogs that are most at risk.

Urate stones can occur in dogs with metabolic defects, and Dalmatians are most prone. They have a metabolic problem with uric acid, similar to gout in people. As uric-acid levels rise in the blood, they spill over into the urine and can result in stone formation. In time, Dalmatians can also develop changes in their haircoat, referred to as Dalmatian bronzing syndrome. This, too, is related to the defect in uric-acid metabolism. The best nutritional approach to these cases is to feed a diet low in a certain class of proteins called purines and to increase the pH of the urine. These diets can be purchased commercially or made at home. In some cases, drugs such as allopurinol are needed to control the problem, but dietary intervention is successful in most cases.

RECOMMENDATIONS:

Dogs are prone to many different types of urolithiasis, and nutritional management is often rewarding if a proper diagnosis is made. Some conditions require altering the pH of the urine up or down, depending on the nature of the urolith involved. Natural substances such as potassium citrate or ascorbic acid can be used to change the pH of the urine as needed. For most cases, a diet can be formulated that produces the least amount of problem-causing substance. Supplements should be used cautiously and only on the advice of a veterinarian. Various reports have suggested that the herb hydrangea may be useful in helping to dissolve urinary-tract stones.

IN SUMMARY

There are over 60,000 dogs affected yearly by bloat (GDV). Diet may be a factor that attributes to this serious and life-threatening problem.

It is thought that feeding ad libitum (free choice of food) and high caloric content in the diet may increase the incidence of hip dysplasia.

In some research studies, decreased caloric intake reduced the incidence of breast cancers, skin tumors, and leukemia.

A dog with heart disease needs to consume a diet that is very similar to a human diet for heart problems. A low-sodium diet and an increased amount of antioxidants are needed to help the heart function optimally.

A dog with liver disease should be on a diet of high-quality (easy-to-digest) carbohydrates, moderate in protein (high quality), low in fat, and with decreased amounts of fiber.

Obese dogs are at risk of developing diabetes mellitus, decreased resistance to infection, and anesthetic complications during surgeries.

A reward that your dog enjoys just as much as a dog biscuit is companionship.

Diet is the major contributor to pancreatitis. Other causes of pancreatitis are drug reactions, trauma, and hereditary factors (some breeds are more susceptible).

If 2 percent of the calories in the diet are provided by linoleic acid, the essential fatty acid requirement for healthy skin will be met if all other aspects of nutrition are also met.

ADDITIONAL READING

Abood, S.K., and Buffington, C.A.T., "Enteral Feeding of Dogs and Cats: 51 Cases (1989-1991)." *Journal of the American Medical Veterinary Association.* 1992; 201(4): 619-622.

Ackerman, L., "Adverse Reactions to Foods." *Journal of Veterinary Allergy and Clinical Immunology, 1993;* 1(1): 18-22.

Ackerman, L., "Dermatologic Uses of fatty acids in dogs and cats." *Veterinary Medicine,* 1995; (12): 1149-1155.

Ackerman, L., "Nondermatologic indications for fatty acid supplementation in dogs and cats." *Veterinary Medicine,* 1995; (12): 1156-1159.

Ackerman, L., Nutrition and Behavior. In, Ackerman, L; Landsberg, G; Hunthausen, W (Eds). "Dog Behavior and Training...Veterinary Advice for Owners." T.F.H. Publications, Neptune City, New Jersey, 1996; 117-123.

Ackerman, L.," Nutritional Immunology." *Advances in Nutrition,* 1993; 1(4):8-10. Ballarini, G., *Animal Psychodietetics.* Waltham Symposium No. 13; 1989; March: 49-58.

Batt, R.M., "*Relationships Between Diet and Malabsorption in Dogs.*" Waltham Symposium No. 13; 1989; March: 16-20.

Bauer, J.E., "*Liver Disease and Diet.*" Waltham Symposium No. 18, 1990; March: 12-15.

Bauer, J.E., "EIT-induced Alterations of Lipoprotein Metabolism." *Journal of the American Veterinary Medical Association,* 1992; 201(11): 1691-1694.

Bella, J.A., "Principles of Nutritional Therapy for Dogs and Cats."*Compendium on Continuing Education for the Veterinary Technician.* 1989; 10(3): 152-162.

Brown, R.G., "Dealing with Canine Obesity." *Canadian Veterinary Journal.* 1989; 30: 973-975.

Burrows, C.F., and Ignaszewski, L.A., "*Canine Gastric Dilatation-Volvulus.*" Waltham Symposium No. 13; 1989; March: 21-27.

Cabre, E., and Gassull, M.A., "Nutritional Therapy in Liver Disease." *Acta Gastro-Enterologica Belgica,* 1994; 57(1):1-12.

Diez, M., Leemans, M., Houins, G., Istasse, L., "Specific-purpose food in companion animals. The new directories of the European community and practical use in the treatment of obesity." *Annales de Medecine Veterinaire,* 1995; 139(6): 395-399.

Dodman, N.H., Reisner, I., Shuster, L., et al., "Effect of dietary protein content on behavior in dogs." Journal of the American Veterinary Medical Association, 1996; 208(3): 376-379.

Donoghue, S., "Diet and Hip Dysplasia." *AKC Gazette,* 1994; July: 18-19.

Dwyer, J.T., "Diet and Nutritional Strategies for Cancer Risk Reduction." *Cancer,* 1993; 72(3):1024-1031.

Elmwood, C.M., Rutgers, H.C., Batt, R.M., "Gastroscopic food sensitivity testing in 17 dogs." *Journal of Small Animal Practice,* 1994; 35(4): 199-203.

Fernstrom, J.D., "Dietary amino .acids and brain function." *Journal of the American*

Dietetic Association, 1994; 94(1): 71-77.

Finco, D.R, "Effects of Dietary Components on Progression of Renal Failure." *Proceedings of the 10th ACVIM Forum*, 1992, pp. 460-462.

Gedek, B.R., "Probiotic agents for regulation of intestinal flora." *Tierarztliche Umschau*, 1993; 48(2): 97-104.

Gentry, S.J., "Results of the Clinical Use of a Standardized Weight-Loss Program in Dogs and Cats." *Journal of the American Animal Hospital Association*, 1993; 29(4): 369-375.

Gey, K.F., "Prospects for the prevention of free radical disease, regarding cancer and cardiovascular disease." *British Medical Bulletin*, 1993; 49(3): 679-699.

Guilford, W.G., "Nutritional Management of Gastrointestinal Tract Diseases." *Proceedings of the 10th ACVIM Forum*, 1992; pp. 66-69.

Halliwell, R.E.W., "Comparative Aspects of Food Intolerance." *Veterinary Medicine*, 1992; September: 893-899.

Hamlin, R.L., and Buffington, C.A.T, "Nutrition and the Heart." *Veterinary Clinics of North America: Small Animal Practice*, 1989; 19(3): 527-538.

Heber, D., "Nutrition in the Prevention and Treatment of Cancer." *Current Opinion in Gastroenterology*, 1994; 10(2): 199-202.

Hill, D.L., and Grubbs, C.J., "Retinoids and Cancer Prevention." *Annual Review of Nutrition*, 1992; 12: 161-181.

Kallfelz, F.A., and Dzanis, D.A., "Overnutrition: An Epidemic Problem in Pet Animal Practice?" *Veterinary Clinics of North America*, 1989; 19(3): 433-445.

Kealy, R.D., et al., "Effects of Limited Food Consumption on the Incidence of Hip Dysplasia in Growing Dogs." *Journal of American Veterinary Medical Association*, 1992; 201(6): 857-863.

Kealy, R.D., et al., "Effects of Dietary Electrolyte Balance on Subluxation of the Femoral Head in Growing Dogs." *American Journal of Veterinary Research*, 1993; 54(54): 555-562.

Kurie, J.M., Lippman, S.M., and Hong, W.K., "Potential of Retinoids in Cancer Prevention." *Cancer Treatment Reviews*, 1994; 20: 1-10.

Leaf, A., and Hallaq, H.A., "The Role of Nutrition in the functioning of the Cardiovascular System." *Nutrition Reviews*, 1992; 402-406.

Leib, M.S., "Dietary Management of Chronic Large Bowel Diarrhea in Dogs." *Veterinary Economics*, 1992; June: 24-32.

Messina, M.J., Persky, V., Setchell, K.D.R., Barnes, S., "Soy intake and cancer risk— A review of the in vitro and in vivo data." *Nutrition and Cancer—An International Journal*, 1994; 21(2): 113-131.

Miller, S.J., "Nutritional Deficiency and the Skin." *Journal of the American Academy of Dermatology*, 1989; 21(1): 1:30.

Mortensen, S.A., "Perspectives on Therapy of Cardiovascular Diseases with Coenzyme Q_{10} (Ubiquinone)." *The Clinical Investigator*, 1993; 71: S116-S123.

Nelson, R.W., "The Role of Fiber in Managing Diabetes Mellitus." *Veterinary Medicine*, 1989; December: 1156-1160.

Ogilvie, G.K., "Alterations in Metabolism and Nutritional Support for Veterinary Cancer Patients: Recent Advances." *Compendium on Continuing Education for the Practicing Veterinarian,* 1993; 15(7): 925-936.

Pociot, F., Reimers, J.I., and Andersen, H.U., "Nicotinamide—Biological Actions and Therapeutic Potential in Diabetes Prevention." *Diabetologia,* 1993; 36: 574-576.

Polsin, D.J., et al., "Dietary Management of Canine and Feline Chronic Renal Failure." *Veterinary Clinics of North America: Small Animal Practice.* 1989; 19(3): 539-560.

Rackett, S.C., Rothe, M.J., and Grnt-Kels, J.M., "Diet and Dermatology." *Journal of the American Academy of Dermatology,* 1993; 29: 447-461.

Schmidt, E.B., Dyerberg, J., "Omega-3 fatty acids—Current status in cardiovascular medicine." *Drugs,* 1994; 47(3): 405-424.

Schoenthaler, S.J., et al., "Applied Nutrition and Behavior." *Journal of Applied Nutrition.,* 1991; 43(1): 31-39.

Sheffy, B.E, and Williams, A.J., "Nutrition and the Immune Response." *Journal of the American Veterinary Medical Association,* 1982; 180(9): 1073-1076.

Silverman, J., "Nutritional Aspects of Cancer Prevention: An Overview." *Journal of the American Veterinary Medical Association,* 1981; 179(12): 1404-1409.

Simpson, J.W., Maskell, I.E., Quigg, J, and Markwell, P.J., "Long-term Management of Canine Exocrine Pancreatic Insufficiency." *Journal of Small Animal Practice.,* 1994; 35(3): 133-138.

Slater, M.R., Scarlett, J.M, and Donoghue, S., "Diet and Exercise as Potential Risk Factors for Osteochondritis Dissecans in Dogs." *American Journal of Veterinary Research,* 1992; 53: 1749-1751.

Stefanovic-Racic, Stadler, J., and Evans, C.H., "Nitric Oxide and Arthritis." Arthritis and Rheumatism, 1993; 369: 1036-1044.

Tanaka, T. , Ichiba, Y., and Miura, Y., et al., "Canine Model of Chronic Pancreatitis Due to Chronic Ischemia." *Digestion,* 1994; 55(2); 86-89.

Wallin, M.S., and Rissanen, A.M., "Food and Mood: Relationship Between Food, Serotonin and Affective Disorders." *Acta Psychiatrica Scandiinavica,* 1994; 89 (Suppl. 377): 36-40.

Watson, P., Simpson, K.W., Bedford, P.G.C., "Hypercholesterolemia in Briards in the United Kingdom." *Research in Veterinary Science,* 1993; 54(1): 80-85.

White, P.D., "Essential fatty acids: Use in management of canine atopy." *Compendium on Continuing Education for the Practicing Veterinarian,* 1993; 15(3): 451-457.

White, S.D., Rosychuk, R.A.W., Reinke, S.I., Paradis, M., "Use of tetracycline and niacinamide for treatment of autoimmune skin disease in 31 dogs." *Journal of the American Veterinary Medical Association,* 1992; 200(10): 14997-1500.

White, S.D., Rosychuk, R.A.W., Scott, K.V., et al., "Use of isotretinoin and etretinate for the treatment of benign cutaneous neoplasia and cutaneous lymphoma in dogs." *Journal of the American Veterinary Medical Association,* 1993; 202(3): 387-391.

Willard, M.D., "Effects of Dietary Fructooligosaccharide (FOS) Supplementation on Canine Small Intestinal Bacterial Populations." In, Carey, D.P., Norton, S.A., Bolser, S.M. (Eds)., *Recent Advances in Canine and Feline Nutritional Research: Proceedings of the 1996 Iams International Nutrition Symposium, Orange Frazer Press,* Wilmington Ohio, 1996, pp. 45-52.

Willard, M.D., Simpson, R.B., and Delles, E.K., et. al. "Effects of Dietary Supplementation of Fructo-oligosaccharides on Small Intestinal Bacterial Overgrowth in Dogs." *American Journal of Veterinary Research*, 1994; 55(5): 654-659.
Ziegler, R.G., Byers, T., "Health claims about vitamin C and cancer." *Journal of the National Cancer Institute*, 1994; 86(11): 871-872.

This is where your dog's future begins. Good nutrition for the mother, for the puppy year, and on to adulthood, can help build a champion. Photo courtesy of Clifford Oliver.

APPENDICES

APPENDIX A. NRC MINIMUM NUTRIENT REQUIREMENTS OF DOGS FOR GROWTH AND MAINTENANCE (amounts per kg of body weight per day)

Nutrient	Unit	Growth	Adult Maintenance
Fat	g	2.7	1.0
Linoleic acid	mg	540.0	200.0
Protein			
Arginine	mg	274.0	21.0
Histidine	mg	98.0	22.0
Isoleucine	mg	196.0	48.0
Leucine	mg	318.0	84.0
Lysine	mg	280.0	50.0
Methionine-cystine	mg	212.0	30.0
Phenylalanine-tyrosine	mg	390.0	86.0
Threonine	mg	254.0	44.0
Tryptophan	mg	82.0	13.0
Valine	mg	210.0	60.0
Dispensable amino acids	mg	3,414.0	1,266.0
Minerals			
Calcium	mg	320.0	119.0
Phosphorus	mg	240.0	89.0
Potassium	mg	240.0	89.0
Sodium	mg	30.0	11.0
Chloride	mg	46.0	17.0
Magnesium	mg	22.0	8.2
Iron	mg	1.74	0.65
Copper	mg	0.16	0.06
Manganese	mg	0.28	0.10
Zinc	mg	1.94	0.72
Iodine	mg	0.032	0.012
Selenium	mcg	6.0	2.2
Vitamins			
A	IU	202.0	75.0
D	IU	22.0	8.0
E	IU	1.2	0.5
Thiamin	mcg	54.0	20.0
Riboflavin	mcg	100.0	50.0
Pantothenic Acid	mcg	400.0	200.0
Niacin	mcg	450.0	225.0
Pyridoxine	mcg	60.0	22.0
Folic Acid	mcg	8.0	4.0
Cobalamin	mcg	1.0	0.5
Choline	mg	50.0	25.0

APPENDIX B.. PROPOSED OPTIMAL NUTRIENT ALLOWANCES FOR GROWING AND ADULT DOGS (amounts per kg of body weight per day)

Nutrient	Unit	Growth	Adult Maintenance
Fat	g	4.0	1.5
Linoleic acid	mg	600.0	220.0
Protein			
Arginine	mg	584.0	40.0
Histidine	mg	118.0	27.0
Isoleucine	mg	236.0	58.0
Leucine	mg	382.0	106.0
Lysine	mg	392.0	70.0
Methionine-cystine	mg	297.0	42.0
Phenylalanine-tyrosine	mg	468.0	105.0
Threonine	mg	305.0	55.0
Tryptophan	mg	115.0	20.0
Valine	mg	252.0	72.0
Dispensable amino acids	mg	4,097.0	1,520.0
Minerals			
Calcium	mg	710.0	265.0
Phosphorus	mg	545.0	205.0
Potassium	mg	392.0	145.0
Sodium	mg	35.0	13.0
Chloride	mg	55.0	20.0
Magnesium	mg	38.0	14.0
Iron	mg	3.56	1.32
Copper	mg	0.43	0.16
Manganese	mg	0.30	0.11
Zinc	mg	5.94	2.2
Iodine	mg	0.08	0.03
Selenium	mcg	6.54	2.42
Vitamins			
A	IU	295.0	110.0
D	IU	27.5	10.0
E	IU	2.45	1.1
Thiamin	mcg	68.0	25.0
Riboflavin	mcg	120.0	60.0
Pantothenic Acid	mcg	450.0	225.0
Niacin	mcg	500.0	250.0
Pyridoxine	mcg	75.0	25.0
Folic Acid	mcg	8.5	4.2
Cobalamin	mcg	2.4	1.2
Choline	mg	76.0	28.0

APPENDIX C. NUTRIENT STANDARDS FOR DOG FOODS

Nutrient (drymattee basis)	Units	Growth, Reproduction (Minimum)	Adult Maintenance (Min./Max.)
Protein	%	22.0	18.0
Arginine	%	0.62	0.51
Histidine	%	0.22	0.18
Isoleucine	%	0.45	0.37
Leucine	%	0.72	0.59
Lysine	%	0.77	0.63
Methionine-cystine	%	0.53	0.43
Phenylalanine-tyrosine	%	0.89	0.73
Threonine	%	0.58	0.48
Tryptophan	%	0.20	0.16
Valine	%	0.48	0.39
Fat	%	8.0	5.0
Linoleic acid	%	1.0	1.0
Minerals			
Calcium	%	1.0	0.6/2.5
Phosphorus	%	0.8	0.5/1.6
Potassium	%	0.6	0.6
Sodium	%	0.3	0.06
Chloride	%	0.45	0.09
Magnesium	%	0.04	0.04/0.3
Iron	mg/kg	80.0	80/3,000
Copper	mg/kg	7.3	7.3/250
Manganese	mg/kg	5.0	5.0
Zinc	mg/kg	120.0	120/1,000
Iodine	mg/kg	1.5	1.5/50
Selenium	mg/kg	0.11	0.1/2
Vitamins			
Vitamin A	IU/kg	5000.0	5000/50,000
Vitamin D	IU/kg	500.0	500/5,000
Vitamin E	IU/kg	50.0	50/1000
Thiamin	mg/kg	1.0	1.0
Riboflavin	mg/kg	2.2	2.2
Pantothenic acid	mg/kg	10.0	10.0
Niacin	mg/kg	11.4	11.4
Pyridoxin	mg/kg	1.0	1.0
Folic acid	mg/kg	0.18	0.18
Cobalamin	mg/kg	0.022	0.022
Choline	mg/kg	1,200.0	1,200.0

Presumes an energy density of 3.5 kcal ME/g DM. Rations greater than 4.0 Kcal/g should be corrected for energy density.
From: "Nutrient Profiles for Dog Foods." Association of American Feed Control Officials, 1990.

APPENDIX D. CALORIC REQUIREMENTS FOR ADULT DOGS

Weight		Calories Required			
Kg	Lb	House dog	Sick dog	Active Dog	Working Dog
2.3	5	200	240	250	300
4.5	10	400	480	500	600
6.8	15	600	720	750	900
9.1	20	650	780	815	975
11.4	25	700	840	875	1,050
13.6	30	840	1,010	1,050	1,260
15.9	35	930	1,115	1,225	1,470
18.2	40	1,120	1,345	1400	1,680
20.5	45	1260	1,510	1,575	1,890
22.7	50	1,400	1,680	1,750	2,100
25.0	55	1,540	1,850	1,925	2,310
27.3	60	1,680	2,015	2,100	2,520
29.5	65	1,820	2,185	2,275	2,730
31.8	70	1,980	2,375	2,450	2,940
34.1	75	2,010	2,520	2,480	2,990
36.4	80	2,025	2,430	2,515	3,060
38.6	85	2,040	2,450	2,550	3,150
40.9	90	2,160	2,590	2,700	3,240
43.2	95	2,280	2,735	2,850	3,420
45.5	100	2,400	2,880	3,000	3,600
47.7	105	2,520	3,025	3,150	3,780
50.0	110	2,640	3,170	3,300	3,960
52.3	115	2,760	3,310	3,450	4,140
54.5	120	2,880	3,455	3,600	4,320
56.8	125	3,000	3,600	3,750	4,500
59.1	130	3,120	3,745	3,900	4,680
61.4	135	3,240	3,890	4,050	4,860
63.6	140	3,360	4,030	4,200	5,040
65.9	145	3,480	4,175	4,350	5,220
68.2	150	3,600	4,320	4,500	5,400

These are average daily calorie requirements, calculated as kilocalories of metabolizable energy per day. "House dog" represents sedentary pet. "Sick dog" requirements are for minor to moderate illnesses. "Active dog" are those with routine exercise availability. "Working dog" requirements are for animals with regular and intensive exercising. Modified from several sources, including "Caloric Requirements for Adult Dogs Based on Physical Activity and Breed Size," in *Current Veterinary Therapy* XI. W. B. Saunders Co., 1992, pg 1349.

APPENDIX E. CVMA STANDARDS FOR CERTIFIED DOG FOODS

Nutrient	Unit	Minimum Standard	Suggested Upper Limit
Protein	%	22.0	55.0
Fat	%	5.0	50.0
Linoleic acid	%	1.0	—
Calcium	%	1.1	4.0
Phosphorus	%	0.9	—
Potassium	%	0.6	—
Sodium chloride	%	1.1	—
Magnesium	%	0.04	—
Iron	mg/kg	60.0	1,500.0
Copper	mg/kg	7.3	—
Manganese	mg/kg	5.0	—
Zinc	mg/kg	50.0	—
Iodine	mg/kg	1.54	—
Selenium	mg/kg	0.11	10.0
Vitamin A	IU	5,000.0	37,100.0
Vitamin D	IU	500.0	4,000.0
Vitamin E	IU	50.0	1,000.0
Vitamin K	IU	—	2,000.0
Thiamin	mg/kg	1.00	1,000.0
Riboflavin	mg/kg	2.20	44.0
Pantothenic acid	mg/kg	10.0	2,000.0
Niacin	mg/kg	11.4	—
Pyridoxine	mg/kg	1.0	50.0
Biotin	mg/kg	0.10	1.0
Folic acid	mg/kg	0.18	—
Cobalamin	mg/kg	0.022	7.80
Vitamin C	g/kg	—	10.0
Choline	mg/kg	1,200.0	—

From: "Nutrient Standards for the CVMA Pet Food Certification Program." *Canadian Veterinary Journal*, 1987; 28(12): 744-745.

APPENDIX F. THINGS YOU CAN DO FOR THE PICKY EATER

1. Moisten the food with warm water if you are using dry food. This tends to make hard foods tastier and more chewy.

2. Most dogs prefer the flavor of beef, chicken, pork, or lamb rather than vegetable protein such as soy, corn, and wheat. Choose a dog food that provides these more desirable ingredients.

3. Heating the food in an oven or microwave can enhance the flavor. Do not make the food hot enough to burn the dog's mouth. Gentle heating only is required.

4. Add flavor enhancers to the diet such as liver or poultry broths or bouillon cubes.

5. Consider adding very small amounts of cooked garlic to the food. Use small amounts of cooked garlic cloves, not garlic oil. Don't get carried away—just add small amounts!

6. Add fresh fruit purées as a topdressing on the food. Mashed apples or bananas are good choices to try first. If necessary, the same effect can be gained by adding small amounts of artificial sweeteners such as aspartame.

7. Add some fresh-cooked food (hamburger, liver, chicken, etc.) to the diet to encourage picky dogs to eat. Slowly wean them off the fresh-cooked food onto the commercial ration.

8. Try a super-premium dog food that provides increased levels of protein and fat. Dogs need to eat less of these foods to achieve their daily requirements.

9. Add small amounts of commercial cat food to the dog food diet. Cat food has many more flavor enhancers, and is high fat, high protein and loaded with B vitamins. Many dogs find it very appealing.

10. Limit treats to the picky dog. Many people who think they have a picky dog really have a dog that fills up on treats rather than his dinner. Think about it.

APPENDIX G. TEN STEPS TO DETERMINE HOW MUCH TO FEED YOUR DOG

At one time or another, every dog owner questions their veterinarian about how much dog food they should be feeding. The answer is never an easy one because each dog is an individual and there is so much variability in dog foods. As a general guideline, veterinarians and nutritionists often advise to feed enough food to maintain normal weight; add more food if the dog is underweight and cut back if he is overweight. For those who want to know exactly how much they should be feeding, here is a formula for you.

1. Determine the ideal weight of your dog, not how much he currently weighs.

2. Look up that weight on Table 4 to determine the daily calories needed for your dog's particular situation.

3. Determine the caloric density (Kcal/g) of the dog food you are using. This is usually not on the label but can be provided by the manufacturer. You will also need to know the percentage dry matter in the food. Rough approximations are as follows:

Type of food	Caloric Density	Dry Matter
Dry	3.67 Kcal/gDM	90%
Canned, Regular	4.59 Kcal/gDM	20-25%
Canned, Lite	3.67 Kcal/gDM	20-25%
Canned, Premium	5.25 Kcal/gDM	20-25%
Biscuit Treats	3.60 Kcal/gDM	90%

4. Decide how many treats you plan to give daily and multiply that number by the weight of the biscuit, then by the caloric density, and then by the dry matter divided by 100.

5. Subtract the caloric contribution of the biscuit treats from the daily caloric need (step 2 above). This gives the amended caloric need to be provided by the dog food.

6. Divide the amended caloric need (step 5 above) by the caloric density of the food (step 3 above). This tells you how much of the food (by dry weight) to feed.

7. To determine the dry matter factor to use, divide 100 by the percent dry matter in the diet you're using.

8. Multiply the dry weight needed (step 6 above) by the dry matter factor (step 7 above). This tells you how much of the food you are using (by actual weight) needs to be given on a daily basis.

9. Divide the total daily food intake (step 8 above) by the number of meals fed daily to determine the weight of food to give at each meal. Convert to pounds if you need to by dividing by 454, since one pound equals 454 grams.

10. Feed your dog and relax!

EXAMPLE:

You have an 80-lb Greyhound that is reasonably active and you are feeding him a dry extruded diet (kibble). He eats twice a day and gets a biscuit treat (25 grams) after each meal. You realize that he really should be 70 lbs and you think you may be over-feeding him.

Step 1	His ideal weight is 70 lbs.
Step 2	You look up "70 lbs" and "active" on Table 4 and determine that he really needs 2450 Kcal/day.
Step 3	His dry food is 3.67 Kcal/g dry matter and is 90% dry matter.
Step 4	He gets 2 treats x 25 grams each x 3.6 Kcal/g x 90/100 = 162 Kcal.
Step 5	Subtract 162 Kcal from 2,450 Kcal. The food must provide 2,288 K/cal.
Step 6	Divide 2,288 Kcal by 3.67 Kcal/g dry matter = 623.4 g dry matter.
Step 7	The dry matter factor is 100 divided by 90 or 1.11.
Step 8	Multiply 623.4 grams x dry matter factor of 1.11 = 692 grams.
Step 9	Divide 692 grams by 2 because he's fed twice a day. Thus, he needs 346 grams or just over 3/4 lb (0.76 lb) of food with each meal.
Step 10	Feed your dog and take a well-deserved rest.

ABOUT THE AUTHOR

Lowell Ackerman D.V.M., Ph.D. is a nutritional consultant and board-certified veterinary dermatologist. He is the past editor of *Advances in Nutrition* and has authored 66 books and more than 150 articles in various professional journals and periodicals. Dr. Ackerman also manages an Internet Pet Site on the World Wide Web (http://www.pet-zone.com). Dr. Ackerman is a member of the American Academy of Veterinary Nutrition, the International Academy of Nutrition and Preventive Medicine, and the American Institute of Nutrition. He has lectured and written extensively on the subject of nutrition across the United States, Canada, and Europe. He recently presented some of his nutritional research findings at the World Veterinary Congress, which was held in Durban, South Africa.

INDEX

dextrose, 208, 211-212
diabetes mellitus, 205-206
diabetic(s), 57, 98, 126, 144, 151, 165, 205-206, 225
dicalcium phosphate, 127
dietary anion gaps (DAG), 199, 201
dietary electrolyte balance (DEB), 200
diet-related, 198, 212, 214
digestibility(ies), 4-5, 9, 13, 16, 29, 44, 57, 60, 114
digestive-enzyme, 166
digestive-tract disease, 206, 210
digitalis, 78, 162, 173, 215-217
digoxin, 217
dihomogamma-linolenic, 52
dilatation, 47
dilatation-volvulus, 197
dilate(s)(ed), 163, 181, 198, 216-217
diltiazem, 217
dimethylglycine (DMG), 37, 84, 163-164, 188, 199-200, 204-205, 217, 221, 227
dioxin, 62
discoid lupus, 187
dispensable amino acids, 10
diuretics, 78, 93, 215-217
DL-phenylalanine, 164-165
DNA, 61, 82, 86, 93, 189
DNA-linkage, 96
Doberman Pinscher(s), 94, 96, 177, 197, 216
docosahexaenoic acid (DHA), 52, 203
dog-food, 5, 15, 76, 94, 105, 107, 110, 113, 117-118, 128, 213
Doxorubicin, 204
dry-food, 122
dry matter (DM), 115, 122
duodenum, 206
dwarfed, 95
dysplasia, 22, 85, 164-165, 185, 199-201
dysrhythmia, 198

easy-to-digest, 137, 221, 232
Echinacea angustifolia, 174, 188
echinacen, 174
echinacoside, 174
echocardiography, 163
E coli, 209
edema, 215, 221
eicosapentaenoic acid (EPA), 50, 52, 147, 169-170, 203, 229
elderly, 27-29, 78, 134, 170, 172, 181
electrocardiograms, 163
electrolyte(s), 74, 199-200, 207-208, 211-212, 227
electron(s), 189
elimination, 199
ELISA, 214

emulsion, 219, 221
endemic, 99
endorphins, 164
endoscopy, 207, 209
energy-dense, 31-32, 34, 47, 112, 135
enkephalinase, 164
enteral, 37, 210-212
enteral/parenteral nutrition, 210-212
enteritis, 206-210
enterocolitis, 213
enteropathy, 207
environment, 7, 22, 131, 186, 199
environmental, 48, 190, 198-199, 222
enzymes, 12
eosinoophilic gastroenteritis, 207
epidermolysis bullosa simplex, 187
epithelial tissues, 70
eriodictyol, 171
essential fatty acids (EFAS), 63, 168
esophagus, 206
ethoxyquin, 11, 117, 118-119, 124, 202
etodolac, 201
Etogesic, 201
etretinate, 183
Eukanuba, 52, 229
evening primrose, 13, 33, 49, 52-53, 170, 218, 221, 225, 229
excretion, 74, 95, 206, 217
exercise(s)(ed)(ing), 26, 28, 47, 198, 201, 223
exocrine pancreatic insufficiency (EPI), 226
exorphine(s), 196-197
extract(s), 36, 72, 174, 175, 226
extranutritional, 196
extrusion, 109
eyebalm, 175

fasting, 209
fat-containing, 227
fat-promoting, 12
fatigue, 36, 222-223
fattening, 54, 223
fatty-acid, 12, 49-54, 168-169, 221, 223, 225
fear, 83, 85, 196, 202
feather(s), 114, 124
fecal, 167, 209, 226
feces, 14, 214
feedings, 21-22, 135, 212
Feldene, 201
femoral, 199
ferment, 81, 198
fertility, 99
fiber(s), 13, 57, 60, 177
fibrosarcoma, 171
fillers, 154, 214
flatulence, 26, 47-48, 58-59, 212

flavonoids, 171
flavor(ed)(ing), 51, 117, 147, 196, 214
flax, 52
flaxseed, 28, 33, 38, 49-51, 111, 114, 130, 140, 168, 218, 225, 228
flea(s), 33, 172
flora, 175
flour(s), 26, 55, 59, 75, 114, 117, 124, 129, 179, 186, 221-222
fluid(s), 30, 57, 60-61, 74, 91-93, 101, 207-208, 211, 215-216, 221
fluoride, 61, 98
fluorine, 14, 98
folacin, 82
folate, 82, 84, 181, 185, 207
folic-acid, 82-83, 210
food alergy/intolerance, 212-215
FOS, 57-58, 207
foxglove, 162, 173
free radical, 13, 160, 189
freeze, 129, 145
freeze-dried, 174
fried, 148, 213
frozen, 80, 108, 119, 128-129, 145, 213
fructooligosaccharides (FOS), 57-58, 207
fructose, 55, 205-206
fruit, 58, 98, 127-128, 205-206
fry(ing), 129, 135, 148
fuel-efficient, 45
fungal, 175
fungi, 166
fungus, 179
fur, 33, 41, 168, 182, 184
furosemide, 217

gallbladder, 27, 95, 168-169, 206-207, 220
gamma tocopherol, 11, 74
gamma-linolenic, 33, 52-53, 169-170, 190, 201-202, 229
garlic, 57, 173-175, 179, 188, 191
gas, 14, 21, 26, 45, 47, 59, 197-198
gastric, 47, 197-198
GDV, 197-199, 232
gelatin, 44, 166, 229
generally regarded as safe (GRAS), 118
genetic(s), 2, 10, 61, 68, 81-82, 94-95, 177, 198-199, 222
genetic code, 82
geriatric, 18, 27-28, 38, 78, 134
German Shepherd Dog, 111, 166, 197, 207, 223, 226
germanium, 174, 179, 188, 199-200, 204-205, 217, 221, 227
gestation, 30, 38, 106
Giant Schnauzers, 6
giant-breed, 197
Giardia, 209